Hosts and Guests

Eric Crystal

Lewis I. Deitch

Nelson H. H. Graburn

Davydd J. Greenwood

Alice Shear Lepie

Laurence D. Loeb

Philip Frick McKean

Dennison Nash

Theron Nuñez

John Gregory Peck

Rayna Rapp Reiter

Oriol Pi-Sunyer

Valene L. Smith

Max E. Stanton

Margaret Byrne Swain

Charles F. Urbanowicz

HOSTS AND GUESTS

The Anthropology of Tourism

Valene L. Smith, *Editor*

University of Pennsylvania Press
1977

Library of Congress Cataloging in Publication Data

Main entry under title:

Hosts and guests.

    Bibliography: p.
    Includes index.
    1.   Tourist trade. I.   Smith, Valene L.
G155.A1H67   338.4'7'91   77-81447
ISBN 0-8122-7728-7

Contents

Hosts and Guests

Introduction

VALENE SMITH

Tourism has burgeoned since World War II and eclipsed more traditional industries to become one of the world's largest, which, in 1975, generated US$41.5 billion in international revenues alone (Waters and Patterson 1976). If national or domestic tourism are also included, in 1976 the industry is estimated to pump 80 billion dollars into the total world economy. Ever alert to potential income, government agencies at every level from UNESCO and the World Bank to local Chambers of Commerce have so thoroughly analyzed the characteristics and flow of visitors that tourism may well be the best-researched single topic in history. But the nature of tourism and its effects on the people involved—those in tourist areas who become the hosts, and the tourists who become their temporary guests—remains heretofore essentially unstudied.

Anthropologists have observed the growing impact of tourism throughout the world but buried their data in field notes and only occasionally published peripheral articles, as if tourism were not a scientific or scholarly subject. The history of anthropological analyses of tourism is brief; 1963 marks the first published article (Nuñez 1963). The following year, James Silverberg organized a regional session on tourism in conjunction with the Milwaukee meetings of the Central States Anthropological Society. The first national symposium, to which this volume owes its genesis, was held in Mexico City in 1974 in conjunction with the meetings of the American Anthropological Association toward the goal of legitimatizing the study of tourism as an academic subdiscipline. Subsequently there have been two other national anthropological symposia (1975, 1976), and two regional symposia on Pacific tourism—one organized by Ben Finney and Karen Watson at Honolulu's East-West Center, and the other by Brian Farrell at University of California, Santa Cruz—which have yielded a growing body of literature, and are indicative of the mounting scientific and global concern with the impact of tourism and the stresses it may generate.

In a pioneering work it is not possible to outline a systematic methodology of touristic research or present an overview of all types of host-guest relationships. The individual case studies offer a sampling of the variety of

1

anthropological research on tourism and suggest lines of inquiry that could lead to still more fruitful research in the future. The book is organized into five parts: Tourism and Leisure; A Theoretical Overview; Nascent Tourism in Non-Western Societies; Tourism in European Resorts; Tourism in Complex Societies; and Tourism in Anthropological Perspective. The themes are individually considered at the beginning of each section. In addition, I have also included some preliminary typologies concerning the impact of tourism, to stimulate further investigation and discussion. The bibliography is broadly based in the social sciences but omits economic studies that are primarily statistical in nature.

Types of Tourism

Tourism is difficult to define because business travelers and convention-goers can combine conferences with tourist-type activities; but in general, a tourist is a temporarily leisured person who voluntarily visits a place away from home for the purpose of experiencing a change. Tourism as a form of leisure activity structures the personal life cycle to provide alternate periods of work and relaxation (Graburn, chapter 1). As work gives way to leisured mobility, individuals find re-creation in a variety of new contexts. Different forms of tourism can be defined in terms of the kinds of leisured mobility undertaken by the tourist, and may be identified as five types:

Ethnic tourism is marketed to the public in terms of the "quaint" customs of indigenous and often exotic peoples, exemplified by the case studies on the Eskimo, the San Blas Indians of Panama, and the Toraja in Indonesia. Destination activities that stimulate tourism include visits to native homes and villages, observation of dances and ceremonies, and shopping for primitive wares or curios, some of which may have considerable intrinsic value to the art historian. Frequently these tourist targets are far removed from the "beaten path" and attract only a limited number of visitors motivated by curiosity and elite peer approval. As long as the flow of visitors is sporadic and small, host-guest impact is minimal.

Cultural tourism includes the "picturesque" or "local color," a vestige of a vanishing life-style that lies within human memory with its "old style" houses, homespun fabrics, horse or ox-drawn carts and plows, and hand rather than machine-made crafts. Destination activities include meals in rustic inns, folklore performances, costumed wine festivals, or rodeos reminiscent of the Wild West. This is peasant culture, illustrated by the case studies on Bali and Spain. Host-guest stresses may be maximal because the rural peasant areas are often readily accessible from tourist resorts, and large numbers of visitors come for the very purpose of observing and photographing the lives of peasants who become objects of study *per se*.

Historical tourism is the Museum-Cathedral circuit that stresses the glories of the Past—i.e., Rome, Egypt, and the Inca. Favored destination activities include guided tours of monuments and ruins, and especially light and sound performances that encapsulate into a brief drama the life-style and key events that textbooks record. Historical tourism tends to attract many education-oriented visitors, and tourism is facilitated because the targets are either in or readily accessible to large cities. An institutionalized tourist industry, or "tourist culture," usually exists to cater to a stream of visitors, and host-guest contacts are often impersonal and detached, and primarily economic rather than social, as shown by the case study on the Iranian Jewish merchants.

Environmental tourism is often ancillary to ethnic tourism, attracting a tourist elite to remote areas such as Antarctica to experience a truly alien scene. Because environmental tourism is primarily geographic, many education-oriented travelers enjoy driving through mountains and countryside to observe man-land relationships. Popular destination activities include tours of local industries such as tea farms and processing plants in Japan or Ceylon, or salmon canneries in Alaska. One of the recognized bases for the popularity of the Polynesian Cultural Center is the tourist's ability to "visit the Pacific"—to see how material culture adapts to environment as well as to sample native foods and see a variety of dances—within an hour's drive of Waikiki. Host-guest contacts in this category vary widely and must be assessed locally.

Recreational tourism is often sand, sea, and sex—promoted by beautiful color pictures that make you want to be "there"—on the ski slopes, the palm-fringed beaches, the championship golf courses, or sunning in a deck chair, and attracts tourists who want to relax or commune with nature. Destination activities center upon participation in sports, curative spas, or sunbathing, as well as good food and convivial entertainment. Las Vegas epitomizes another type of recreational center: gambling, "name" shows, and the away-from-home freedom to indulge in the new morality. Again, host-guest relationships vary widely but may be influenced by the seasonality of some types of recreational tourism, which may require imported labor to handle massive influxes, or by radical changes in land values when favored sites are converted to a monetarily more profitable use, as in the case studies of the three North Carolina coastal towns and the French Alpine commune.

The Impact of Tourism

Tourism is a powerful medium affecting culture change, and central to its anthropological study is the impact between hosts and guests. To become one of the world's largest industries—sponsored by governments, regulated by international agencies, and supported by multinational enterprises as well as local businesses—presupposes that tourism is a positive or beneficial force. But whom does it benefit? Dependent upon the type of tourism, the expectations of the tourists, and the host's ability to provide appropriate facilities and destination activities, the effects of tourism can be assessed along a continuum from a highly positive relationship that benefits all, to a highly disruptive, negative interraction fraught with conflict. The two major bases for conflict and stress appear to be economic and social and are individually considered.

For many nations (and states such as Hawaii), mass tourism is the economic mainstay, generating wage employment, yielding valuable foreign exchange, and sustaining necessary transportation networks by augmenting their payloads. To analyze the entire economic process is beyond the scope of this book, but individual chapters provide insight into aspects of the economic impact. Several case studies such as Bali, the French Alpine commune, the Polynesian Cultural Center and the San Blas Indians illustrate the positive economic gains from the tourist trade. The data suggests that tourism can economically benefit a community if individual participation and local involvement are broadly based. Interpersonal conflict between hosts and guests is minimal when their respective standards of living are similar, as in urban European centers, Switzerland, or Australia and New Zealand. Here, hosts have the economic capacity and social incentives to travel, to become guests in some other land.

Where wide economic disparities exist and tourists are perceived to be "rich" simply because they are leisured, severe stress is often apparent. Native populations are attracted to jobs in tourism for the benefits of upward social mobility and fuller participation in a westernizing cash economy. As the case studies on Bali, the French Alpine commune, and the Eskimo show, many potential employees discover that only a limited segment of their population—either already-established leaders or bilingual, bicultural "marginal men"—can truly profit in their new roles. Hiring policies are often discriminatory, favoring those who have the linguistic skills to cater to tourists, and management positions are frequently reserved for Western-trained hoteliers and chefs. Further, the contrasts between well-appointed hotels and resorts only serve to heighten the awareness of poverty on the part of those who wait on the tourist but may still live in one-room shacks. The strains are often manifest by the "have nots" who make scapegoats of tourists either by the persistent cry in India for "baksheesh," the pickpockets who frequent crowded tourist centers, and the double-pricing of goods and services. For cultures in which bargaining etiquette is unlearned or disapproved (as in the United States), or where language barriers leave him defenseless, the tourist is often trapped into paying the asked-for price but carries a bitter aftertaste that he's been "had."

The tourist industry can have a negative effect upon a community through the disruption of the local economic system. The problems cited in part in the Tongan case study can be replicated in many locales where a native population, in order to acquire greater cash income, abandons subsistence agriculture to enter the tourist labor force, with the result that local food production declines. Imported products are required to feed both hosts and guests, all other services increase in cost, and inflation commences its upward spiral. The industry itself further contributes to inflation when inn-keepers and tour operators often pay higher wages, to procure the best possible personnel to meet visitor demands for superior service, than could be earned for the same services on the local economy. Tourism is also often seasonal, leaving hotels empty, carriers and tour operators with idle wheels, and employees jobless. Unless a pervasive sound economic base exists, individuals who are tied to tourism either feast or famine, as suggested in part by the Balinese example. Tourism can also be very sensitive to external variables over which the local industry has very little control, including fluctuations in currency values and the political climate. Tourists flock to centers where their purchasing power makes travel a "good buy" and avoid tensional areas where terrorism and political activities might threaten their lives.

The advent of large-scale tourism often necessitates the transfer of local control to a central government, which has the power to compete internationally for the tourist trade by offering concessions in the form of favorable taxes or negotiated land values to induce major hotel chains to construct facilities. A well-developed tourist industry is a powerful international lobby involving carriers in fare structures and the distribution of routes, and a powerful domestic lobby with effective control of regional planning and budgets. When the tourist industry is managed by outsiders, to whom profits flow, tourism becomes a form of imperialism (Nash, chapter 2) and may often develop into a neo-colonialism. The case studies indicate that the San Blas Cuna have to date retained local control of their economy, but the construction of the Los Gruyos project may ultimately place them in the position of the Eskimo, where tourism has been controlled by the air carriers. Government at all levels also has the ability to selectively develop tourism and benefit one area vis-a-vis another when a potential tourist "attraction" is recognized. In the Toraja example, the central government expended large sums to construct roads and hotels to provide tourist access to interior villages where they could see the elaborate funeral rituals. As Crystal notes (chapter 7), from the *local* perspective the money might better have been spent on agricultural aid and endemic health problems since tourism would benefit only a few individuals locally. In a similar vein, the local manipulation of power to favor recreational tourism over more basic subsistence industries in the French Alpine commune proved divisive, and split a once cohesive community into political factions.

The economic effects upon the arts and crafts industries merits men-tion. Although McKean suggests that tourism to Bali encourages a regeneration of their traditional industries, it must be pointed out that due to its location, Bali is visited by a comparatively few, affluent tourists who have both the interest and the means to purchase quality crafts. Deitch (chapter 12) similarly shows that tourism has been important in the renascence of Indian arts in the Southwest USA and Loeb (chapter 13) discusses religious art, but none of the authors discuss the "trinketization" of aesthetics created by the marketing in curio shops of cheap goods of nonnative manufacture. Again, the question must be asked: who benefits, and in what proportion? The alien manufacturer, or local entrepreneurs who have the capital to buy, inventory, and sell this "airport art"?

Statistical analyses, the hallmark of the economist and the planner, frequently cite the gross profits to be derived from tourism but gloss the real human costs of tourism residual in the disruption of locally-functioning economic systems without providing sustained, proven alternatives.

The social impacts of tourism are the most fundamental and of particular concern to anthropologists and other social scientists because established scholarship stresses the validity of maintaining group cohesion as a bulwark against disruption with its accompanying internal conflict and stress. In contrast to the dramatic charts of economic growth, the effects of tourism upon the lives and world view of an indigenous population are subtle, and usually recognized only by the people themselves and the anthropologist who was there before-and-after tourism.

The tourist trade does not have to be culturally damaging. Many tourists genuinely want to "get to know the people," and given the ideal circumstances of infrequent visitors who share mutual interests and a common language, tourism can be a bridge to an appreciation of cultural relativity and international understanding. However, catering to guests is a repetitive, monotonous business, and although questions posed by each visitor are "new" to him, hosts can come to feel that they have simply turned on a cassette. Especially late in "the season," it becomes progressively harder to rekindle the spontaneity and enthusiasm that bids guests truly welcome. If the economic goals of mass tourism are realized and the occasional visitor is replaced by a steady influx, individual identities are blurred in the phrase "tourists' who, in turn, may be stereotyped into national character images (Pi-Sunyer, chapter 10) Guests become dehumanized objects to be tolerated for economic gain, and tourists are left with little alternative other than to look upon their hosts with curiosity, as objects. To fulfill social needs, overseas visitors in particular find identity by congregating with their compatriots in bars and lobbies, thereby creating their own reality—their "tourist bubble"—of being physically "in" a foreign place but socially "outside" the culture.

Ethnic and cultural tourism promise to the visitor the opportunity to see at least some portion of the indigenous culture, and apparently some culture traits can be effectively shared with outsiders without disruption. In the several positive examples provided by the case studies, including Balinese rituals, Toraja funerals, and the dances of the King Island Eskimo, the presence of tourists as paying guests heightened local enjoyment and widened participation. However, these were in essence already public rituals. Social stress becomes apparent when tourism invades the privacy of daily lives, as among Kotzebue Eskimo or when, by government fiat, a substantive sacred ritual—here, the *Alarde* of Fuentarrabia, Spain—is made public. To protect the integrity of their value system as the basis of group solidarity, the people whose culture is the object of tourism may try to transfer what Nuñez (part V) terms "front stage" in their lives to a private sector, removed from tourist view. Failing that, their culture is commoditized and sold "by the pound" (Greenwood, chapter 8), making of individuals and their traditions little more than the "quaint customs and queer ideas" of a so-called "primitive" people. The once-proud and independent Masai of Ngoronogoro Crater, who now charge a "£ a car" to visit their mud huts and be photographed, are among many now in that sad plight.

Host-guest relationships are further strained by the mutual failure to understand social roles within respective cultures. Because the tourist *is* leisured, visitors to formerly colonial areas are often perceived to be elite or politically powerful and may be addressed as "Chief" or "Boss," as Pi-Sunyer notes for the British who are dubbed "lor" for milord in Catalan towns. Aboard luxury cruise ships, cabin "boys" and dining stewards of non-White ethnic origins are often regarded as impoverished villagers who have found employment in this lonely life. However, we found on one vessel that the properly silent and unassuming "servants" were Javanese university students from locally prominent families who competed for the temporary positions for language proficiency and for the educational breadth of foreign travel. Uniforms, personality, or glibness are spurious status markers, and subservience can be assumed for varied personal goals.

In this context, even the title of this volume—suggested by Professor Nuñez—may be inappropriate, for "hosts and guests" presupposes social reciprocity between equals. In most of the case studies in parts II and III, considerable social distance obtains between indigenes and visitors, at least in their contact roles, for the latter are leisured and served, albeit for a fee, by the former. Even in complex societies (part IV) in which economic disparities may be mitigated, the tendency to view visitors as "outsiders" is evident. Further research in tourism may provide considerable insight into the locally-perceived social boundaries that delineate, and separate, functioning entities within a larger social group.

Tourism can be disruptive when it reinforces the desire for socioeconomic aspirations that are not locally attainable. Luxurious hotels—the shrines of the Nacirema with big bathrooms, daily clean linens, and sumptuous meals—often stand in stark silhouette against local standards. Thoughtless guests who haul out wallet photos to display their big homes, private pools, or luxury boats only reinforce the personal schisms. The expensive gadgetry that most tourists carry creates new host demands, and provokes new behaviors, ranging from the childish "give money" to the desire for unearned Western status symbols, as among young men in Third World nations who solicit university class rings.

Still more subtle are the effects of tourism upon local social systems as young people in traditionally closed societies observe the freedom of movement of tourists, especially among Western women traveling alone. McKean (chapter 6) suggests that in Bali the economic benefits of tourism simultaneously reinforce family structures, but this topic needs extensive research. Even the so-called "simple" life style of youthful travelers (Teas 1976; Vogt 1975) poses multiple problems. Natives in villages along their overland route through the Middle East to Nepal repeatedly complain that supposedly impoverished "hippies" move in with local families and drain their limited resources, increase the rate of prostitution, and, among local youths, create new and deviant behavioral norms including the use of narcotics. Politically powerless at the local level to rid themselves of these human "parasites," villagers form negative images of Western culture that no amount of government propaganda can mitigate. Other conflicts and stress arise over differences in value systems. The puritan-missionary ethic of Tongans preclude work and drinking on Sunday but the ever-present tourist and his needs, and wishes, have to be met. Everywhere, owners of souvenir shops who want a day "off" are ambivalent about the economic necessity of being open on Sunday or festival days.

Come One or All: The Effects of Numbers

To a host population, tourism is often a mixed blessing: the tourist industry creates jobs and increases cash flow but the tourists themselves can become a physical as well as a social burden, especially as their numbers increase. In addition to the types of tourism suggested earlier, it appears a touristic typology can be drawn, accounting for their numbers, their goals, and their adaptations to local norms (Figure 1).

Explorers quest for discovery and new knowledge but in a shrinking planet, their numbers are sharply restricted. By definition, they are not tourists and traditionally are almost akin to anthropologists living as active participant-observers among "their" people. They easily accommodate to local norms in housing, food, and life-style, bolstered by an amazing array

Figure 1
Frequency of Types of Tourists and Their Adaptations to Local Norms

Type of Tourist	Numbers of Tourists	Adaptations to Local Norms
Explorer	Very limited	Accepts fully
Elite	Rarely seen	Adapts fully
Off-beat	Uncommon but seen	Adapts well
Unusual	Occasional	Adapts somewhat
Incipient Mass	Steady flow	Seeks Western amenities
Mass	Continuous influx	Expects Western amenities
Charter	Massive arrivals	Demands Western amenities

of Western technology including "walkie-talkies," dehydrated foods, portable chemical toilets, oxygen tanks, and medicine.

Elite tourists are few in number and usually include individuals who have been "almost everywhere" and who now, for example, choose to spend us$1500 for a week, to travel by dugout canoe, with a guide, on the Darien River in Panama. They overnight in Cuna Indian homes, sleep in hammocks, get thoroughly bitten by chiggers, eat native food, and chance the tourist "trots." They differ from explorers because they are "touring"—irrespective of whether they planned the trip in great detail in advance or not, they are using facilities that could be prearranged at home by any travel agent. However, they adapt easily with the attitude that "if they [the natives] can live that way all their lives, we can, for a week."

The Off-beat tourist includes those who currently visit Toraja Regency to see the funerals, "trek" in Nepal, or go alone to Point Hope as part of an Alaskan tour. They seek either to (1) get away from the tourist crowds, or (2) heighten the excitement of their vacation by doing something beyond the norm. In general, they adapt well and "put up with" the simple accommodations and services provided for the occasional tourist.

The Unusual tourist visits South America on an organized tour, and buys an optional one-day package tour to visit the Cuna Indians, as an alternate to a day of shopping in duty-free Panama. By chartered small plane, tour members fly to a coastal airstrip where an American guide provides a motorboat to tour two or three off-shore villages; shopping for *molas* (chapter 4) is encouraged and, for a fee, tourists may photograph the women and/or the interiors of their houses. The tourist tends to be "interested" in the "primitive" culture but is much happier with his "safe" box lunch and bottled soda rather than a native feast.

Incipient Mass tourism is a steady flow of people, and although the numbers are increasing, they usually travel as individuals or in small groups. The tourist industry is only one sector of the total economy, and hotels usually have a mix of guests including domestic travelers and businessmen as well as tour groups. This phase of tourist activity is exemplified by many "popular" destinations such as Guatemala, or the summer visitors to the Arctic, the latter secure in their guided tour, heated buses, and modern hotels. These tourists seek Western amenities, and, totally ignoring the fact that at great expense the hotel room in the Arctic has a private bath, many of these visitors would complain about the "ring around the bathtub."

Mass tourism is a continuous influx of visitors who inundate Hawaii most of the year, and other areas at least seasonally, including the European resorts (part III), and Northern Hemisphere "winter vacation" lands such as coastal Mexico and the Caribbean. Mass tourism is built upon middle-class income and values, and the impact of sheer numbers is high. Because of the diversity of individual tastes and budgets, in Europe, for example, the tourists are everywhere—hitchhiking at the roadside, riding trains with their Eurailpasses, or huddled around a guide who is attempting to be heard above the voices of other guides in some crowded museum. With a "you get what you pay for" attitude, they fill up hotels of every category, pensions, and hostels *but*, as a common denominator, they expect a trained, multi-lingual hotel and tourist staff to be alert and solicitous to their *wants* as well as to their needs. The "tourist bubble" of Western amenities is very much in evidence.

Charter tourists arrive en masse, as in Waikiki, and for every 747 planeload, there is a fleet of at least ten big buses waiting to transfer them from the airport to the designated hotel, in the lobby of which is a special Tour Desk to provide itineraries and other group services. Should an individual ask even a simple, "What time does the tour bus go?," the immediate answer is, "What *group* are you with?" The "you" in the reply is spoken as to a "living thing" and not as to a personality. Charter tourists wear name tags, are assigned to numbered buses, counted aboard, and continually reminded: "Be sure to get on the right bus." Given the requisite organization that makes charter tourism a high-volume business, to avoid complaints tour operators and hotels have standardized the services to Western (or Japanese) tastes, and there are "ice machines and soft drinks on every floor." For charter tourists, even destination may be of very little importance, especially if they won the trip as part of an incentive sales program, or it coincides with tax-free convention travel.

The frequency of tourist types seems to approximate a pyramid (Figure 2), in which the bold triangle is a scale of increasing numbers, from top to bottom. An inverse triangle suggests the role of the host culture penetrated by the increased flow of tourists. Explorers and Elite travelers, by virtue of their limited numbers, usually make little impact upon the indigenous culture, for hotels and other services are seldom

Figure 2

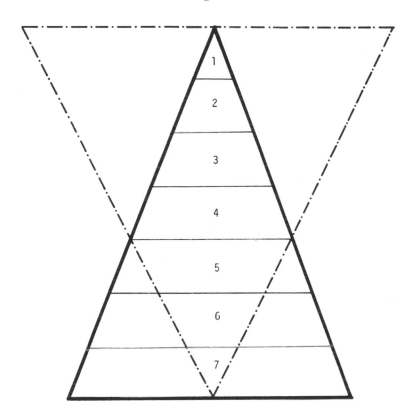

Touristic impact upon a culture ($\triangle$) and local perceptions of visitors ($\triangledown$), expressed in types of tourism: 1. Explorer; 2. Elite; 3. Off-beat; 4. Unusual; 5. Incipient Mass; 6. Mass; 7. Charter.

required. Their presence may be unnoticed except by the few who meet and serve them. The Off-Beat and Unusual tourist commonly stays at roadhouses or hotels that locals also use, and gets about by local transportation (including the use of the school bus, for the very occasional groups who visit). The money they spend is a welcome addition, their presence is seldom disruptive, and children may delight in "talking English" with someone other than their teacher.

However, as the number of tourists progressively increases, it appears different expectations emerge, more facilities are required to handle them, and the native view of outsiders also changes: tourists cease to be individuals and become stereotypes. When charter tourism appears, I suggest that nationality is no longer locally significant, for the only economic base able to generate charter tourism is Western society, whose members are fast approaching cultural and economic homogeneity.

The stressful contacts between hosts and guests also appear to increase, proportionate to the larger numbers. I believe that the critical point in the development of a successful tourist industry occurs at or near the intersection of the two triangles, when members of Incipient Mass tourism "seek" Western amenities, with the result that these facilities begin to be economically or even visually important, as "tourist hotels" and privileged parking places for tour buses. The local culture is probably at the "Y" in the road, and should decide whether to (a) consciously control or even restrict tourism, to preserve their economic and cultural integrity; or (b) to encourage tourism as a desirable economic goal and restructure their culture to absorb it. The first choice has been made by the economically powerful but socially traditional oil states adjacent to and including Saudi Arabia who refuse tourist visas; but elsewhere, given the Third World tendency to "modernize" and their need to provide increased service-type employment for a growing population, tourism will probably expand along the second course. Therefore cultural impact studies are needed to ascertain what elements of a specific culture are "public" and can be marketed as "local color" without serious disruption. The case study by Crystal (chapter 7) is particularly germane because the Indonesian government and travel industry "discovered" that Torajan rituals were a marketable commodity. As a consequence, and without careful planning, Toraja has moved from elite to charter tourism in only five years. At this critical stage, applied anthropologists could assist in assessing the potential social impacts of tourism, the nature of the stresses that may arise, and alternative solutions.

If a group can survive the transition from incipient to full-blown mass tourism, then it may ultimately achieve what Kemper (1976) has termed "tourist culture," or a process of full accommodation, so that large numbers of tourists are part of the "regional scenery," as in charter tourism to Hawaii.

Two other important but unstudied questions emerge from the diagram and the need for planning. To what degree, if any, are the tourists a significant agent of culture change? Impressionistic data suggests that the small numbers of tourists prior to Incipient Mass tourism are of little effect. In 1957, I escorted one of the first American tour parties to visit Nepal. Then, only three vintage vehicles (that had been transported over the mountains by bearers, in parts, and later reassembled) were available for public transport. Fifteen years later, thanks to a highway linking India with Nepal, thousands of cars were in evidence driven by Nepalese for a variety of business and pleasure purposes, and tourism had grown manyfold. However, it was a government decision that opened Nepal to the West, sanctioned economic development and tourism, built the road, and brought in Western goods—not the tourists, most of whom still fly to Kathmandu. Even in the Spanish Basque case, the changed attitude toward the *Alarde* was initiated by the government acting as a culture broker, and not by the tourists.

Therefore, to what degree are the tourists the real culprits for economic and social stress? Or are they visible scapegoats for deep-seated problems of acculturation or, more basically, the problems created by population growth occasioned by better medical care and the associated underemployment. The case study on Tonga is instructive here. Urbanowicz (chapter 5) points out that the islands are overpopulated and that the importation of goods erodes the economy, triggering inflation. Here, tourism is weighed as potential panacea. However, were the strictures of careful scientific analysis removed, it would be easy to conclude that because of forty-four thousand visitors, food prices soared. It is patently easier to blame a nameless, faceless foreigner who comes (and goes) than it is to address and solve fundamental problems.

The Future of Tourism

Tourism is not new. In brief historical perspective, Herodotus collected "ethnographies" about foreign peoples and Augustine emphasized the educational value of travel in his dictum: "The world is a book; he who stays at home reads only one page." However, mass tourism is the product of the post-World War II air age, which has figuratively shortened world distances by expressing them in hours of travel time rather than mileages. The parallel advances in industrial technology have radically altered the human life-style in Europe, America, and Japan by providing both blue and white collar workers with longer vacations, earlier retirement, and more surplus income to spend away from home. The brokers of tourism—governments, carriers, and tour operators—have expertly translated the expanding economy into marketable tour packages, low-cost charters, and off-season fares designed to encourage and sustain foreign travel. These masters of advertising have "psyched" millions of people into mass tourism on the premise that "to take a vacation" means to "go someplace," and that to "stay home and do nothing" is almost immoral and/or an acknowledgement of low economic status (Graburn, chapter 1).

If tourism is not new, neither is it past tense. Those who doubted the Wright brothers' sanity in 1903 could scarcely have envisioned successful manned lunar landings, and some skeptics still doubt interplanetary travel, colonies, and tourism. The human motives for travel are universal, and as more nations achieve industrialization, an increase in tourism can be expected, especially since Kruschke (1974) shows that mass transit and jumbo jets minimize energy consumption while maximizing economic flow. In future decades, greater numbers of Asians and Africans will probably become tourists, just as mass tourism among the Japanese has emerged as a phenomenon of the seventies and great touristic mobility is evident within eastern Europe.

The study of tourism is already almost salvage ethnography. The *Alarde* cannot be restored to its original meaning, and many stereotypes cannot be erased. In this first survey, it appears that the existent forms of tourism tend overall to be more negative than positive in impact, but this is not irremedial. The concept of "progress" is irreversibly moving even so-called Stone Age people in New Guinea and the Amazon into the mainstream of a cash economy, and the visible presence of outsiders who bring and spend money reinforces the ongoing total process of culture change. Anthropologists can gather data, devise more sophisticated typologies, and seek solutions to the problems of stress and conflict, even as I have proposed on the basis of Eskimo data the construction of "model cultures" such as the Polynesian Cultural Center, which preserve the traditional heritage and remove the tourist from interference in local lives. As applied anthropologists, we can examine and plan, through governments and business, a tourist industry that will create true hosts and guests, and benefit both.

Part I

Tourism and Leisure:
A Theoretical Overview

Tourism as a manifestation of leisure presupposes a socioeconomic milieu in which money and time-away-from-work can be accumulated to be spent at will. Tourism as a form of mobility suggests that culturally-sanctioned reasons exist for leaving home to travel. In this theoretical introduction to the nature of tourism, Nelson Graburn in chapter 1 traces the history of tourism and discusses why tourism arose in the forms in which it exists today. In chapter 2, Dennison Nash considers the economic bases for tourism, and why tourism arose in the places where it is found today. Both authors treat tourism as an organized industry, catering to a clientele who have time and money and want to spend them, pleasurably, in leisured mobility or migration.

1

Tourism: The Sacred Journey[1]

NELSON H. H. GRABURN

The human organism ... is ... motivated to keep the influx of novelty, complexity, and information within an optimal range and thus escape the extremes of confusion [This is Tuesday, so it must be Belgium] and boredom [We never go anywhere!].

D. Berlyne (1968, p. 166)

The anthropology of tourism, though novel in itself, rests upon sound anthropological foundations and has predecessors in previous research on rituals and ceremonials, human play, and cross-cultural aesthetics. Modern tourism exemplifies that part of the range of human behavior Berlyne calls "human exploratory behavior," which includes much expressive culture such as ceremonials, the arts, sports, and folklore; as diversions from the ordinary, they make life worth living. Tourism as defined in the introduction does not universally exist but is functionally and symbolically equivalent to other institutions that humans use to embellish and add meaning to their lives. In its special aspect—travel—it has antecedents and equivalents in other seemingly more purposeful institutions such as medieval student travel, the Crusades, and European and Asian pilgrimage circuits.

[1] This paper is derived from a series of revisions made of the remarks that I delivered as a discussant to the Symposium on Tourism, organized by Valene Smith at the American Anthropological Association meetings in Mexico City, November 1974. A draft of this chapter was presented as "The Anthropology of Tourism" in June 1975 and discussed at a meeting of the faculty of the Department of Anthropology at the University of California, Berkeley, to whom I direct my gratitude for many suggestions and criticisms. In addition I owe particular thanks to Sheldon Rothblatt and Ian Dengler of the Department of History at Berkeley, for suggestions concerning the development of tourism in European history, and to Valene Smith I owe special gratitude for her stimulating pursuit of this new branch of anthropology and for particular insightful comments on the nature of travel itself, which are incorporated in this chapter.

17

All Work and No Play Makes Jack a Dull Boy

A major characteristic of our conception of tourism is that it is *not* work, but is part of the recent invention, *re*-creation, which is supposed to renew us for the workaday world, a point emphasized by Nash (chapter 2). Tourism is a special form of play involving travel, or getting away from "it all" (work and home), affording relaxation from tensions, and for some, the opportunity to temporarily become a nonentity, removed from a ringing telephone. Stemming from our peasant European (or East Asian) traditions, there is a symbolic link between staying:working and traveling:playing, which may be expressed as a model (Figure 1).

Figure 1

	Stay "Doing nothing" at home	*Travel* Tourism and/or Recreation
Voluntary	*Stay* "Doing nothing" at home	*Travel* Tourism and/or Recreation
Compulsory/ *Serious*	Work (including school-work and housework)	Occupations requiring travel

Norbeck (1971) points out that in Western society and Japan, and particularly in Northern European-derived cultures, the work ethic is so important that very strong moral feelings are attached to the concepts of work and play, including an association of what is "proper" in time and place. From the model, compulsory or serious activities such as making a living properly take place in the workaday world and preferably "at home." Conversely, "proper" travel is voluntary, does not involve routine work, and therefore is "good for you." A majority of Americans and Europeans see life as properly consisting of alternations of these two modes of existence: living at home and working for longish periods followed by taking vacations away from home for shorter periods. However, some sanctioned recreation is often another kind of "hard work," especially in the rites-of-passage or self-testing types of tourism such as those of youthful travelers. (Teas 1976; Vogt 1975) Many tourists admittedly return home to "rest up" from their vacations.

The model also indicates that staying at home and *not* working is considered improper for normal people. Many would complain that to not go away during vacations is "doing nothing" as if the contrasting "something" must take place away from home or it is "no vacation at all." The very word vacation comes from the Latin *vacare*, "to leave (one's house) empty," and emphasizes the fact that we cannot properly vacation at home.[2] People who stay home for vacation are often looked down upon or pitied, or made to feel left behind and possibly provincial, except for the aged and infirm, small children, and the poor. Within the framework of tourism, normal adults travel and those who do not are disadvantaged.

By contrast, able-bodied adults who do not work when living at home are also in a taboo category among contemporary Western peoples. If they are younger or poorer they are labelled "hippies," "bums," or even "welfare chiselers"; otherwise they may be labelled the "idle rich." In both cases, most people consider them some kind of immoral parasites.

The other combination—work that involves compulsory travel—is equally problematic. Somehow, it is improper to travel when we work, as it is improper to work when we travel. The first category includes traveling salesmen, gypsies, anthropologists, convention goers, stewards, and sailors, and our folklore is full of obscene jokes about such people— for their very occupation is questionable, whatever their behavior! Alternately, people on vacation don't want to work, and justifiably complain about their "busman's holiday." Among them are housewives whose families, to save money, rent a villa rather than stay in a hotel; doctors who are constantly consulted by their co-travelers; and even anthropologists who are just trying to vacation in a foreign country.

To Tour or Not to Tour: That is the Problem

Tourism in the modal sense emphasized here is but one of a range of choices, or styles, of vacation or recreation—those structurally-necessary, ritualized breaks in routine that define and relieve the ordinary. For the present discussion our focus is consciously on the more extreme examples of tourism such as long distance tours to well-known places or visiting exotic peoples, in the most enchanting environments. However, the most minimal kinds of tourism, such as a picnic in the garden, contain elements of the magic of tourism. The food and drink might be identical to that normally eaten indoors, but the magic comes from the movement and the nonordinary setting. Furthermore, it is not merely a matter of money that separates the stay-at-homes from the extensive travelers. Many very wealthy people never become tourists, and most "youthful" travelers are, by Western standards, quite poor.

---

[2]Though the sense of "leaving one's house" now implies a holiday or tourism, it was originally intended to describe the itinerant work of people such as craftsmen, apprentices, and circuit judges. Such changes in meaning from: holiday = to celebrate a holy day in the home community, and vacation = to go off to work, to the present usage reflects the post-Renaissance changes in ideology that account for the rise of modern tourism.

The stay-at-home who participates in some creative activity such as remodeling the house, redoing the garden, or seriously undertaking painting, writing, or sports activities, shares some of the values of tourism in that recreation is involved that is nonordinary and represents a *voluntary* self-indulgent choice on the part of the practitioner. Still others who, through financial stringency or choice, do not go away during vacations but celebrate the released time period by making many short trips, take the nonworkaday aspects of the vacation and construct events for the satisfaction of their personal recreational urges. Even sending the children away to camp may count as a vacation for some parents. Though not tourism in the modal sense, camping, backpacking, renting a lake cottage, or visiting relatives who live far away function as kinds of tourism, although their level of complexity and novelty may not be as high.

The Sacred and the Profane, or A Change is as Good as a Rest

Taking our cue from Berlyne, who suggests that all human life tries to maintain a preferred level of arousal and seeks "artificial sources of stimulation . . . to make up for shortcomings of their environment" (Berlyne 1968, p. 170), tourism can be examined against its complement: ordinary, workaday life. There is a long tradition in anthropology of the structural examination of events and institutions as markers of the passage of natural and social time and as definers of the nature of life itself. This stems partly from Durkheim's (1912) notions of the sacred—the nonordinary experience—and the profane. The alternation of these states and the importance of the transition between them was first used to advantage by Mauss (1898) in his analysis of the almost universal rituals of sacrifice, which emphasized the process of leaving the ordinary, i.e., sacralization that elevates participants to the nonordinary state wherein marvellous things happen, and the converse process of desacralization or return to ordinary life.

Leach (1961, pp. 132–36), in his essay on "Time and False Noses," suggests that the regular occurrence of sacred-profane alternations marks important periods of social life or even provides the measure of the passage of time itself. The passing of each year is usually marked by the annual vacation (or Christmas), and something would be wrong with a year if it didn't occur, as if one had been cheated of time. "The notion that time is a 'discontinuity of repeated contrasts' is probably the most elementary and primitive of all ways of regarding time. . . . The year's progress is marked by a succession of festivals. Each festival represents a temporary shift from the Normal-Profane order of existence into the

Abnormal-Sacred order and back again." The total flow of time has a pattern, which may be represented as in Figure 2.

Figure 2

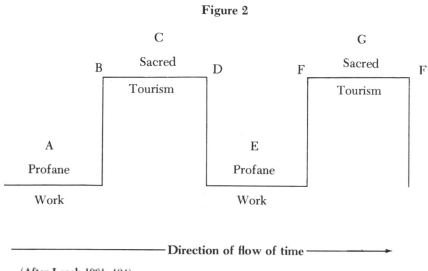

(After Leach 1961: 134)

Vacations involving travel, i.e., tourism, since all "proper" vacations involve travel, are the modern equivalent for secular societies to the annual and lifelong sequences of festivals for more traditional, God-fearing societies. Fundamental is the contrast between the ordinary/compulsory work state spent "at home" and the nonordinary/voluntary "away from home" sacred state. The stream of alternating contrasts provides the meaningful events that measure the passage of time. Leach applies the diagram to "people who do not possess calendars of the Nautical Almanac type," implying that those who have "scientific" calendars and other tacit reminders such as newspapers, radio, and TV rely on the numerical calendar. I believe the "scientific, secular" Westerner gains greater meaning from the personal rather than the numerical in life. We are happier and better recall the loaded symbolic time markers: "That was the year we went to Rome!" rather than "that was 1957," for the former identifies the nonordinary, the festive, or ritual.

Each meaningful event marks the passage of time and thus life itself. Each secular or sacred period is a micro-life, with a bright beginning, a middle, and an end, and the beginnings and endings of these little "lives" are marked by rituals that thrust us irreversibly down life's path. Periods A and C in Figure 2 are both segments of our lives but of a different moral quality. The profane period, A, is the everyday life of the "That's life!" descriptive of the ordinary and inevitable. The period of marginality, C, is another life, which, though extraordinary, is perhaps more "real" than "real life." Vacation times and tourism are described as "I was really living, living it up ... I've never felt so alive," in contrast to the daily humdrum often termed a "dog's life," since dogs are not thought to "vacation." Thus, holidays (holy, sacred days now celebrated by traveling away from home) are what makes "life worth living" as though ordinary life is not life or at least not the kind of life worth living.

Our two lives, the sacred/nonordinary/touristic and the profane/workaday/stay-at-home, customarily alternate for ordinary people and are marked by rituals or ceremonies, as should the beginning and end of lives. By definition, the beginning of one life marks the end of the other. Thus, at time B, we celebrate with TGIF (Thank God it's Friday) and going-away parties, to anticipate the future state and to give thanks for the end of the ordinary. Why else would people remain awake and drink all night on an outbound plane enroute to Europe when they are going to arrive at 6:40 A.M. with a long day ahead of them? The re-entry ritual, time D, is often split between the ending-party—the last night in Europe or the last night at sea—and the welcome home or welcome back to work greetings and formalities, both of which are usually sadder than the going away.

In both cases the transition formalities are ambivalent and fraught with danger or at least tension. In spite of the supposedly happy nature of the occasion, personal observation and medical reports show that people are more accident prone when going away; are excited and nervous, even to the point of feeling sick; and Van Gennep (1914) suggests that the sacralization phase of symbolic death lies within our consciousness. It is implied in phrases such as, "Parting is such sweet sorrow,": or even, "To part is to die a little." Given media accounts of plane, train, and automobile accidents, literally as tourists we are not sure that we will return. Few have failed to think at least momentarily of plane crashes and car accidents or, for older people, dying while on vacation. Because we are departing ordinary life and may never return, we take out additional insurance, put our affairs in order, often make a new will, and leave "final" instructions concerning the watering, the pets, and the finances. We say goodbye as we depart and some even cry a little, as at a funeral, for we are dying symbolically. The most difficult role of a travel agent is to hand someone their tickets to travel to a funeral, for the happy aspect of the journey is entirely absent, leaving only a double sorrow.

The re-entry is also ambivalent. We hate to end vacation, and to leave new-found if temporary excitement; on the other hand, many are relieved to return home safely and even anticipate the end of the tense, emotion-charged period of being away. We step back into our former roles (time E), often with a sense of culture shock. We inherit our past selves like an heir to the estate of a deceased person who has to pick up the threads, for we are *not* ourselves. We are a new person who has gone through re-creation and, if we do not feel renewed, the whole point of tourism has been missed.

For most people the financial aspects of tourism parallel the symbolic. One accumulates enough money with which to vacation, much as one progressively acquires the worries and tedium of the workaday world. Going away lightens this mental load and also one's money. Running out of money at the end of the holiday is hopefully accompanied by running out of cares and worries—with the converse accumulation of new perspectives and general well-being. The latter counteract the workaday worries with memories of the more carefree times. In turn, they stimulate the anticipation and planning for the next vacation, and F and G will be different from B and C because we have experienced times A through E.

While traveling, each day is a micro-model of the same motif. After the stable state of sleep, the tourist ventures forth to the heightened excitement of each new day. Nightfall is often a little sad for the weary tourist; the precious vacation day is spent. Perhaps the often frantic efforts at nightlife on the part of tourists who may never indulge at home are attempts to prolong the "high"—to remain in the sacred, altered state—and delay the "come down" as long as possible.

The Profane Spirit Quest: The Journey Motif in Tourism

Life is a succession of events marked by changes in state. It is both cyclical, in that the same time-marking events occur day after day, year after year, and it is progressive or linear in that we pass through life by a series of changes in status, each of which is marked by a different (though similarly structured) rite of passage. An almost universal motif for the explanation and description of life is the journey, for journeys are marked by beginnings and ends, and by a succession of events along the way.

The travel involved in tourism is more than geographical motion or a symbolically-altered state. For Westerners who value individualism, self-reliance, and the work ethic, tourism is the *best* kind of life for it is sacred in the sense of being exciting, renewing, and inherently self-fulfilling. The tourist journey is a segment of our lives over which we have maximum control, and it is no wonder that tourists are disappointed when their chosen, self-indulgent fantasies don't turn out as planned.

A journey is seldom without purpose, but culturally-specific values determine the goal of travel. In many American Indian societies, a young man left the camp alone to travel and suffer, and to meet the right spirit in order to advance to the next higher status on the journey through life. In India, in medieval Europe, and in the Islamic world, people made difficult pilgrimages to find spiritual enlightenment. Visitors to Las Vegas are also enlightened and often return home with a flat wallet, having sacrificed dearly for their pleasures.

Even if one regards tourism as voluntary, self-interested travel, the tourist journey must be morally justified by the home community. Because the touristic journey lies in the nonordinary sphere of existence, the goal is symbolically sacred and morally on a higher plane than the regards of the ordinary workaday world. Tourists spend substantial sums to achieve the altered state—money that could be invested for material gain or alternately used to buy a new car or redecorate their home.

"Human exploratory behavior," says Berlyne (1968, p. 152), "is behavior whose principle function is to change the stimulus field and introduce stimulus elements that were not previously accessible." Thus, as art uplifts and makes meaningful the visual environment, so tourism provides an aesthetically appropriate counterpoint to ordinary life. Tourism has a stated, or unstated but culturally determined, goal that has changed through the ages. For traditional societies the rewards of pilgrimages were accumulated grace and moral leadership in the home community. The rewards of modern tourism are phrased in terms of values we now hold up for worship: mental and physical health, social status, and diverse, exotic experiences.

In medieval Europe, travel was usually for avowedly religious purposes, as were pilgrimages and crusades; for ordinary people travel was difficult and dangerous, and even for the ruling classes, who also traveled for reasons of state, travel required large protective entourages. Those who could afford it often retired to retreats or endowed religious institutions in their spiritual quest for the ultimate "truth." It was the Renaissance that changed the world view by bringing forth the kind of consciousness that provides the cosmological foundation for modern tourism: the idea that truth lay outside the mind and spirit. In all fields this outward, materialist turning, this urge to explore and understand, showed up in such new forms as the new astronomy, the explorations, the new historical and scientific investigations of the fifteenth and sixteenth centuries. Means of land and sea transportation improved, and curiosities and exciting tales of discovery were brought back from all over the world.

By the seventeenth century the aristocracy and the wealthy were traveling to and in Europe to see the evidence of old historical truths and to converse with the discoverers of the new geographical and scientific ones. For eighteenth-century England the Grand Tour became a fully developed institution; the tourist motive for going abroad was not only cultural but highly educational and political. The post-medieval decline of the universities and the great public and grammar schools as institutions of liberal learning meant the rise of alternative means of instruction: the tutor and the tour were the two principal ones. Milord went abroad not only to see the classical sights, but to learn languages, manners and accomplishments, riding, dancing, and other social graces. The tour was deemed a very necessary part of the training of future political and administrative leaders, as well as patrons of the arts.

The Industrial Revolution took hold at the end of the eighteenth century and set in motion further changes affecting travel and tourism. It enhanced the need for scientific exchange and learning, for trade and raw materials, and for imperial expansion. (See Nash, chapter 2.) In addition it gave rise to the romanticism that glorified nature and the countryside, ideas stemming partly from the formerly neoclassical pastoral games of British and French aristocracy. As the Grand Tour in its elitist form declined in significance, new modes of transportation and new political arrangements made travel safer and cheaper for the bourgeoisie.

Thomas Cook, a Baptist minister and social reformer, taking advantage of the new railway system, in 1842 organized an all-inclusive tour to a temperance meeting. Other successful and morally uplifting tours followed; Cook combined his visions of democratic travel and the promotion of sobriety, with the chance to profit financially from the opportunities for taking townspeople to the countryside or abroad. His tours expanded from the Lake District, Wales, the Isle of Man, and Scotland, to reach France, Italy, and the glories of the Middle East by the 1870s. Promoting railway expansion everywhere, and the standardization of hotels and restaurants, Cook's coupons and later traveler's checks made travel easy for the masses, opening approved parts of the world to the inspection and edification of the educated middle classes. Imitators arose in Europe and America and travel-made-easy followed closely on the heels of imperial and commercial expansion.

Displaced from their command of the historical and cultural centers of Europe and the Far East, the aristocracy pioneered another form of tourism, which was later to become a form of mass escape: the ruling families and the very wealthy began to leave their palaces and their homes for recreational and health reasons on a regular, yearly basis. Not since Roman times had this been done on such a massive scale. Prior to the eighteenth century the royal families regularly moved between their several castles, for the hunting and falconry seasons; and after the Renaissance a larger part of the ruling stratum began to take "cures" at spas within their own countries, such as at Bath or Baden-Baden. These were the forerunners of the strongly re-creational theme in tourism.

Starting in the eighteenth century and becoming the mode in the nineteenth century, luxurious rivieras were built along the Mediterranean and Adriatic shores to house the royalty and idle rich from the nations of Northern and Eastern Europe. Like the national health spas they displaced, these resorts were often only thinly-disguised excuses for gambling and more lascivious pleasures. As the winter abodes for the Northerners were opened in the warmer South, this pleasure-seeking trend led to the establishment of Monte Carlo and other casino resorts. By the beginning of the twentieth century even rich Americans came to partake of the idle winter life-style, and great liners and trains made long distance travel safe all over the world for those who could afford to pay.

The final cultural revolution that set the stage for the mass tourism of today was prompted by the First World War. Not only did this catastrophe pauperize the elite rivieras, but it did away with many of the ruling families and other European aristocrats whose fortunes had fueled the life-style. By the 1920s the newly wealthy Americans came to be the dominant tastemakers, not only in Paris but along the Cote d'Azure. The winter vacation retreats of the elitist "international set" became summer pleasure resorts. No longer was nature shunned and white skin universally admired. American experience in Florida and the Caribbean, along with an increasing realization of the healthy aspects of exposure to sunlight (pioneered by the discovery of Vitamin D and German experiments in World War I) made the suntan fashionable. An air of freedom from the old mores and the overthrow of the (superficially) stuffy old aristocracies brought out the excesses of the 1920s in every sphere of life. Features of the life-style of common people were studiedly imitated, folk music and jazz were heard, and a snobbish kind of "slumming" that equated dark skins and sexuality provided a spark for these changing attitudes, which are now well nigh universal. During this period aspects of "ethnic" tourism and anthropology itself became popular. Though the Depression put a lid on some of the excesses, the themes of nature, recreation, and ethnic interest were securely added to the previous cultural, historical, and educational motivations that underlie tourism today.

Nature Tourism and Cultural Tourism

Symbolically, Nature tourism has two different manifestations, both of which are strongly with us. The purest form is represented by Environmental tourism (McKean, chapter 6) where varied aspects of the land, sea, and sky perform their magical works of renewal—it's the "pure" air, the soothing waters, or the vast vistas that are curative. In its most extreme form the absence of humans is a factor: "There I was, the only person for miles . . . alone in the woods." If Nature is curative, performs magical recreations and other miracles otherwise assigned to Lourdes, God, or *gurus*, the medicine is weakened by the presence of other humans. To share is to lose power. Recently, Environmental tourism has bifurcated into Ecological tourism (see Figure 3), wherein the tourist tries to leave as little effect from his visit as possible—concentrating perhaps on photographs and tape recordings—rather than the variant, Hunting and Gathering tourism. The latter includes environmental tourism and nature appreciation, including hunting, wherein little thought is given to impact, and at least some souvenirs are brought home.

To others, however, Nature in the "raw" is nice but somewhat boring because there is no dialogue; Nature is unresponsive even when threatened by capture on film or violation by campfire. Another way to get close to Nature's bosom is through her children, the people of Nature, once labelled Peasant and Primitive peoples and considered creatures of instinct. Interaction with them is possible and their naturalness and simplicity exemplifies all that is good in Nature herself. What more exciting and uplifting experience could one imagine than to share a few words or, even better, a meal and a bed with such delightful people? Again, the magic is spoiled by the presence of too many other tourists. The approach to Nature through Her People is Ethnic tourism (Swain, chapter 4, Smith, chapter 3), whereas the use of Nature for her specified attributes of sun (tanning), wind (sailing), snow (skiing), surf (fishing), and sky (gliding) is Recreational Tourism.

The relation between the various forms of tourism is diagrammed in Figure 3.

Figure 3

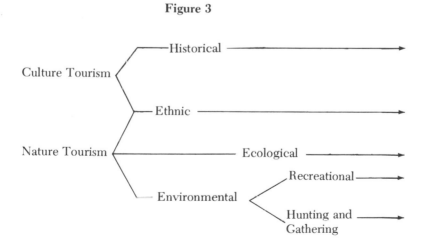

Each touristic type has its own special scale of values and its hierarchy of prestigious places, i.e., those having more "magic." However, two or more kinds are frequently combined in one trip. For instance, one might visit the museums and cathedrals in Europe (Historical) and then go to Northern Scandinavia to see the Midnight Sun (Environmental) and the Lapps (Ethnic), or one might combine the Historical, Cultural, and Ethnic by touring India. Certain types of tourism are closer in fact and function than others; for instance, Ethnic tourism is a combination of Culture and Nature tourism. Others are conceptually further removed, such as Cultural tourism, with its emphases on the great traditions, in contrast to Hunting and Gathering tourism represented by African hunting safaris. Within these categories of tourism, there are an almost infinite variety of substyles including class, and ethnic and national variations. The rush of urban Germans to the southern and western coasts of Europe is different from the Scandinavians' junket to the Adriatic; the French take to their countryside quite differently than do the British to theirs. The levels of preferred arousal and the nature of the touristic goals vary almost as much by age group and personality as by national origin and sex, and cannot all be described here.

The Holy Grail: Symbols and Souvenirs

Few tourists come home from a vacation without something to show for it, whether it is matchcovers, folk art, or rolls of exposed film. The type of vacation chosen and the proof that we really did it reflect what we consider "sacred." The Holy Grail is the myth sought on the journey, and the success of a holiday is proportionate to the degree that the myth is realized.

Souvenirs are tangible evidences of travel that are often shared with family and friends, but what one really brings back are memories of experiences. As Carpenter (1973, p. 17) puts it so well:

> The connection between symbol and things comes from the fact that the symbol—the word or picture (or artifact)—helps give the 'thing' its identity, clarity, definition. It helps convert given reality into experienced reality, and is therefore an indispensable part of all experience.

The chosen style of tourism has its counterpart in types of souvenirs. The Environmental tourist is usually content with pictures and postcards but the Hunter and Gatherer wants rocks and sea shells, or even pieces of an archaeologic ruin. Bolder members bring back heads or even whole animals to stuff, to testify to their vacation glory. The Ethnic tourist rarely has the opportunity to bring home the "whole Primitive" but is content with arts or crafts, particularly if they were made by the ethnic for his/her own (preferably sacred) use. Items made specifically for the tourist market have much less symbolic appeal, and this authenticity is often overstated (Graburn 1976).

The limitations of tourist travel, especially for jet-setters who cover so much ground so fast, diminishes experienced reality and the momentos and souvenirs serve as cues by which to relive the experience at a slower pace. In photography, to get oneself in the picture is common to tourists of both Occidental and Oriental origins as evidence of identity and placement. If they are not afraid of soul-loss, native peoples often project themselves into tourist's pictures as a momentary escape from their environment and as a means of "getting into" the imagined happiness and affluence of the tourist's home situation. As one improverished African in a remote ex-colonial country said to the anthropologist who was taking last-minute photos of all his informants, "And when you develop the photo, please make me come out white."

"Wish you were here"

Tourists almost ritualistically send postcards from faraway places to those whom they wish to impress as well as to those they love. Partly, it is to let the latter know they are well and enjoying themselves, and partly to be remembered and awaited. Conversely, the sacred charisma rubs off; those left at home feel partly uplifted, though perhaps jealous, when they receive such cards and may even display them near their work desks or on bulletin boards. The next best thing to traveling is to know someone who did.

Yet if they did go along, had already been there, or were about to visit the same area, there would be heightened excitement in sharing, which parallels Huizinga's (1950, p. 12) observations about play:

> The [co-traveling] community tends to become permanent even after it is over . . . the feeling of 'being apart' together in an exceptional situation, of sharing something important, or mutually withdrawing from the rest of the world and rejecting the usual norms, retains its magic beyond the duration . . . surrounds itself with an air of secrecy . . . dressing up . . . disguised together as other beings.

Even aboard jets, we all know the "stranger on the train" phenomenon, or the "shipboard romance" that didn't last. The magic of sharing a touristic activity lasts only when (1) the event is really nonordinary; (2) participants initially share similar value systems; and most importantly, when (3) they already know each other or are in the same profession or institution. The popularity of conferences (held in vacation settings such as Hawaii or Disneyland), or touring groups of farmers or attorneys as well as "in-house" travel planned for factory workers, attest to the fact that the magic of tourism is enhanced by group identity and, later, reliving the experience with associates. Analogous to the truism that "Distance is to love as wind to fire; it enflames the great and puts out the feeble," experiences shared at a distance strengthen relationships between the like-minded but may push others further apart.

Tourism is rife with snobbery, and within each of its basic forms hierarchies of rank and prestige exist that illustrate the continuum and the contrast between the ordinary/nonordinary. Obviously, what is extraordinary for some—for a rural Britisher, a trip up to London to the theater—may be an almost daily affair for others (a London suburbanite). Thus one man's excitement may be another man's boredom and threshold from which the more urbane measures his sacred.

To measure the hierarchies of prestige, the journey motif suggests that the further removed from the ordinary, the better; the sacred/profane motif suggests that the more extra-ordinary, the better; while the time measuring aspect suggests that the longer the period or more frequent the trips, the better. Each theme can be translated into the one-upmanship of the genre of tourists. For the young, rebellious Ethnic and Environmental tourist (or nontourist as they proudly claim), distant and exotic places such as Kathmandu or Goa are "in," and prestige is enhanced by the length of uninterrupted travel.

Others of a more rugged bent, the elite tourists, emphasize the struggle against Nature, and gain their prestige through solitude, and a high degree of self-reliance in the communion. Driving alone from Cairo to Capetown, or daring raft trips down wild rivers are pale imitations of what were once rugged individual efforts worthy of Explorer's Club membership.

A common theme in these contrasting examples of Ethnic and Environmental tourism is the emphasis on the "spirit quest" or the self-testing, often maturing, pioneer endurance that they both effect in their different ways. This spirit quest may be imagined, for Cohen (1973) suggests that modern drifter-tourism is as safe and commonplace as riding a New York subway. Nevertheless, these apparently dangerous and effortful styles of tourism seem to attract the young, as a kind of self-imposed rite of passage to prove to themselves and to their peers that they can make their own way in life—probably never to repeat it later on. Or, this high adventure attracts the affluent, often highly-educated middle-aged for whom social constraints and a Depression denied their youthful wanderlust. Money is not the criterion of prestige. For the youthful traveler, Cohen (1973) notes that voluntary poverty is the sacred/non-ordinary quality of tourism for the middle-class "Nomads from Affluence".

In sharp contrast is the tourism of the timid—often parents of the youthful travelers—who have money and don't mind spending it, as long as they can carry the home-grown "bubble" of their life style around with them. They rely on the advice and blandishments of tourist brokers in order to live as comfortably as at home or even more luxuriously, for the holiday is nonordinary, and one should eat, drink, and spend beyond the rules of the ordinary. Though undoubtedly enchanted by the view of God's handiwork through the pane of the air-conditioned bus or the porthole, they worship "plumbing that works" and "safe" water and food. The connection with the unfamiliar is likely to be purely visual, and filtered through sunglasses and a camera viewfinder. These tourists are likely to have the greatest impact on the culture and environment of the host peoples both by virtue of their greater numbers and by their demands for extensions of their home environments for which they are willing to pay handsomely. Cohen (1973) points out that mass drifter-tourism stimulates the hosts to maintain specially designed receptive institutions, even if the travelers are unaware of the degree to which they are being catered.

Although the outward rationale for tourism has as many variations as there are tourists, the basic motivation seems to be the human need for re-creation. Tourism is one manifestation of the fulfillment of this need—one, that because of the more affluent economic status of the developed world, is enabling many people to see "how the other half lives."

University of California, Berkeley

2

Tourism as a Form of Imperialism[1]

DENNISON NASH

A concern with tourism by anthropologists would seem to be related to a general interest in culture contact and sociocultural change that has animated so much of our sociocultural inquiry in recent years. The tourist, like the trader, the employer, the conqueror, the governor, the educator, or the missionary, is seen as the agent of contact between cultures and, directly or indirectly, the cause of change particularly in the less developed regions of the world.

Recent analyses of culture contact have suggested that an understanding of the immediate contact situation may not be enough to fully comprehend it. Some reference to larger contexts may be required. Adams (1974, p. 240), for example, states, "Both social change and social continuity require interactive processes with the significant interactions in some respects confined to single communities, in others to multiple groups in time ordered settings, in others to whole regions, in still others to interregional contacts whose historical role was far out of proportion to their limited scale and frequency." And Magubane (1973) has pointed out the too-restricted scope of many studies of culture contact in Africa, and called for a consideration of the broader context of colonialism in which such contact occurs. He is one of a number of scholars who have brought theories of imperialism to bear on the kind of contact situation that has tended to preoccupy anthropologists. Though his and much other anthropological work on imperialism tends to be of Marxist persuasion and on the side of the underdogs in the Third World and elsewhere, one need not be a Marxist or a revolutionary to see the easy applicability of concepts of imperialism to such situations.

[1] The author wishes to thank Robert Bee, Scott Cook, James Faris and Bernard Magubane for discussions that helped in the preparation of this chapter. Assistance also was provided by the University of Connecticut Research Foundation, the Camargo Foundation, and the Centre des Hautes Etudes Touristiques (Rene Baretje, director) in Aix-en-Provence.

33

Imperialism

At the most general level, theories of imperialism refer to the expansion of a society's interests abroad. These interests—whether economic, political, military, religious, or some other—are imposed on or adopted by an alien society, and evolving intersocietal transactions, marked by the ebb and flow of power, are established. Such transactions will have various consequences for the societies involved. As I have indicated elsewhere (Nash 1970), a formulation of the imperialistic process at the present state of our knowledge does not require the acceptance of a particular interest (e.g., the economic) as crucial, nor does it require the notion of the unwanted imposition of some interest on an alien society. The possibility of voluntary acceptance by a native people and voluntary participation in transactions that further expatriate interests are an essential part of this conception of imperialism.

Changes in the relative power of the partners in an imperialistic transaction can transform or even lead to the breakdown of the relationship between them. Whatever happens between the partners will have greater or lesser consequences for their societies. The trading of such consequences in the less powerful partner society is, as this book demonstrates, grist for the anthropologist's mill. It is the nature of the sociohistorical processes which lead to these consequences which is less well understood.

Tourism as a Form of Imperialism

If the investigation of tourism is to be truly anthropological, it should not be confined to a narrow range of societies or contact situations but should endeavor to comprehend the phenomenon wherever it occurs. Perhaps it will not be possible to consider all tourism in a single theoretical scheme, but theoretical formulations of tourism should be as broadly applicable as possible. Since there appears to be no *a priori* reason why the principles governing internal tourism and external tourism should differ, the field of investigation ought, at least at the outset, to include both. An anthropologically useful theory of tourism would have the potential to embrace such varied events as skiing at St. Moritz, vacation activities on the Black Sea, New York's special relationship with the Catskill Mountains, the Victorian English winter community in Nice, ancient Romans in their country villas, thermalism in Ancient Greece, and possibly Muslim pilgrimages. In all such cases the focus of the inquiry ought to be on tourist-host relationships involving transactions between groups.

The association of tourism with industrial or modern society has been noted by a number of authors (Boyer 1972; Enzenberger 1962; Greenwood 1972; Nuñez 1963). However, if one takes tourism to imply leisured migration and all that is associated with it, as does Boyer, then it is difficult not to find it in preindustrial societies (Sigaux 1966, pp. 9–19). There is a problem in isolating leisure in hunting and gathering societies, but some aspects of their perpetual migrations (e.g., the visit to religious places by Australian aborigines) might be considered a sort of proto-tourism. In Ancient Athens, where citizens had much leisure time, Duchet (1949) states that people traveled for pleasure or education, sport, religious purposes (festivals or pilgrimages to sanctuaries), and reasons of health (spas). Ancient Romans vacationed in country villas. Medieval pilgrims, a possible variety of tourist, overcame obstacles to travel to visit religious centers. And some French monarchs in what was an essentially agricultural society were noted for their visits to and between country châteaux. It seems clear, therefore, that tourism is not totally confined to industrial or modern society; but it also is true that only in such a society does it become a pervasive social phenomenon.

The necessary cause of tourism, as it has been defined here, appears to be a level of productivity sufficient to sustain leisure. If productivity is the key to tourism, then any analysis of touristic development without reference to productive centers that generate tourist needs and tourists is bound to be incomplete. Such metropolitan centers have varying degrees of control over the nature of tourism and its development, but they exercise it—at least at the beginning of their relationship with tourist areas—in alien regions. It is this power over touristic and related developments abroad that makes a metropolitan center imperialistic and tourism a form of imperialism.

It may be useful to have an extreme, almost ideal-typical example in mind in beginning to explore the touristic process. The North American vacationer who insists on American fast-food hamburgers, coffee with his meals, hot running water in his bedroom and the use of the English language is a familiar image. Here is a person from a highly industrialized country expecting, even demanding, that his vacation life abroad meet expectations he has come to take for granted at home. Beyond this vacationer there often stands a metropolitan touristic infrastructure that, in effect, sees that his expectations are met. The tourist and his supporting infrastructure engage in transactions with a native people. Such transactions, which are marked by a disparity of power, may involve not only individuals of a given touristic phenomenon but will depend also on the relative significance of different social structures for understanding it.

The touristic process involves the generation of the touristic impulse in productive centers, the selection or creation of tourist areas to serve their needs, and the development of transactions between the productive centers and tourist areas. These transactions, centering on the host-guest relationship, have various consequences for the parties involved and develop according to laws we have yet to discover. This chapter makes some preliminary observations about different aspects of this touristic process and suggests some research questions that are likely to provide significant information about it.

The Generation of Tourism

As mentioned above, the origins of tourism are to be found in conditions of higher productivity, especially in industrial society. It is questionable if there is tourism among hunters and gatherers, and there is only a slight amount in agricultural societies. Higher productivity, associated with technological advances, has made possible the development of leisure classes as well as an improved material apparatus for travel. Tourism arises when people use the available means of travel for leisure-time pursuits. At the point in the industrial cycle where significant tourism appears, people are beginning to live in a society where productivity is great enough, the horizons broad enough, and the social mobility significant enough to nourish the touristic impulse. Though people could stay home in their spare time, they now have the desire and an increasing opportunity to tour. Who has the opportunity will, of course, depend on the distribution of leisure and resources in a society, but in an advanced industrial society widespread tourism is to be expected. Many people in such a society have come to expect a trip or a vacation away from home at some point in the year. Such expectations may be temporarily frustrated by economic conditions, political events, or military developments, but the aspirations have been normalized and are not likely to disappear so long as the industrial base remains.

What are the factors which generate the touristic impulse? It would seem advisable to divide this question into two parts: (1) What are the factors that tend to produce leisure? (2) What are the factors promoting migration during leisure time? Undoubtedly, productivity is associated with leisure, and attention to economic factors, as a somewhat ethnocentric Veblen (1899) has shown, is important in explaining it. One might posit a universal need for variation or "recreation" in humans, as does Graburn in this volume, but unless people are freed from the work routine by adequate productivity, there will be no possibility of satisfying that need. Also, such a need probably would be to some extent acquired and therefore would vary with social conditions. Here one is reminded of the characteristics of the so-called modern mentality that a number of authors (Inkeles 1969; Lerner 1958) have attempted to describe. A "modern" person has broader horizons and is prone to travel. If he lives in a modern city he may want to flee from its problems, a point emphasized by those authors (Boyer 1972; Duchet 1949) who implicate urbanism with tourism. Whether or not he migrates in his leisure time will depend on opportunities and facilities to travel abroad.

Without facilities for travel, of course, there would be no migration and hence no tourism. In the Middle Ages travelers had to move on poor roads, cross innumerable frontiers, pay many tolls, endure brigands, and put up with scarce and inadequate lodging. Indeed, as Gaulis and Creux (1975, p. 11) point out, *Pendant les siècles, le voyage n'était qu'une suite de contretemps* ("Throughout the centuries, travel was a series of difficulties"). Modern means of transport have changed all this and have opened up vast touristic possibilities. Boyer (1972, p. 134) has argued that the coming of a railroad usually produced a dramatic increase in visitors to a tourist area. Improved means of transport also would seem to be related to an increasing desire to travel.

In summary, the factors associated with the appearance and development of tourism are an increased productivity that creates leisure, psychological mobility associated with broadened horizons, and improved transport and communication facilities. Obviously, these factors are interrelated, but a greater weight probably should be assigned to productivity than to the others. Any so-called touristic "need" ought to be derivable from these factors. As indicated above, I believe that positing a universal need for variation of experience takes us only a short way in our attempt to explain tourism. Any such need probably varies with social conditions operating on the potential tourist in a negative way, as does a crowded, alienating urban existence, or positively, as with a modern, liberal education.

The Creation of Tourist Areas

Touristic expansion takes place according to the needs and resources of productive centers and their people. What tourist realms tend to be selected or created, and what purposes they will serve, vary with their accessibility as well as with the character of the centers involved. More southern regions, for example, often have become vacation meccas for the peoples of northern industrial nations; and the kind of services they are expected to perform or wishes they must fulfill often are given in the travel literature. The young Goethe (1962) thought that Italy offered a particular kind of fulfillment for romantic northern souls, and Thomas Mann (1930) saw Venice as a place where constricted northerners opened up and came apart. One cannot begin to account for the character of the Costa del Sol without reference to northwestern Europe; turn-of-the-century Nice without reference to England and Csarist Russia; or Miami Beach and the Catskills without referring to New York City. Of course, tourist areas are not entirely the creation of metropolitan productive centers. Native peoples sometime take the initiative and often actively collaborate in their establishment. Even then, however, they take as a significant point of reference the availability and needs of certain metropolitan centers. To the extent that they take these into account, they are collaborating in the touristic expansion (and thus the imperialism) of such centers.

What are the factors causing certain alien regions to become touristically linked with specific metropolitan centers? Undoubtedly, cost must be considered. Forster (1964, p. 219) points out that adequate and cheap transport must be available and that the tourist area must have a slightly lower standard of living than the region from which it draws tourists. Though this generalization would seem to fail in a number of cases where tourists migrate to urban or more industrialized areas, it does point to the significance of cost in accounting for the selection or creation of tourist areas. Forster also suggests that such places must be different enough to satisfy the touristic impulse. Such differences, however, must be compatible with the touristic needs of specific metropolitan centers. Such compatibility sometimes is described as charm, beauty, or excitement, but it must always be assessed in terms of metropolitan expectations or needs. Not too many years ago, Puerto Vallarta was a relatively isolated, sleepy little fishing village, but it became the answer to some metropolitan touristic dreams involving sun, sea, and an unspoiled, picturesque landscape inhabited by a friendly, easy-going people. At the close of World War II the area that is now Vail, Colorado, was a mountain wilderness distinguished by, among other things, its deep and long-lasting snow cover. Its potential for satisfying the needs of a nation experiencing the beginnings of a skiing boom was recognized by a group of entrepreneurial businessmen who mobilized the necessary resources to transform the area into a modern ski resort. Both Puerto Vallarta and Vail had features of potential touristic significance for certain metropolitan centers. They were chosen and, with the collaboration of their inhabitants, developed because of their compatibility with metropolitan dreams. Their fate thus became linked with exogenous forces over which they were to have less and less control.

We need to know more about the forces that generate specific touristic aspirations because they will tell us which places in the world are likely to come under what metropolitan touristic pressures. The boom in pleasure skiing is an example. How did it come about? What needs in a society and its people does skiing serve? If we know that people want to feel free and daring and that they can feel that way on skis, it is possible to chart the areas of the world where appropriate ski resorts might arise. Whether or not they would be developed would depend on a number of factors, among them transportation, skiing technology (including cable cars, snow making machines, ski equipment, etc.), the collaboration of native people, and certain economic resources. In considerations of this kind one might want to probe deeply into motivations and their sources. If, as Farber (1954) has suggested, travel is conceived to be a "magic helper," why is a certain kind of travel to a certain place thought to be more efficacious? Or if, as Enzenberger (1962) has argued, one function of tourism is to help people flee from distasteful work roles, why is flight in a certain direction thought to be more desirable? Here, methods of the market researcher, such as those being used in studies commissioned by the United States Travel Service (U.S. Department of Commerce 1972), can be of use in making predictions.

In any transactional view of imperialism one cannot forget the role played by native peoples. I have suggested above that some native peoples may be rather active partners in the creation of tourist resorts. What are the forces causing them to seek out or consent to touristic development? Where disparities of power are very great, as in the case of military conquest, such a question may be of little significance, but it is not possible to ignore the fact that the development of a tourist area usually depends on some local cooperation. This is especially apparent when a powerful country such as Soviet Russia chooses not to cooperate. In the post–World War II period when other countries eagerly pursued the tourist "dollar," the Russians resisted the intrusion of international tourism into their homeland; they began to cooperate only after a relaxation of the Cold War and their own development of what they considered to be adequate touristic controls and facilities.

A society may use its power not only to prevent or promote the establishment of touristic relationships, but also to select what for it seem to be advantageous ones. Some kind of maximizing model such as that used by Barth and his associates (1963; 1967) would be particularly helpful in analyzing early and later choices of indigenous peoples in the development of tourism in their societies. With time, their power to shape the course of touristic transactions with metropolitan centers would vary. This in turn would affect the existence and nature of the tourism that depends for its development on their cooperation.

Touristic Transactions

With the creation of a tourist realm, various social interactions are set up between tourists, their hosts, and the organizations and societies they represent. These transactions, which can be long or short term, cyclical (e.g., seasonal) or noncyclical, and simple (as in a tourist-host relationship) or complex (involving an elaborate touristic organization), come to be based on understandings about how the parties involved will treat each other and on the conditions that could bring about the termination of the relationships. If a native people are murderous, nasty, disease-ridden, or embroiled in political conflict, the relationship could be threatened by metropolitan dissatisfactions. If, on the other hand, the brokers of tourism attempt to interfere in internal political affairs or desecrate local institutions, the hosts might seek to end the touristic relationship. Guerrilla fighters sometimes deliberately violate the implicit terms of a touristic contract in order to further their political aims, and metropolitan centers may restrict or end the flow of tourists to a given area if the terms of their contract are not honored. Similar to any other social relationship, the relationship between tourists and their hosts includes certain understandings that must be agreed and acted upon if it is to be maintained. What are these terms, and what are the conditions defining them?

Touristic transactions are defined, first, by the condition of strangerhood. The tourist is almost an ideal-typical example of what Simmel (1950, pp. 402-7) had in mind when he formulated his conception of the stranger. Simmel saw the stranger as a temporary sojourner who does not share the essential qualities of host group life. As a result, interaction between him and the hosts tends to take place on a more general, impersonal level. Simmel (p. 407) says, "Strangers are not really conceived as individuals, but as strangers of a particular type." The tendency to generalize or categorize, which also characterizes strangers' conceptions of their hosts, suggests the type of relationship common in the modern world.

Not only do strangers and their hosts treat each other as types but also as objects. Where disparities of power are great, as in the early stages of colonialism, this can lead to prejudice and discrimination by the colonizers and a variety of familiar responses among the colonized (Fanon 1968). People who treat others as objects are less likely to be controlled by the constraints of personal involvement and will feel freer to act in terms of their own self-interest. This tendency often is tempered by the development of controls involving force or legal mechanisms and the intervention of external agencies such as governments or military bodies. This is one reason why transactions involving tourists usually cannot be successfully analyzed without reference to broader social structures with which they are connected.

Strangers are notable also for their tendency to clump together with their fellows (Nash 1970, pp. 108-22). Finding themselves uninvolved and often confused in a foreign situation, they may begin to build a familiar social network involving people from home. As the gap between this stranger group and the hosts solidifies, certain intergroup specialists such as the diplomat, the community relations expert, and the concierge, or organizations such as the World Association of Travel Agents, must be mobilized if successful stranger-host relationships are to continue. These mediators, who have been called "culture brokers" play an increasingly important role as social differentiation proceeds. Any analysis of the tourist-host relationships, therefore, probably will require a consideration of some group of stranger-tourists and the agents and organizations that mediate their relationships with the hosts.

The terms of tourist-host transactions are defined not only by the condition of strangerhood but by the nature of tourism itself. As a tourist, a person is at leisure, which means that he is not bent on shaping the world, only experiencing or toying with it. If the tourist is to pursue peculiarly touristic goals, others must perform more utilitarian functions. To put it more succinctly, others must serve while the tourists plays, rests, cures, or mentally enriches himself. Accordingly, he finds himself separated from those in the touristic infrastructure who serve him by the different, if complementary, nature of the activities specified in the touristic contract. The hosts can be a nation of hotel-keepers perfectly adapted to service, as in Switzerland, or Muscovite waitresses grudgingly performing it, but the work-leisure distinction continues to separate them from their guests. Even if they come from the same cultures and understand each other perfectly, the basic attitudes they bring to their relationship with each other are distinguished along lines specified by the differences between work and leisure. The difficulties attendant upon the development of liaisons between hotel guests and employees provide an illustration of the social barriers involved. Even in new club-style resorts, where the difference between host and guest is minimized, it cannot be eliminated.

In sum, tourists are separated from their hosts by the facts of strangerhood, the work-leisure distinction, and whatever cultural differences obtain in a particular situation. Any viable touristic contract must take into account these facts and make some provision for dealing with them. The tourist is not usually expected to make the adaptations necessary for involving himself in the essential life of the host society. This "privilege," which is resented by some tourists, may be one reason for the combination of envy and disdain shown by more acculturated expatriates for their tourist countrymen (Nash 1970, p. 129). But if the tourist is not expected to make the adaptations necessary for him to get along in a more or less foreign situation, who is? That burden tends to fall on the hosts, and it is one of the prices they pay for having tourists in their midsts. It is apparent that many of them willingly—even eagerly—pay this price. Here again, some kind of maximizing model derived from exchange theory would assist in understanding host calculations; but the fact that native people usually "choose" to take on the additional responsibilities of adjustment necessary for dealing with tourists suggests that the incentives or constraints in the direction of touristic development are very great and that the tourist benefits in his adaptations vis-a-vis hosts from the considerable economic, political, or military power of the metropolitan center he represents. Of course, calculations may go awry, and what may have appeared to be a very profitable venture may turn out in the end to be extremely costly. The decision to expand tourism may be seen by certain entrepreneurial hosts to require some compromises with tourists and their way of life, but the additional compromises demanded by developing tourism may not be foreseen. When the hosts find themselves dealing also with hotel-keepers, transportation people, travel and publicity agents, sanitary engineers, and the like, and making adjustments in the areas of life these represent, they may begin to have second thoughts about the wisdom of their initial calculations.

What kind of research endeavors would be appropriate for the analysis of touristic transactions? Microsociological analyses of tourist-host and tourist-tourist relationships using, perhaps, some variation of Goffman's (1959; 1967) approach to social relationships would give us some insight into the immediate social world of individual tourists and their hosts. In addition, institutional analyses of the nature of tourism would be essential for understanding why individual relationships take the form they do. Finally, some kind of exchange theory would help us understand why in a given situation certain forms of touristic transactions emerge. Such investigations would assume the generation of certain forms of tourism by particular metropolitan centers.

The Consequences of Tourism

Anthropologically viewed, the consequences of tourism may be seen to flow from the peculiar nature of the intergroup contact involved. Since that contact often (but not always) involves representatives of groups differing in degree of productivity and power (the tourist area usually being the less productive and powerful), investigations focusing on the modernization, urbanization, or development of a tourist area (Nuñez 1963) or the effects of exploitation by the dominant metropolitan center (Pérez 1973-74) ought to be of considerable scientific value. However, an alternative approach that focusses on touristic universals and their consequences for the individuals and societies involved also would seem to be indicated.

Since the touristic transaction is a two-way street involving interaction between metropolitan centers and tourist areas, there is no *a priori* reason to rule out a consideration of consequences to both ends of the relationship. Anthropologists' sympathies may lie with the underdog and the exotic, but they must recognize that one-sided transactional analysis is necessarily incomplete no matter how unequal the relationship being studied. Here, Hallowell's (1957) paper concerning the effects of the frontier is instructive.

In the tourist area the consequences of tourism derive from the introduction from outside of a new sociocultural reality. This reality, to which the native people and their social system must adapt, amounts to a transiently populated, externally based leisure class and its accompanying goals or expectations. The principal social adaptations that the hosts must work out in regard to this reality are between groups or societies and classes. The touristic arrangements created to deal with the foreign guests invariably include a serving class whose mission it is, first of all, to deal with strangers from other groups or societies. As Boyer (1972, p. 171) points out, the development of tourism is reflected in the local occupational structure by an expansion of the service center of the economy. Tourists must be transported, accommodated, and assisted with the many problems of getting along in a foreign place. Secondly, some provision for their leisure activities must be made. Such provisions may be extremely simple, as in providing access to a beach in the Canary Islands, or elaborate, as in the construction of Tivoli in Copenhagen. Investigations of the consequences of tourism in tourist areas ought to begin from an analysis of the individual and collective adaptations made by a host people in regard to these inevitable service functions. Such adaptations may be considered the primary consequences of tourism.

Though it probably is too early to begin to generalize confidently about touristic adaptations, one would expect them to be accompanied by at least some psychological and social conflict. In the tourist area, the necessity for at least some of the hosts to function as marginal men or culture brokers in order to deal with tourists and their metropolitan sponsors creates a pressure for acculturation in the direction of metropolitan cultures, learning how to carry on superficial, objective transactions, and providing for leisure needs. The acquisition or reinforcement of such qualities (including unfulfilled aspirations) could lead to social conflict among hosts, between hosts and guest, and also create intrapsychic conflict between incompatible personality dispositions. Additional social and psychological conflict could emerge as a result of competition over, or differential involvement in, the touristic enterprise. Examples of such conflicts have been provided by Lewis (1972), Nuñez (1963), and several chapters in this volume. The individual and social mechanisms that are developed to resolve these conflicts and thus facilitiate the adjustment of the host society to touristic imperialism could be an important factor in social change. Any investigation of the dynamics of the touristic process would have to consider them in some detail.

On the metropolitan side, the consequences of tourism derive from the creation and existence of a mobile leisure class and the infrastructure supporting it. As indicated above, tourism can serve a variety of social and psychological functions for a metropolitan center and its people. Does a vacation on the Baltic Sea, in Montecatini Terme, Acapulco, or the mountains of Hokkaido revive flagging energies, release threatening impulses, satisfy wanderlust, or assist or confirm vertical mobility? How do tours to distant places serve the economic, political, military, or religious needs of a people? Is it possible that the principal psychological consequence of tourism for the metropolitan side is an awakening or heightening of discontent (They'll never get me to go back to Indianapolis!)?

Where industrialization is far advanced and tourism widespread, a travel "industry" emerges, concerned with travel as an end in itself. It would be appropriate in such cases to speak about the institution of travel. Such an institution may be seen to serve certain social and psychological needs, but it also will develop needs of its own. What these self-serving needs are and how their fulfillment affects other institutions in the metropolitan society and with tourist areas would be an interesting subject for anthropological inquiry. In any study of the evolution of tourism, such an investigation would be essential, especially in accounting for its metropolitan-dictated development.

The Evolution of Tourism

So far, the implicit model underlying this analysis of tourism is not unlike that proposed by Malinowski (1945), who saw the world of contact and change in the colonial situation as consisting of three orders of sociocultural reality: the native or traditional, the modern or industrial, and the transitional. Such a model may be appropriate for treating early tourist contacts where tourism involves only some of the people on each side and the consequences of the interaction are not far reaching. But with continued contact, the transitional may engulf the traditional. In such circumstances the contact model proposed by Gluckman (1947) or Balandier (1951) for colonial situations would seem to be more appropriate. It would then be possible to speak of a transitional touristic social system emerging out of touristic contact. This system, which would center on the tourist-hosts relationship and the roles played in it, would be populated by transient tourists and all those hosts and metropolitans who participate in tourism. It would involve associative and dissociative social relationships by more or less committed maximizing people. There would be agreement and disagreement about the touristic goals of the system and the means used to attain them. The system's economic structure would be based on touristic service functions, and other social structures would reflect this. Finally, there would be power centers directing the system's development. Such a system, which could be a part of other systems (e.g., the colonial), might involve whole societies as in the U.S. Virgin Islands, and be multinational in scope as in the Pan American Airways empire.

Gordon Lewis, in his discussion of the U.S. Virgin Islands, provides an almost ideal-typical example of a touristic social system. For him (Lewis 1972, p. 129) the Virgin Islands "can be seen as a prime illustration of the general character of Caribbean parasitical tourism. They belong to the Caribbean subgroup of pure tourist economies, like Bermuda and the Bahamas, which are dependent almost entirely upon their ability to sell themselves to North American affluent societies." Lewis describes in some detail the conflicts that have developed over tourism and the various interests involved, but points out (p. 130) that "all . . . differences yield to a united front when the total image of the economy is challenged."

Lewis (pp. 137–38) implies that all present-day tourist areas dependent on North American metropolitan centers are evolving along a path leading to the kind of "anti-civilization" found in San Juan or Las Vegas. It would be premature to suggest, however, a universal evolutionary scheme for analyzing the development of touristic systems. Forster (1964, p. 218) points out that there is no inevitability in the process of tourist development. A brief survey of specific cases would seem to bear him out. How can one make general statements that would include the development of the touristic systems of Cannes, Leningrad, Acapulco, Davos, Miami Beach, Paris, Promised Land, Pennsylvania, Stratton Mountain, San Sebastion, Sochi, or Kiawah Island?

Any attempt to make broad or narrow generalizations about the evolution of touristic systems requires an identification of those parameters that are especially significant in sociocultural change. Among these are the needs of the metropolitan center(s), the distribution of power in the system, the economic base, and the social divisions relating to tourism. Some discussion of metropolitan touristic needs already has been given above. Here the role that these needs and their development play in the evolution of a touristic system must be added.

Because a tourist system, once established, must meet the touristic needs of one or more metropolitan centers, it will inevitably reflect in its evolution the development of such needs. Moreover, if we assume a competitive situation and maximizing human beings, there will be a pressure towards increasing responsiveness to metropolitan events. This means that the modernization or rationalization of a tourist area, which may have begun with a major effort to attain the minimal level necessary for interesting, accommodating, and serving tourists, will continue as a reflection of subsequent developments in this dimension in the metropolitan center. How exact a reflection it will be will depend on where the power lies in the touristic system. If considerable power is retained by those whose goals are at variance with metropolitan needs (as, for example, in Moscow, Paris, and New York), developments in the touristic system will reflect such needs with lesser fidelity. On the other hand, if power is entirely in the hands of metropolitan expatriates or their local agents, the touristic system will develop along a line that is increasingly dictated by metropolitan needs and their development.

As was suggested above, the economy of any tourist system will tend to become externally oriented and concerned with those service functions that provide for touristic needs. Cohen (1974, p. 250) points out that an expansion of a group's resource base outside its boundaries will alter the degree of dependence of occupational roles on outside resources. In the case of tourism the outside resource is the tourist. The adaptive response to his presence on the economic level is the development of the necessary service occupations to deal with him. The expansion of the service sector, in particular those jobs whose primary or secondary function is attending to transient expatriates and their sponsors, has implications for the economy as a whole and for the rest of the society. I will not attempt here to assess the practical desirability of such a development nor discuss the advisability of balanced economic development. Such important questions can be answered by the economist, more particularly, the economist in his role as advisor.

Insofar as other aspects of social organization are related to the economic structure, changes in that structure ought to be followed by other noneconomic changes. Not only would there be a strain towards consistency with the new economic arrangements, as in the Virgin Islands where even the churches tend to support the touristic "line" (Lewis 1972, pp. 128–29), but inconsistency or conflict between sectors of the touristic system, notably between the better and lesser served by the touristic economy, would arise as well. In some cases the introduction of tourism will exacerbate existing social cleavages; in others new cleavages will appear. Such conflict and associated psychological conflicts can generate additional changes in the touristic system as people work out ways of coping with them.

To sum up, the evolution of a touristic system is seen here to be subject to the actions of both exogenous and endogenous forces. Exogenous forces, which emanate from one or more metropolitan centers, involve the generation of touristic needs and tourists, the selection or creation of tourist areas, and the establishment of direct and indirect tourist-host transactions. The people of a tourist area may enter into a developing tourist system with varying degrees of enthusiasm. Their principal adaptation involves the development of a service economy and the necessary socio-cultural changes to go with it. This service economy is externally oriented and focussed on providing for the needs of transient, leisured strangers. Such developments will tend to produce inter- and intrapersonal disjunctions constituting the principal endogenous sources of change in the touristic system.

It is not possible at this point in the anthropological study of tourism to make significant general statements about the evolution of touristic systems, but if investigations are confined to narrower classes of historical circumstances, as in the studies of Forster (1964) and Greenwood (1972), it may be possible to begin to build an empirically-based theory of tourism within the conceptual framework of imperialism suggested here. The need for such a theory will grow as tourism grows, and since that growth is intimately related to industrialization, that need would seem to be very great indeed.

University of Connecticut

Part II

Nascent Tourism
in Non-Western Societies

The endeavor to record the customs of exotic societies before they vanish into the mainstream of a one-world culture has engaged a growing body of anthropologists for more than a hundred years. Popular accounts of "primitive peoples," rather than scholarly ethnographies, have penetrated school curriculums at every level, and laid the foundation for the tourist's quest to adventure. The powerful, modern taste-makers—the media with its travelogs, and especially the National Geographic Society with its magazine and documentaries—have created strong visual images that beckon the tourist. The culture brokers have converted the anthropologist's "hidden corner" of the world into a focal point for ethnic tourism. In each of the following case studies, tourism to the area is still nascent due to its limited numbers or seasonality.

Each author develops an individual theme: in chapter 3 I have chosen to examine tourism among the Eskimo in terms of locally-differentiated impact; Margaret Swain in chapter 4 analyzes tourism primarily in terms of sex roles; Charles Urbanowicz assesses the economic problems of Tonga in chapter 5, and Philip McKean in chapter 6 and Eric Crystal in chapter 7 provide interesting comparisons and contrasts in their two Indonesian case studies. Hindu Bali with its millenia-old ceremonial traditions seems better able to receive and cope with continuous visitors than the more isolated Toraja, for whom tourism is still new. Both authors, however, note that for diverse reasons tourism to Indonesia apparently strengthens local social bonds.

3

Eskimo Tourism:
Micro-Models
and Marginal Men

VALENE L. SMITH

The air age opened the once nearly inaccessible Alaskan Arctic to tourism. Two coastal communities, Kotzebue and Nome, each with a population of 2,500 residents, are the targets for a seasonal, summer, mass tourism that brought ten thousand visitors to the area in 1974, with as many as three hundred in one day. Because of a vast popular literature and many films descriptive of their customs, Eskimo culture is now an attraction—an ethnic commodity of commercial value—but one that no longer exists in its traditional form. Progressive modernization has transformed Eskimo villages into what I term "white man's towns where Eskimo also live." In contrast to the material and social aspirations of most Eskimo townsmen to live on a wage economy and in Western style, only "marginal men" (the aged and the out-group) are involved in the tourist industry.

The stereotype of the harsh Arctic climate and its snow-covered vastnesses, which once repelled all but explorers and "get rich quick" adventurers, is now an environmental asset. Tourists want to see the "midnight sun" and momentarily experience the geographic conditions in the "Last Frontier" of America. It is ironic that tourism is seasonal in summer when warm, sunny days, flowering tundra, and ice-free seas are nearly the antithesis of tourist expectations. Moreover, in contrast to most other areas where environmental tourism flourishes, the Arctic offers few recreational opportunities, especially now that polar bear hunting is outlawed. For most tourists, the Arctic is a once-in-a-lifetime visit. Despite industry efforts to promote off-season winter tourism, few individuals participate because they fear the very conditions they wish to know.

Tourism has had a different impact on each of the two target communities, Kotzebue and Nome, because of variances in local traditions and group involvement. Analysis of the disparities may be insightful to a clearer understanding of tourism on the micro-level. One cannot consider "Eskimo tourism" in general, but rather tourism in individual Eskimo centers, including the incipient desire of small outlying villages to participate for anticipated economic benefits.

Interpretations of the data base of 1975 are necessarily retrospective. The future of tourism in the area must clearly reflect two facts: the nationwide renascence of ethnic and native identity is a powerful and possible re-creative or regenerative force; and Eskimos have major financial reserves derived from land claims and oil leases that now give them the capability to restructure and to control the local tourist industry. Changes are imminent, and the Eskimo ability to effectively interface requisite outside support—especially, the air carriers and the package-tour wholesalers of the "lower 48" states who advertise, promote, and sell Arctic tourism—with their own values and monetary resources will require able, dedicated leadership and farsighted planning. Creation of a model culture might best serve both host and guest.

Eskimo Contacts with Outsiders

The Eskimo of the Bering Straits area are noted for their long tradition of involvement in aboriginal intercontinental trade with Siberians, and their interecological trade with other Eskimo subgroups along the coast and in the hinterland. They became entrepreneurs *par excellence*, made long sledge journeys for the purpose of trade, and developed a minimally-stratified society that accorded considerable status to shrewd traders (Smith, 1968). To receive strangers (albeit from within the Arctic) and to turn a profit through barter are part of their heritage that may go back a thousand years.

Contacts each summer with hundreds of whaling schooners and White traders date to 1850, augmented by the arrival of tens of thousands of miners in the Gold Rush of 1898. Traditional skills enabled the Eskimo to serve as buffers of survival for the outsiders, and Eskimo hunted, fished, trapped, and sewed as they had always done. This time, they received non-Arctic strangers and turned a cash profit. Few members of this alien horde gained much knowledge of Eskimo ethos, but they returned home imbued with respect for the native culture and disseminated the image of the Eskimos' unique ability to survive in the far north. These transient in-migrants of nearly a century ago laid the foundation for the present ethnic tourism.

Christian missions were founded in most Alaskan coastal villages in the 1890s. Once again, Eskimo in general welcomed these newcomers, and if there was no cash profit, the presence of missions was considered a positive influence. Christianity *per se* is not incongruous with many values inherent in the Eskimo world-view, and the church reinforced native sanctions against the widespread and disruptive use of alcohol. In many instances, missions provided much-sought medical help, started schools to equip Eskimo with the suddenly mandatory skills of English and arithmetic to cope with a new, patently irreversible world, and distributed welfare to the needy. Aging Eskimo who personally knew the first missionaries accord to them profound respect.

The missions also had a negative effect upon Eskimo culture. The church hall, for instance, superceded the traditional men's house, the *karigi*, as a meeting place, and prayer meetings and Christmas parties replaced the aboriginal Messenger Feasts. Very important to Eskimo tourism is the role and attitude of the dominant sects toward native dancing. To name a pertinent few, the fundamentalist churches at Kotzebue and Nome effectively suppressed all native entertainment; the Episcopal mission at Point Hope and the Roman Catholic mission at King Island encouraged Eskimo aesthetics and constructed meeting halls to replace the *karigi* as a dance place; the Presbyterians at Gambell were passive, and dancing persisted. The "marginal men" of Eskimo tourism reflect this philosophical division.

Following sixty years of massive outside contact (1850–1910), the Arctic coast settled into a quiet rut for the next forty years. Intercontinental trade ceased, in 1926, by government fiat, and interecologic trade sharply declined, then faded. Unlike the transient predecessors who had relied upon Eskimo products, the few, new outsiders were salaried government employees who came to stay and work in the newly-developing schools, hospitals, and allied services. Annual supply ships imported their needs of stateside origin. The Eskimo enterpreneurs were still there, but the marketplace was empty.

About 1950, Wien Airlines initiated tourism to support their "bush" service. Small wonder that Eskimo thronged to the airport to greet the little planes and the occasional tourists who would restore the market for native handicrafts and services, but the initial thrust proved disappointing.

Analysis of Arctic Tourism

Tourism to the Arctic is mass tourism in summer but, despite industry promotion, nonexistent in winter. Elite tourists who count countries as status symbols may have visited this area once, but they have long since literally "sailed away" on specially-outfitted cruise ships to visit the "real" Arctic in Greenland or Antarctica. Visitors to the Alaskan Arctic are predominantly middle-aged and middle-class, representing the John

Does who "campered" their way north along the dusty Alaska Highway, or cruised through the Inside Passage. They visit the Far North as an extension, a highlight, of a longer trip. Seldom demanding or critical, they are satisfied with simple accommodations and plain fare. Most are pleased to sample Arctic char (a bland fish) or reindeer stew; few would even taste more exotic native foods such as frozen black *muktuk*, or raw whale skin and blubber. Non-Americans are rare, except for a few Japanese with interests in the fisheries. Because the only access is by air, and comparatively expensive, youthful travelers are uncommon.

In the jet age, most visitors arrive on one of the almost identical two-day "packages," which for US$200 include air transportation from Anchorage or Fairbanks, accommodations, and sightseeing. One group overnights at Kotzebue, the other at Nome; their paths cross, midair, in the hour's flight between the two. Each group arriving at the destined hotel is outfitted in bright-hued cotton parkas, which serve to heighten their tourist identity and their visibility. Despite their commonly-stated desire "to see how the Eskimo really live," most tourists when actually set down in a native town are visibly ill-at-ease, and quite content to be whisked around by bus to gain a kaleidoscopic impression, with a White guide to explain native culture. The guide is commonly a college student, hired for the season, with no prior Arctic experience. Few tourists have face-to-face interaction with Eskimos aside from the few natives hired to serve and entertain them, and then only in passing.

The tour program is highly structured and includes a dog-team ride (in a sled with rubber tires), an exhibition of native crafts (skin-sewing, ivory carving), and climaxed by a blanket toss and a short performance of native dancing. Brief periods of leisure are allotted for shopping in White-owned curio stores but purchases are mostly souvenirs—postcards, small books, and either "fake" art made in Japan or the cheapest products of Eskimo crafts, now carved in bone rather than traditional ivory. The comparative expense of the tour, the mass market, and its middle-class orientation generate few true "collectors" of art forms having considerable intrinsic value but little-known outside the Arctic.

Tourism to the Arctic has been almost exclusively an external operation, financed and managed to benefit the air carriers by providing a passenger load. The host population, whose environment and culture are commodities, have profited only tangentially. The increased air services, with their payloads, have probably helped maintain lower fares for passengers and cargo, indirectly benefitting the Eskimo who are dependent upon these air links; and from among the host culture, a few "marginal men" have found summer wage employment. Generalities end here, and the impact of mass tourism can be assessed only in the context of each target community or micro-model.

Tourism in Kotzebue

Kotzebue lies just north of the Arctic Circle on the Bering Sea coast, and by virtue of location is the administrative and transportation center for northwest Alaska (Figure 1). Archaeologic sites suggest a continuous occupancy from the fourteenth century (Van Stone 1955), and the local Eskimo, the *Kikitarukmiut*, were very active in and probably controlled the extensive aboriginal trade that centered here. Their success as entrepreneurs provoked jealousies with contiguous groups, and it is germane to note that this is one of two reported Arctic sites where slat armor (indicative of warfare) is recovered. Legends particularly emphasize hostility as recently as one hundred fifty years ago with Eskimo from Point Hope, a different dialect group with a slightly variant, more truly maritime economy.

The historic town of Kotzebue, with an estimated 300 Eskimo population, was founded with the advent of the mission in 1897, and so great was its influence, within a few months all local Eskimo had joined the California Yearly Meeting of Friends and sworn abstention from alcohol, tobacco, *and* dancing. Gold Rush activity enticed other Eskimo to Kotzebue, but the residual aboriginal power then mandated to in-migrants a two-year probationary residence based on strict adherence to the established Christian tenets as a prerequisite to permanent settlement. Aboriginal dancing and music was effectively suppressed for all early Eskimo in Kotzebue.

Transformation of the aboriginal village into a modern metropolis seemingly parallels urban growth elsewhere. The indigenous Eskimo replaced sod igloos with frame houses on their traditional homesites, the most-favored for sea mammal hunting. The increasing in-migrants, attracted to the growing town for proximity to schools, hospital, and other desired services, of necessity built their homes on the periphery. The persistence of strong family ties and minor dialect differences in their native tongue created enclaves of "foreign," or ethnic, subgroup settlements at less favored beachline locations or on back roads, and formed the basis for community factionalism (Smith 1968).

When tourism commenced in 1950, few native Kotzebue Eskimo were available to serve as brokers for their culture because of religious sanctions. However, tour operators readily found their dancers among the small colony of Point Hope Eskimo who, as Episcopalians, had maintained their aesthetics. Thus, a historically-disliked, ethnic out-group of "marginal men" became the cultural entrepreneurs and entertained tourists for a profit. The same, progressively aging individuals have dominated local tourism since its inception twenty-five years ago. Among them, a gregarious male Eskimo with a long record of White association

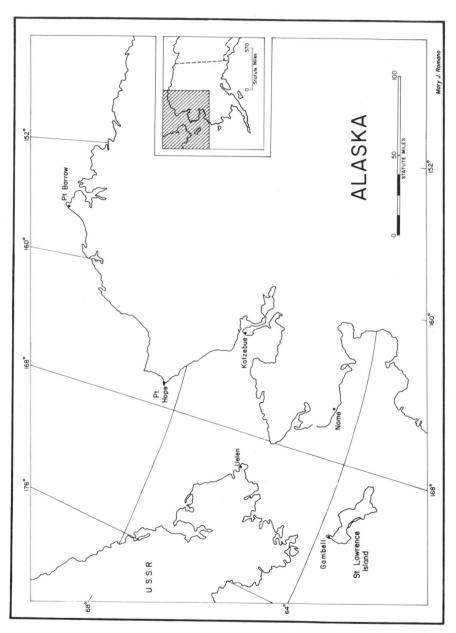

Figure 1. The Map of the Arctic

as a reindeer herder and better-than-average bilingualism assumed the leadership role (Seveck 1973). In 1953, the airlines salaried him on an annual basis and then sent him on winter promotion tours throughout the United States, Hawaii, Mexico, and Japan to dance and generate tourism.

As the numbers of visitors slowly increased, Kotzebuers became proportionately more disenchanted with tourism in general and with Point Hopers in particular. Considerable alienation seems centered on the brief, half-hour dance show. In the early years, the dance performances were sporadic, staged only when justified in terms of the numbers of tourists in town. Then quite a number of Kotzebue Eskimo trickled in to watch, for acculturation had lessened their ties with the church, and older members among them vicariously enjoyed reliving the days of their youth, although they were not made welcome to participate. As the town grew and daily mass tourism began, the numbers of Eskimo spectators at the now-nightly summer dances increased, straining facilities. At this point, nonperforming Eskimo were openly discouraged at the door, and finally a us$2.50 admission fee was levied. From the anthropological perspective, it is unfortunate that the tour operators were insensitive to a widening spectrum of involvement, but the employer/employee bonds were firmly established.

Handicrafts for tourist sales is another source of alienation. Aboriginal Kotzebue Eskimo became entrepreneurs because their resource base was limited, especially in ivory, and they were inferior carvers. However, tourist contacts readily indicated to the Point Hopers that an excellent market existed for "old things" easily obtained by raiding the archaeologic site only three miles south of town. In violation of the National Antiquities Act, Point Hopers (and some white residents) almost systematically plundered Eskimo graves for salable "loot." Considering the half-forgotten tales of pitched battles between two aboriginal villages, this was a signal affront.

Spatial geography is another salient aspect of this micro-model. During the early years, tourists were housed in makeshift quarters above the airlines office, situated at the *south* end of town in a so-called central business district—a complex of buildings housing trading post, coffee shop, theater, and post office—that met tourist needs. The few overnight visitors seldom ventured much beyond this area, and their impact was minimal.

A decade later, the airline constructed an enlarged Alaska-style roadhouse at the *northern* end of the traditional village and on a very slight curve in the beachline. To reach the essential services of the business center, tourists walked round-trip past traditional Kotzebue homes, with the obvious opportunity to "snap photos" of daily life. Further, from the hotel's second-story verandah, guests looked south over the entire length

Plate 1. The view southward from the Wien Airlines' tourist hotel at Kotzebue, Alaska, with Eskimo hunting and fishing activities visible.

of the beachline with a commanding view directly onto the vestiges of Eskimo activity, including butchering (Plate 1).

One of the environmental aspects of Arctic tourism is to "stay up and see the Midnight Sun." After the dance performance finished at 9:00 P.M., the increased number of tourists strolled the beachline, at the very hour when hunters returned and butchering commenced. Tourist expectations were suddenly met—these were the things they came to see, and the pictures they wanted, of Eskimo doing "Eskimo things." But Eskimo wearied of answering repetitive questions and complained about tourists who took muktuk and fish from drying racks, smelled it, and threw it on the ground as if it were garbage. Above all, the many Eskimo passengers aboard airplanes that included tour parties overheard the departing visitors brag about the "pictures I got," and interpreted the remarks as ridicule, which cuts deep into native ethos. In response, Eskimo women began to refuse would-be tourist photographers, then erected barricades to shield their work from tourist eyes, and some finally resorted to hiring a taxi to haul seals and other game to the privacy of their homes for processing (Plates 2, 3).

In summary, tourism in Kotzebue has been minimally directed and insensitive in that it denied a participatory role to the indigenes in favor of financial benefits accorded to an ethnic minority.

Tourism in Nome

The townsite of present-day Nome is on the windy, often storm-battered southern coast of the Seward Peninsula. Native subsistence resources appear to have been minimal, and no archaeologic settlement is known. Nome was founded as a White town during the Gold Rush era when thirty thousand miners created a flourishing frontier city. The Eskimo who now live there are in-migrants from a widespread region attracted to the wage economy of mining, barging, and other services. With one exception, no core group occurs. Several religious sects maintain churches, but most Eskimo appear to be drawn to the fundamentalist Covenant Mission, which discourages native aesthetics although it operates a radio station of region-wide importance because of partial programming in Eskimo.

Mass tourism began in the early 1960s with the construction of first one, then several, good hotels reflecting the dominantly White orientation of the town. Promotional materials stress the historic component of tourism and focus on the "days of '98," with the opportunity to pan for gold. However, since outside capital and management control the tourist industry, local White residents appear disinterested in tourism and have not even developed a "honky-tonk" bar to entertain seasonal visitors. It

Plate 2. To screen their seal butchering from tourist eyes, Eskimo women in Kotzebue erected makeshift barricades.

Plate 3. Butchering was traditionally a time of Eskimo socialization and cooperation. Under the impact of tourism, some Eskimo women now hire taxis to drag carcasses home, to be butchered in privacy.

might prove fruitful to compare Nome with another Alaskan "ghost town," Skagway, where historic tourism appears to involve much of the White community with substantial monetary gain.

By a fortunate coincidence, ethnic tourism became possible in 1959 with the permanent resettlement of Eskimos from King Island, as a result of the closing of their BIA (Bureau of Indian Affairs) school. More traditional and subsistence-oriented than most groups, indicated by their continued use into 1976 of *umiaks* (skin-covered boats), the King Islanders are a dialect and residential group. They clustered their houses around a government-built Council Hall that functioned as a surrogate *karigi* for male ivory carvers (an art form in which they excel) and as a dance place. The Catholic Mission, to which most belong, had long encouraged dancing, and King Islanders have a rich repertoire of elaborate masked dances as well as the commonplace social styles.

Tourism in the Nome micro-model is also highly structured, but with significant, positive differences. King Island village is a discrete unit, situated about a mile east of Nome., Tourists are bussed to the village at 7:00 P.M. for an anticipated hour's visit that includes the usual craft demonstrations, blanket toss, and dancing, and then are immediately returned to their hotel with little opportunity to wander among homes or to observe and photograph other facets of the native life-style. In essence, visitors make a short stay in a "model culture," are entertained, and go away. Since the arrival is anticipated, and since the Eskimo are in their own milieu, a discernible host-guest relationship exists. Most King Island Eskimo attend the dances regularly as a cohesive social activity, and juveniles and youths frequently join the dances spontaneously as fully functioning members of their culture. Impressionistic data suggests that the tourists on this program are more satisfied with their exposure to Eskimo culture for, although there is still little face-to-face contact, the participation of a larger group of all ages lends credulity to the visit.

Comparable to Kotzebue, the ethnic entrepreneurs are an outgrowth both in dialect and tradition and, because of their continued and heavy reliance upon subsistence pursuits, are the object of some adverse comment (verbalized jealousy) by the more urbanized, noncohesive Nome Eskimo. Among King Islanders, touristic leadership is vested in an individual with marked bilingualism whose salary and airlines-sponsored promotion tours are not completely compatible with persistent male norms.

Tourists who overnight in Nome have more time to shop in the White-owned curio stores stocked with crafts of King Island origin and apparently buy more, thus indirectly contributing greater cash flow to local Eskimo touristic income.

Elite Tourism in the Outlying Villages

In the early 1960s, the airlines advertised "Off-Beat" tours to Point Hope and Gambell, remote small villages accessible by air from Kotzebue and Nome, respectively. A few elite tourists—rugged individuals with interest, time, and money who disdained minimal accommodations and services—pioneered tourism to these areas. However, the tours were discontinued after several unsuccessful seasons because there was little to attract these "pathfinders." Those who hoped to see a "real Eskimo village" were disappointed because habitations were the same weathered frame houses, and in summer most of the active hunting families had moved to camps located miles away. The villages were semi-deserted with minimal subsistence activity. Even if a dance performance could be arranged, the fee was fifty dollars. Further, adverse flying conditions frequently prevail in both areas, and to be "weathered" for several days is often disruptive to a travel itinerary.

Elite ethnic tourism was a failure for the visitor, but villagers did not comprehend the reasons. They only recognized that when people came, they spent money that, no matter how limited, added to the minimal cash flow. To encourage more tourism became village goals but differentially expressed, according to the local micro-model.

Twice in the course of my field work, the Point Hope Village Council formally sought guidance to expand their latent tourist industry. They perceived three hallmarks of success. First, their relatives and friends living in Kotzebue were making a good living from tourism, and it could be lucrative to the entire village if transferred to Point Hope. Second, they had copies of the brochure prepared by the (White-dominated) Chamber of Commerce in Kotzebue and naively assumed that this was the advertising that brought thousands of tourists to Kotzebue each summer. Third, Point Hope villagers enjoy the five days each June when they host with great success the several hundred Eskimo who come by chartered plane to celebrate the traditional whaling festival. The practical considerations of capital to build a suitable hotel, the inordinate costs of food and other supplies, and the summer ground fogs and adverse flying weather all fell on unhearing ears. They did not recognize the touristic requirements vis-a-vis those of their Eskimo guests who "camped out" or crowded onto the floor of family homes and ate the abundant native foods. Nor could they anticipate the possible village disruption occasioned by mass tourism. Point Hopers perceive tourists as a seasonally constant source of income as well as an interesting influx of outsiders to redeem the monotony of their daily lives.

Gambell, on remote St. Lawrence Island in the Bering Straits, is so subject to severe storms that air services are erratic at best. Comparatively few Eskimo travel from Gambell to Nome, their gateway city, and even fewer have personal ties with Eskimo on the mainland. Even elite tourism had barely touched them.

Suddenly in 1967, with no prior tourist base, national travel trade journals announced an Alaskan Centennial Year Pageant to be held in Gambell on three Saturdays, one each month, that summer. Tourists could join charter aircraft from Anchorage and Fairbanks and for a US$5.00 local fee, visit the village and the Museum (constructed for the occasion), have lunch, and see the dance pageant. The bold plan was inspired and directed by the capable resident White couple whose leadership role as teachers is well-stated by Hughes (1960, p. 314), "The school would therefore seem to have been one of the positive contributions of the White world to village solidarity."

Eskimo built an almost perfect reconstruction of a Siberian house-type to display aboriginal artifacts collected from many homes including some Okvik carvings, stone lamps, and a well-made umiak. Some individuals drafted a traditional story replete with hunter, walrus, seal, puffin, and owls, made costumes, and rehearsed the dances; others cooked and froze gallons of spaghetti; another crew planned for emergency beds in the event guests had to overnight because of bad weather. Word came that the charters were full, but on the appointed June Saturday, locally adverse weather prevented the flights. In July, Alaska's Governor was listed among the distinguished guests but poor weather again precluded their arrival. On the designated August date, a devastating and costly storm spread across Arctic Alaska, and Gambell was inaccessible and forgotten. Determined to do it once, in theatrical tradition, the show "went on," and half a dozen of us, including George-Bandi's archaeologic crew, were privileged to see the closest approximation to truly aboriginal values available to Whites in at least half a century.

Disappointment was keen, especially for the teachers, but Eskimo accepted failure here, as in the food quest, with the resignation that has earned for them the appellation, "phlegmatic." Despite the overt failure, Gambell profited from the endeavor through the strengthening of their social bonds. This obscure micro-model suggests the resiliency of native culture as a potential for future tourism. At least in some locales, the manifest acculturation is superficial—a veneer of White-oriented economic aspirations that have not yet deeply eroded enduring Eskimo values.

The Future of Arctic Tourism

Tourism to the Arctic expanded rapidly in the years 1964–73 (Figure 2), but the rate of growth experienced from 1970 to 1973 has not been

Figure 2
Employment and Wages in Alaska's
Tourist Industry

	1964	1967	1970	1972	1973	1977*
Numbers of Tourists	59,000	86,000	129,000	182,000	215,000	280,000
Tourist Impact (in U.S. dollars)	18,200,000	29,000,000	45,000,000	65,630,000	72,000,000	90,000,000
Nongovernment Employees	1,600	2,400	3,700	5,220	6,100	not available
Total Wages (in U.S. dollars)	9,600,000	15,850,000	22,940,000	34,472,800	40,333,000	not available

Source: Cresap, McCormick and Paget. *A Program for increasing the Contribution of Tourism to the Alaskan Economy,* 1968.

Alaska Division of Tourism, *Alaska Transportation and Purpose of Travel,* 1974.

*Projections based on a study in progress, May 1977, by R.M. Dindinger, Market Coordinator, Division of Tourism, State of Alaska.

sustained in the four subsequent years primarily because of the pipeline construction. The "boom towns" of Anchorage and Fairbanks with their inflated cost of living generated by the extraordinarily high wages paid for construction have discouraged some potential visitors.

The statistics compiled by the State of Alaska are not broken down by region but Robert M. Dindinger, Market Coordinator, Division of Tourism, State of Alaska, observed that Arctic tourism in the years 1970–73 was one of the fastest growing segments of Alaska travel. However, tourism to the Arctic slumped somewhat in 1975 and 1976, to perhaps no more than six thousand total visitors per year. The explanation is probably economic, due to the higher overall costs for travel to and in Alaska. However, in the face of a well-established industry that in 1977 will generate an estimated us$90,000,000 in income to Alaska, it is apparent that the Eskimo whose environment and culture are the real targets in the North have received a very small slice of the economic pie.

Heightened American interest in the Arctic because of its economic development is a strong stimulus to increased numbers of tourists in future years. Travel industry observers generally feel that once the pipelines are completed, an expensive "normalcy" may prevail in Alaska, and an increased flow of tourism may be expected. However, the pattern will probably remain the same—a summer stream of short-term visitors who make the trip once and, with curiosity satisfied, do not return. New National Parks to be established on lands currently being allocated for this purpose may stimulate more recreational tourism in the future.

1976 may ultimately prove to have been a turning point in Arctic tourism, at least for the two target micro-models, Kotzebue and Nome. Eskimos of northwest Alaska have suddenly become wealthy from land-claim settlements and revenues from oil leases. Continuing oil exploration throughout the area may prove other deposits and contribute further to their economic reserves. Fortunately, the Eskimo who now fill important leadership roles are well-educated, sophisticated in their understanding of the ongoing process of acculturation, and dedicated to the development of a new life-style compatible with their resource base.

In Kotzebue, the NANA Regional Corporation (the shareholding entity created to administer accrued native funds) is vigorously entering the tourist business and by 1975 had already purchased the only hotel that was not airlines owned. In November 1975 construction was completed on a new us$2.2 million complex, the Nul-luk-vik Hotel. The 55-room facility offers superior travel amenities including dial phones, color TV, and a gift shop. Primarily built to meet the housing needs of the continuous stream of government visitors, the hotel also immediately became the social center for Kotzebue, for banquets, parties, and conferences. NANA offices are located on the second floor, and throughout the hotel there is a pervasive air of officialdom.

The Nul-luk-vik (Eskimo, "resting place") was available to tourists on the "package tour" in 1976 at a small supplemental charge, but tourist reaction was mixed. The lack of a large lobby, the small coffee shop crowded with Eskimos, the presence of many natives drinking at the bar on the premises, and the general business bustle made many tourists feel ill-at-ease. They could "see the Eskimo," but not in the roles they had anticipated. Many tourists preferred the "bubble" of touristic isolation offered to them in the old-fashioned roadhouse, which was more their image of the "real" Alaska.

John Schaeffer, President of NANA, is a frequent visitor to Hawaii and a great admirer of the principle of cultural conservation stressed at the Polynesian Cultural Center (see chapter 14). In preparation for the 1976 tourist season, NANA reconstructed, five miles south of town at the reindeer camp, a traditional sod igloo and appropriately furnished it to simulate aboriginal living. An Eskimo couple who serve as reindeer herders for NANA's recently instituted herds also served as local guides. Tourists appreciated the opportunity to drive across the tundra, visit the reindeer camp, and see one "old-style" house. This was the ethnic tourism of which they had dreamed.

NANA has other plans to stimulate tourism to Kotzebue by providing interesting destination activities. In 1976, NANA received a gift of several hundred professionally-mounted animals from a now-defunct Anchorage taxidermy store, and in 1977 expects to complete a large building in which they can be displayed in habitat groups. Also under construction in 1977 is a new Pioneer Home for senior citizens, and provision is being made for the lobby to contain craft areas where residents can carve and sew, demonstrating the traditional handicrafts and selling their products. Kotzebue is also ultimately slated to be the headquarters for a new Arctic National Park, with an Interpretive Center that will encompass the biological and social sciences.

In 1976, the dancing performance was transferred from the airlines building to Cudd Hall, the Episcopalian Church center, and local Eskimo were once again made free to attend, though few participated in the dancing aside from the aged, paid Point Hope troupe dominated by Seveck. Five big tour buses, each with their White driver-guide, shuttled the visitors on their scheduled round of activity but encountered some problems of roads "blocked" by stalled cars. The buses suffered an inordinate number of minor mechanical difficulties. A few native houses were splattered with white-wash, "Tourists, Go Home." NANA wants tourism for the economic benefits of jobs and cash flow, but it was evident that an increasing number of young dissidents resented it. In Kotzebue, tourism is being gradually transferred to local, native control but even native leadership to date is unable to counter the adverse image that tourism brings outsiders to "gawk" at native ethnicity. As for the outlying villages now under NANA control, John Schaeffer summarized the native viewpoint in March 1976: "Tourism is an important industry and in Kotzebue, which is a big city, we can handle it without disruption. I am not sure that the outlying villages can withstand the saturation, but we are going to send some small groups to them, to observe the effect."

In Nome, a devastating storm in November 1974 completely destroyed King Island village (miraculously, without loss of life). Prefabricated materials were immediately flown in and houses assembled in a hangar, and within months neat rows of new homes were aligned on streets contiguous to the eastern end of Nome's urban sprawl, and set back from the beachline for safety from high waves. Regrettably, the damaged Council House was not rebuilt and the dance performances were shifted to the basement of a hotel, destroying the former host/guest relation and the group solidarity the performances had reinforced. Ethnic tourism in Nome has disintegrated into the aging out-group of performers who are brought to the hotel by bus to "dance for money" as has been true in Kotzebue for two decades.

Micro-Models and Marginal Men

Tourism is a complex, multi-faceted phenomenon. To understand its scope and the impetus that attracts people to spend time and money away from home, in one area vis-a-vis another selected from the world-wide and therefore enormous range of potential centers, will require many case studies. Although Arctic tourism is environmental and ethnic, the effect is different in each of the host communities. Therefore, micro-models rather than generalized examples may be the primary data source from which a theory of tourism can be developed.

Tourism, especially mass tourism, modifies the local scene and may segment a population in terms of their participation. The sheer presence of tourists may also create new aspirations, for human curiosity about other life-styles is a two-way street. Few among the thousands of annual visitors probably realize that Eskimo are not isolated from travel ads in Alaskan newspapers and, loving warmth and sun, daydream of vacationing in Hawaii (and quite a few have done so, returning with their pictures and souvenirs).

Tourism may also generate a patronizing ethnocentrism (the "ugly American"), as hard-working middle-class citizens on a once-a-year "fling" suddenly perceive themselves as a wealthy and leisured class by comparison to the quaint customs and the lesser standard of living of the indigenes whom they visit. Many Americans are "surprised" to discover that their native guides, even in very remote areas such as Hunza in Pakistan, have lived in or traveled to the United States. They are often equally surprised to learn that many of the tour operators who market the "picturesque" are not bilingual peasants or culture-bound local business-men. They are frequently sophisticated world travelers with extensive communication networks who regularly attend international meetings to promote the travel industry.

"Marginal men" is used here without a specific referent and devoid of prior definitions of ethnicity or minority role to allow freedom to examine various forms of marginality that exist among a host population. The Eskimo data suggests several types that probably have their counterparts in tourism elsewhere. In both target communities, the Eskimo who dance and demonstrate crafts are members of a minimally-defined minority who have overtly retained their aesthetics and are in a position to capitalize upon them. Younger and better-educated Eskimo hold most of the wage jobs in government and business, and have the means to achieve some of their Western aspirations for cars, TV, airplanes, and nice furnishings. They are negative toward being identified with the ethnic stereotype of fur-clad hunters or skin-chewing women, and eschew or ridicule this touristic performance. Consequently, older or aging individuals have entered the marketplace as marginal members of Eskimo culture to sell the one thing they know—their former lifestyle. Their position is not dissimilar from that of American Blacks who, in recent decades, found jobs and success in theater and sports when other employment opportunities were limited. Elsewhere in tourist realms it may be that the Fijian "fire-walkers" and the Tahitian night-club dance troups would also be found to be marginal men of this type.

In Kotzebue and Nome, the cultural brokers are an ethnically distinct out-group, a circumstance with many parallels elsewhere. Loeb (chapter 13) notes in this volume that Jews play a major role in Iranian tourism. Elsewhere (chapter 7), Chinese are the travel brokers in Borneo, and East Indians are important in Fiji, while Anglo-Indians function in India, and displaced East African Moslems are in business in Pakistan. For the sincere ethnic tourist, the implication is evident: is the interpretation about a native culture, when described by a culturally-marginal guide, accurate? This comment seems particularly applicable to archaeologic ruins, interpreted by so-called guides who have never read the site reports.

Bilingualism is essential for the role of spokesman but certain personality traits are apparently also necessary—charisma, charm, wit, gregariousness—which attracts individuals to jobs in tourism who may gain considerable upward mobility in wages and the opportunity for travel. Impressionistic data in the Arctic and elsewhere suggest that touristic leaders may individually differ in experience and background from the norms of their subculture and thus be another variant of "marginal men."

Relationships between host and guest are a blend of value orientations. For the most part, historic Eskimo contacts with American whalers and gold-seekers were positive and financially profitable, which predisposed their initial welcome to American tourists. The historic contacts between Russians and Bering Straits Eskimo are little-documented, but Russian penetration farther south in Alaska and among the Aleuts is associated with cruelty. Suffice to say that Nome and Kotzebue Eskimo are negative toward Russians, although they have seen none in several decades. Had the first tourists been Russians, the reception might have been less cordial. Analagous is the attitude of many Micronesians and Filippinos towards the recent invasion of Japanese tourists. Tolerance and moderation for the financial gain of the host cannot, in one short generation, erase the memory of loved ones lost in battles against a would-be conqueror whose "armies" now come in tour busses. Tourism therefore has an ethnohistoric component, and, since it is seldom a sudden "happening," continuity of field observation may contribute to the study of process.

The Role of Model Cultures and Regional Planning

Model cultures have been successfully developed as reconstructions of an historic past, as at Williamsburg, Plymouthe Plantation, and the many Folk Museums of Europe. Of an ethnographic nature are Fiji's Orchid Island, Bangkok's Rose Garden—(Thailand in miniature), and Hawaii's Polynesian Cultural Center. All are apparently popular and profitable, and merit careful research as a touristic option and a possible panacea to the disruptive aspects of large numbers of tourists imposed directly in the midst of a host population. Models appear to meet the ethnic expectations of tourists, as a reconstruction of the life-style they hope to see, that also accords to them the freedom to wander and to photograph at will. King Island village, as it formerly functioned, suggests some of the merits of a model in that visitations were anticipated and scheduled, leaving to the residents considerable time and privacy for their personal lives.

The spatial relationships between host and guest are also important. Where regional planning can be conducted, possibly tourists should be accommodated in locations where their creature comforts are met, and from which their forays into indigenous life can be structured in time and place.

California State University, Chico

4

Cuna Women and Ethnic Tourism: A Way to Persist and an Avenue to Change

MARGARET BYRNE SWAIN

The impact of tourism as an agent of socioeconomic change reflects the nature of what is marketed to transient visitors and the processes through which this marketing is controlled. The San Blas Cuna Indians of Panama are involved in a form of ethnic tourism: the marketing of tourist attractions based on the local population's traditional way of life. Ethnic tourism is a paradoxical agent of change and continuity for this indigenous group, in that acceptance of tourism simultaneously encourages the maintenance of traditions and provides many stimuli for change.

Problems inherent in Cuna tourism are unique to their situation and address broad questions of changing roles, ethnic identity, and economic survival. This study considers differential female and male participation in tourism and its relationship to the marketing of a primary Cuna attraction: the women's traditional way of life. Modification of traditional sex roles and statuses is expected to correlate with changing occupations, including those stimulated by tourism. The impact of tourism among the Cuna varies with who is in charge of marketing management, as well as with the degree of local socioeconomic isolation.

Geographic and Cultural Background

Approximately twenty-five thousand Cuna live in the *Comarca de San Blas*, a treaty-regulated reserve. The *comarca*, a long narrow area, extends 200 kilometers along Panama's northeastern Atlantic coast, and 15 to 20 kilometers inland to the continental divide. Some thirty-five communities are settled on near-shore (100 to 200 meters) islands within the San Blas archipelago and on the adjacent littoral. Other Cuna groups are located nearby in the Darien interior and adjacent Colombia.

The Cuna are subsistence maize and plantain *milpa* cultivators and raise large quantities of coconuts for cash sale and for barter with Colombian trading boats. Fishing, turtle, and lobster catching are other important sources of food and cash income. Additional activities for cash revenue include some local employment, long term circular migration by the men for jobs in the Canal Zone and Panama, and the women's handicraft industry. Some 90 percent of San Blas homes are without potable water or electricity (1970 National Census of Panama), and the majority of Cuna live at a subsistence level in which malnutrition is significant. Traditionalism in San Blas society is not necessarily only a cultural preference but reflects constraints imposed by the physical environment as well.

San Blas is popularly regarded as a *"jardin anthropologico"* (Herrara 1972): a primitive paradise of palm trees, islands, and exotic people frozen in time. The Cuna have maintained their culture despite centuries of contact with western technological societies. Their efforts include strong prohibitions against intermarriage with other ethnic groups. The *Comarca* population is 97 percent Cuna, reflecting as well territorial sovereignty since their 1925 revolt against Panamanian control. Almost all Cuna speak their Chibchan-derived language, although now at least half of the men and about one-eighth of the women are literate in Spanish (1970 National Census of Panama), and a number of men also have a command of English. All Cuna men are involved in the *congressos*, their democratic political organization that regulates each community's affairs and pan-*Comarca* relations with Panama. Use and elaboration of cultural myths and rituals is another significant function of this indigenous government.

Female and Male Roles in Cultural Adaptation

One of the most striking aspects of Cuna society is the relatively insulated conservatism of most Cuna women with respect to men in matters of travel, Western education, dress, and occupations. Historically, the Cuna have shifted sex roles and statuses in efforts to retain their territory and defend their economic base. After Spanish contact in the 1960s, the Cuna retreated deep into the Darien and changed from a patriarchial class structure to an egalitarian, bilateral, and matrilocal society much as it still functions today (Stout 1947). In order to supplement their subsistence activities, Cuna men began to leave their isolated communities to seek wage employment in cities and aboard ships.

Around 1900 a rapid change in sex roles occurred—from all female to all male *milpa* cultivators—associated with the development of coconut cash cropping by men and trade by women (Brown 1970). This shift in the internal division of labor complemented male migration and female insulation patterns as a further adaptation to culture contact, providing both intersocietal contacts and the maintenance of a traditional social core (Helms 1970, p. 208).

The stability of Cuna society has also reflected a delicate balance between male political control of the society and elements in the Cuna value-system that sanction the desirability of female status through special female puberty rites and earth-mother symbolism (Sanday 1974). Cuna women are partners, not chattels, although they have no political franchise or socially-recognized capacity for handling either complex business or moral matters (Brennan 1973, p. 62). The range of occupations traditionally open to women are in the domestic sphere of child rearing, house keeping, and local bartering. Some women with exceptional interest study to be a midwife, curer, or very rarely a *nele* or clairvoyant. Today, the growing demand for cash in a changing economy and the increased number of girls attending school signal the need and capacity for more diversified local employment for both sexes.

Salaried positions in the San Blas include a variety of government jobs of which Cuna hold over 60 percent, or more than two hundred positions (Herrera 1972); the majority of these jobs are held by men. Ailigandi Hospital is representative in that of 22 government positions, 16 are held by men. Only in teaching are positions nearly equally held by women and men. The other major job sources include church missions, small businesses such as *sociedades*, and tourism.

Sociedades are a post-World War II indigenous adaptation of communal cooperatives, most of which are male organizations, but also include "mixed" *sociedades* with both female and male members. Individuals buy shares to join the organization and then participate in the rotation of paid and unpaid jobs. *Sociedades* are organized for production, import, export, and services (Shatto 1972), and provide employment for both educated youth and older members of a community while maintaining the cooperative aspects of Cuna society.

The tempo of socioeconomic change in San Blas has increased greatly since the late 1960s. National government agencies operate San Blas programs in health, education, and agriculture, while the *Congresso General* has increased efforts to retain traditions through sponsorship of festivals and a cultural center. Opportunities to increase cash earnings and to improve the local standard of living are being carefully weighed in the *Congressos* against the effects of tourism and other economic development on the autonomy and quality of Cuna life.

The Scope of Cuna Ethnic Tourism

Although the San Blas have not yet been included in "South America on $5 and $10 a Day," the possibility of mass tourism increases with every new advertisement about tours to the "remote, exotic, unspoiled habitat" of the Cuna. Marketing emphasis is centered on Cuna women who are promoted as the "colorful, fascinating, and genuine" essence of Cuna culture. Their picturesque appearance (arm and leg beads, gold nose ring, face painting, and "*mola* blouse") is especially noticeable in comparison with men's everyday attire. Cuna women's routine village life and their sewing skills have easily become the main attractions for the ethnic tourist.

Travel literature frequently bolsters the image of Cuna women by referring to them as the "real rulers of their matriarchial society," confusing this mythical stereotype with the fact that the Cuna reside matrilocally. This emphasis is complemented by the fact that the primary tourism symbol of Panama, the *mola*, is solely the product of Cuna women. *Mola* refers specifically to the unique blouse worn by Cuna women, but the term also refers to the unworn panels and other articles made in the same reverse applique technique. For many years Cuna men have sold *molas* in urban areas, and on the islands women have marketed them to outside visitors. *Molas* are now found throughout the world, in museums and in the ethnic art market. This international marketing of Cuna *molas* is both a cause and an effect of ethnic tourism.

The volume of San Blas tourism has been small but visible for a number of years. The first (and for many years the only) hotel and tour service was started during the 1940s by the late "Jungle Jim" Price. Tourism began to increase in the 1960s when several other hotels and resorts were constructed, and continues to grow as air services improve. The Panamanian Institute of Tourism (IPAT) estimated a three-fold increase in these tourists, from 2,000 in 1972 to 6,000 in 1973. Cruise ships also add to this influx. Concurrently, *mola* manufacture and sales have also increased dramatically.

In addition to these developments, IPAT plans a large resort complex at Los Gruyos, an uninhabited San Blas cay. The resort is scheduled to open in 1978, with a projected initial tourist population of 26,000 per year. This area of San Blas will be the first to be linked to the rest of Panama by a road, scheduled for completion in 1975–76. National government plans for San Blas development is currently centered around this area.

In Cuna communities, ethnic group cohesion was maintained through isolation, segregated female and male roles, and cooperative village maintenance. Now Cuna are substituting cash for their communal work obligations and unrest is evident in San Blas villages. Young people are often bored with island life and resent the demands and restrictions of *Congresso*. As the women specifically become more mobile, realignment of female roles with respect to group maintenance becomes a problem for Cuna society and for the Panamanian tourism industry as well. Some Cuna consider themselves permanent residents of Panama, but many

Plate 1. Cuna Indian, Elena Perez, sewing on a small tourist *mola*. (Photo by Walt Swain, Ailigande, San Blas, 1975)

Cuna who have moved out of San Blas and abandoned traditional occupations later returned to their home communities. It is simply easier to be Cuna with other Cuna than to be an Indian in the big city where prejudice and only menial jobs abound.

Culture change induced by economic development could be partially reconciled with ethnic group maintenance through the distinctive attributes of ethnic tourism. If manipulated by the people themselves, ethnic tourism can serve as an "identity maintenance mechanism" for group cohesion (Graburn 1969). The marketing of Cuna heritage might thus provide an economic livelihood and be a rallying point for ideological solidarity. In particular, sustained *mola* production has the potential of being a powerful symbol of ethnic pride to the Cuna while simultaneously being a marketable symbol of the Cuna. Tourism stimulates the manufacture and sale of *molas*, providing essential opportunities for increased local employment (Boserup 1970).

Insitu Tourism Employment

Tourist-related employment includes local services to care for visitors and the export cottage industry occupations. Within each category there are both traditional as well as new male and female roles. Local employment centers around San Blas hotels and resorts, including two hotels run by *sociedades*, The Anai with eight rooms and Las Palmiras with five rooms. The latter, on Ailigandi, is owned by a mixed *sociedad* of three hundred members and was started as a restaurant which is still its main function. Rotating wage jobs employing six women and four men include housekeepers (women) and counter help (women and men). Cooking is traditionally a woman's task, but quantity preparation of non-Cuna food is a skill many Cuna men learn in the Canal Zone and Panama. Most professional chefs are men, but women continue to clean, and wash the laundry.

Resorts in San Blas include Pedirtupu, an established operation that is careful to maintain good rapport with its Cuna neighbors, and Islandia, which was recently demolished by the Ailigandi village after continued friction with the owner. The IPAT resort projected for Los Gruyos expects to allocate one-half of its fifteen hundred total positions to Cuna, including all of the unskilled work (30 percent of the total); none of the administrative personnel is expected to be Cuna (also 30 percent of available jobs); the remaining 40 percent will be mixed. The absence of Cuna in managerial and skilled jobs in particular does not bode well for the ultimate success of the project. Recent unrest in Caribbean tourism (Bryden 1973), and Cuna traditional values, both indicate a strong need for local involvement at all levels if the project is to have any actual developmental impact.

In conjunction with the IPAT project, the government also plans to build artisan schools and introduce some form of quality control in *mola* production. Ideally, these efforts could be an elaboration of present Congresso efforts and the *mola* co-op already in existence. In addition to *mola* sewing, other Cuna crafts such as male-dominated wood carving and basketry could be expanded to meet the enlarged market for aesthetic and ethnic souvenirs.

Roles in *Mola* Manufacturing and Marketing

An IPAT study as well as an informal survey on Ailigandi indicate that most tourists come to San Blas to experience Cuna culture and to buy *molas*. Many other tourists never visit San Blas, but purchase quantities of *molas* from souvenir shops and street vendors in Panama City. The first large-scale effort initiated in San Blas to deal with the growing demand for *mola* work was a Peace Corps-sponsored project started in 1965 on Nargana, the most westernized of all Cuna communities. Very few Nargana women now living have even worn full traditional dress, and simply lacked the skill to sew *molas* (Reynolds 1968, pp. 3–11). Within a few months, the initial sewing course was expanded with classes offered in neighboring communities. Ultimately, the project included 350 women from eight islands organized like community *sociedades*. Ailigandi, then the only one of the islands with permanent tourist facilities, also participated in the project, but some residents sold *molas* directly to tourists at a price below that set by the sewing group. Attendant problems caused this community to withdraw from the Peace Corps *mola* program.

During 1967 a pre-cooperative was officially formed to enable its members to gain legal benefits including co-op education classes from the national government. Initially, the co-op prospered and operated its own retail store in Panama City, but subsequently by 1972 had cut back to wholesale production only. Many problems contributed to breakdowns in communication and, as a result, in supplies reaching the store. A majority of the participating *socias* are traditional and often illiterate women. They have had to rely on a few bilingual, urbanized Cuna women, Cuna men, and diverse government agencies to coordinate and promote their business. Although the co-op now communicates with *Artisania Panamania*, an IPAT affiliate, there is little indication that they will re-expand into a self-contained retail business. The current *mola* co-op president, a bilingual Cuna woman, commutes between San Blas and her home in Panama City to arrange orders with the eight co-op groups.

The amount of income generated by *mola* sewing is difficult to even estimate. Data from the Tigre *mola* co-op (Brennan 1973) show an average monthly earning of us$15 per *socia* in that community. 1973–74 co-op figures show total annual earnings of us$8,900 for 398 *socias*. As this represents an average, for only 5 percent of all adult Cuna women, *mola* work generates a minimum of us$50,000 annual income. Sale of used *mola* work and individual production rates (as in Tigre) pushes the actual figure to something much higher. *Molas* are in great demand throughout the world. Since 1971, wholesale *mola* prices have increased from us$2.50 per panel to us$4.00 (a minimum set by the *Congresso General*), and today the standard price for a fine *mola* is us$20.00.

While the *mola* co-op was being formed, other *mola* businesses also increased. In addition to tourists, commercial buyers have arrived on islands with thousands of dollars at hand to buy or commission *mola* work. Established shops in Panama City often rely on Cuna men to serve as wholesalers and to supply special order items (from *mola* yarmulkas to watch bands). On Ailigandi, the hotel is the headquarters for an IPAT official's bimonthly *mola* buying trips in the islands to supply the national handicrafts store in Panama. Another Cuna *mola* business is operated by a *tienda* on a piece work basis for *mola* necktie manufacture. Using store materials, women receive in wages us$1.50 per tie, which in turn wholesales for us$3.50 and retails at up to us$10.00. The tie business was started by a Cuna man who, like other male Indian wholesalers and the IPAT official, turn their profits in Panama City.

A unique *mola* business was started in the early 1970s to aid the Ailigandi hospital and facilitate the use of *molas* as payment for services rendered to patients. The buyer is a Cuna woman employee, who, although nontraditional in many ways (including dress), is a very fine *mola* sewer in her own right. She assesses and buys *molas* as they come into the hospital, keeping the accounts in her head. During a typical week in October 1974, 62 *turista* panels, 10 used blouses, and 28 patches were collected, representing a minimum of us$500 worth of wholesale purchases. The buyer receives a regular salary, and the *molas* are sold in private homes in Panama City and the Canal Zone.

Several distinctions can be made with respect to the roles of women and men in *mola* marketing. When *mola* products are sold in quantities through a traditional Cuna organization, be it a family or community, the entrepreneur is usually a man. This conforms to the accepted pattern of men dealing with *wagas* or non-Cuna in all matters outside their home territory. A home-based business, such as bartering coconuts or selling individual *molas* directly to buyers and/or tourists on the islands (and now also in the cities), is frequently handled by women. A woman will also sell for her friends and relatives, but there is no indication that this kind of marketing gives rise either to individual or group female enterprise. However, during the past few years, young girls have become much more involved in *mola* sales, reflecting their math and language skills and possibly indicating female entrepreneurs in the future. The few Cuna women directly involved in quantity *mola* marketing, such as the co-op president and the hospital buyer, are bilingual women already removed from traditional female occupations.

Judging from *mola* co-op data, traditional women will learn new skills, given the opportunity and incentive. In addition to economic concerns, female pride is an important factor in structuring group decisions. For example, the *socias* believed their manager should be a woman, and there was much debate when a male *mola* sewer applied for membership in 1970. The *socias* did allow the man to join because the co-op by-laws say nothing about sex.

The co-op structure made it possible for the first time for many women to have a steady income and the opportunity to learn skills in their home communities, by promoting the first female-owned and operated enterprise ever attempted in San Blas. The co-op has had a visible if tenuous effect on the status of Cuna women. Since 1968, the *Congressos* have gradually acknowledged the *mola* co-op as a bona fide women's community and business organization. Brennan (1973) has computed that a *mola* co-op *socia*'s average monthly income (US$15.00) paid for almost 100 percent of a woman's personal needs and approximately half of the household expenses as well. With this income, a traditional woman gained greater economic status than before. There have even been a few cases of co-op trained women becoming vocal in their local *Congressos*. If Cuna women are franchised, major status changes seem certain.

The *mola* is both a vehicle of change for Cuna women, as well as a Cuna ethnic identity symbol. *Mola* sewing is highly evident as an aspect of daily Cuna life. Many young Cuna women and men wear *mola* work on their otherwise western clothing, and it is also used extensively on special outfits such as band uniforms. Women who sew bad *molas* are censured by *Congresso* in some communities; material printed like *molas* is considered a bad influence; and machine done applique is strictly second class. A good *mola* sewer will sew for other Cuna as well as for her family and the tourist trade.

The future of *mola* sewing depends on a complex blending of economics and ideology affecting the society as a whole. *Molas* are unique because of the aesthetic principles with which they are designed and the care with which they are made. Ethnic tourism has stimulated increased *mola* sewing, but the quality varies from excellent products to crude *turista* work. Preservation of fine *mola* sewing will depend on value according by ethnic pride and market demand as weighed by the Cuna women themselves.

Conclusions

Cuna society is on the verge of major socioeconomic changes, which may benefit Cuna group cohesion and cultural continuity, but to do so will

Plate 2. By Cuna standards, *molas* sewn by machine are of low quality; however the work is acceptable to tourists. (Photo of Elizabeth Pacheco by Walt Swain, Ailigande, San Blas, 1975)

require planning and compromise. The Panamanian government is well aware that the introduction of mass tourism into San Blas could have disastrous effects on the culture if an unquantifiable "carrying capacity" is surpassed. Both legal and moral constraints compel them to heed Cuna wishes, although Panama keenly wants the San Blas resort project for its expanding tourism industry. Cuna leaders are divided over the desired extent of tourism.

Ethnic tourism like many other enterprises may best be assimilated into Cuna society through *sociedad* organizations, as seen in the hotel and *mola* co-op. This is not a panacea, but if all business aspects including management and banking are fully integrated into a full cash economy, *sociedades* should be able to handle most aspects of local service. In this respect, Jopling (1974), in her work on female entrepreneurs and manufacturing, noted that if outside management (as in the hospital and co-op *mola* projects) is initially available to share the social and financial risk of pioneering the untried, then it appears likely that the local business will successfully develop as local residents move into managerial roles. *Sociedad*-type organizations seem particularly appropriate for the ethnic tourism industry, which needs assurance of continued group stability.

Field data supports the hypothesis that if Cuna society is to persist, its adaption to culture changes must once again include realignment of sex-defined statuses and roles. In this instance, a more equitable sharing of occupations and of financial and political rights and obligations has been indicated. As female insulation declines, ethnic tourism can become a vehicle for obtaining some of this role adaptation. By providing ample diversified local employment while simultaneously encouraging people to "be ethnic," tourism can benefit Cuna group solidarity. Such benefits will not occur, however, unless government and big business make more direct efforts for education and job diversification, rather than perpetuating both current male dominance of *mola* marketing and the present availability to Indians of mainly unskilled or menial occupations.

With specific reference to women's roles, a number of occupations are now available in San Blas, but few women have the training, especially the literacy, to handle them. In semitraditional mixed *sociedades*, however, women are expanding roles for remuneration within the existent social structure. As businesses now develop with external assistance, both modernized and traditional Cuna women have the opportunity for schooling and to assume new, formerly male responsibilities and statuses.

The effects of ethnic tourism on the quality of San Blas life will ultimately depend on how it is controlled. The *modus operandi* of continued ethnic tourism is continued attractive ethnicity. In the Cuna's case, there must be sufficient reason for the women to continue producing and wearing high quality *molas* for an expanding market, even as opportunities increase for greater income and status in other employment. Their small society's economic and social survival in relation to imminent changes depends largely on the future position of Cuna women.

University of Washington

5

Tourism in Tonga:
Troubled Times

CHARLES F. URBANOWICZ

The Kingdom of Tonga lies in the heart of fabled Polynesia, approximately 550 miles southwest of Samoa and 450 miles southeast of Fiji. The tiny kingdom encompasses approximately 289 square miles and supports an estimated (1975) population of 100,105—an average density of more than 346 persons per square mile. However, the actual usable land available for settlement is only 190 square miles, giving a true population density of 532 persons per square mile. The population is not evenly distributed and the largest island of the group, Tongatapu (100 square miles with a population of 52,000) is the economic center for the archipelago. This island has also been the historic residence of the aboriginal (Royal) leaders, and Nuku'alofa—the largest city, the capital, and the main tourist target—is located there.

Formerly a British protectorate, Tonga achieved independence in 1970 and entered the British Commonwealth of Nations. The Constitutional Monarchy dates to 1875 and the current monarch, His Majesty King Taufa'ahau Tupou IV, acceded to the throne in 1965. Tongan is the official language, English is the second language and most Tongans are bilingual. The population is also ethnically uniform: 98 percent of the population are Tongans, and all are stalwart Christians. The 1966 census listed 77,429 inhabitants, only 61 of whom failed to declare a religious affiliation.

Tourism is nascent in Tonga, but the number of visitors is increasing annually due to extensive overseas promotions that stress, in colorful brochures, the beauty of "unspoiled" Polynesia, where English is spoken and where there is a "real live King (and Queen)." Although Tonga is the last surviving Polynesian Kingdom, it is far from being the "storybook" land of the culture brokers. It is an overpopulated and underdeveloped tiny nation, struggling to maintain its cultural integrity in the face of twentieth-century changes. There are serious internal economic problems in Tonga, for which tourism might be the panacea. This case study examines the impact of tourism on the Tongan economy and the social and cultural problems associated with the advent of recent mass tourism.

The Economic Problem

Tonga is primarily an agricultural nation of small landholders. Despite Government efforts to modernize and increase food production, the natural resources of the islands are inadequate to feed the growing population. For greater cash-flow, primarily to meet Tongan consumer demands for Western products, Tonga has become an exporter of agricultural commodities. It is germane to note, however, that foodstuffs (especially meat and chicken) account for almost a third of Tonga's annual imports. In 1973, for example, total exports amounted to almost us$5,000,000, with copra being the most important export (at us$3,347,000). Dietary inadequacies among Tongans, occasioned by high food costs, are best assessed by the Minister of Health who stated in 1973 that protein-calorie malnutrition is prevalent among young Tongan children to a disturbing degree. In the same year seventeen cases of severe "nutritional deficiency" required hospitalization, two of which became fatalities.

Spiraling inflation has eroded Tongan buying power over recent years, as indicated by the Consumer Price Index (CPI). Established in 1969 with a September base of 100.0, the CPI is based on the purchasing power of a "typical" Tongan family earning less than us$37 per week. Heavily biased towards food items (64 percent of all items on the index), the CPI has risen steadily (Figure 1) to 172.4 in six years. Increases in food prices, both domestic and imported, have consistently contributed most to this upward trend. In one of the largest overall increases, 11.4 percent in the quarter of June–September 1973, the fruit and vegetable component of the CPI increased by 46.9 percent. In the second largest increase, 11.2 percent from December 1972–March 1973, this same sub-group of basic staples increased by 33.1 percent, while the cereal subgroup (bread, flour, and rice) increased by 31.6 percent.

Unemployment is another critical economic problem. In an island world where land is extremely important, many adult Tongans are without land. Although every Tongan male, upon reaching the age of sixteen (and becoming a taxpayer) is entitled to some "bush land" for crops and "town land" for a home, there simply isn't enough to go around. The Assistant Secretary in the Ministry of Finance pointed out that in 1966, 59 percent of all men over sixteen years of age who were entitled to tax allotments were landless and, no doubt, this proportion has increased by 1971. Even if the unused areas are used it may provide employment for about thirty-four hundred men, still leaving thousands unemployed.

Figure 1

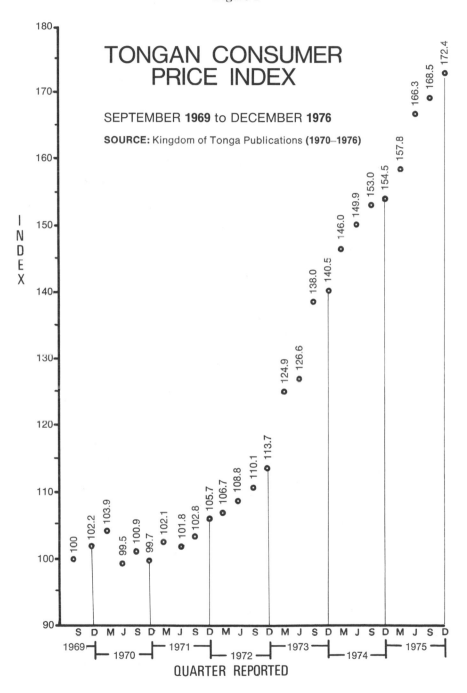

TONGAN CONSUMER
PRICE INDEX

SEPTEMBER **1969** to DECEMBER **1976**

SOURCE: Kingdom of Tonga Publications **(1970–1976)**

The Secretary also noted that every year, only about 5 percent of the Tongans who leave school are able to find employment in the Tongan economy.

To offset this serious lack of domestic employment, thousands of Tongans since 1971 have gone overseas to work, primarily in New Zealand. Their remittances to Tonga have been substantial: in 1971–72 us$1,250,000 and for 1972–73 us$2,000,000. This money, together with donations, gifts, and contributions from other overseas sources (us$2,150,000) have helped to offset the Tongan trade deficit. In addition, individual men, returning to Tonga after the expiration of overseas work permits, often bring back a substantial amount of cash (once estimated to be an average of us$1,800 per man). Although this work program was initiated at the request of the Tongan government, it has been criticized as being a form of economic subservience. The revenues obtained from this unique "export item" (diligent and hardworking Tongans) have, in fact, benefitted the Tongan economy, but they have also created some domestic problems: family life is disrupted for male wage earners who go overseas, and divorce appears to be increasing.

Tonga, as with the rest of Oceania, continues to undergo massive acculturation. The economic problems have aggravated social problems because of the inability of individual Tongans to achieve their Western-induced desires. Housebreaking, theft, and unlawful entry are now prevalent crimes in Tonga and are, unfortunately, apparently increasing at a steady rate. Tongan homes now commonly have barred windows, and families may keep numerous dogs in the yard for protection. Crimes of violence have also increased, especially in attacks by Tongans on non-Tongans. The Tongan Minister of Police openly admits that in view of population pressures and economic side effects, continued potential increase of crime may reasonably be predicted.

In the face of their economic dilemma, it is not surprising that in their 1970–75 development plan, Tonga has assessed tourism as having the greatest economic potential to the Kingdom, both as an employer of labour and also as a source of foreign exchange.

The Economic Role of Tourism

Tourists arrive in Tonga by private yacht, by cruise ships making a one or two-day stop as part of a longer Pacific itinerary, or by air from Samoa or Fiji. Guests to Tonga in 1958 were an elite group, when only three cruise vessels landed passengers at Tongatapu, and some special flights brought a total of sixty-four air passengers from Australia (Figure 2). Subsequently, tourism has grown steadily and rapidly, and more growth is anticipated, including tourism to areas other than Nuku'alofa. In 1973, twenty-four cruise ships also called at Vava'u, approximately 180 miles north of Tongatapu, bringing 9,463 tourists to that island. In 1975, 17,500 tourists visited Vava'u as part of their cruise itinerary.

Figure 2
Tourists to Tonga by Ship and Plane: 1958 to 1975
(Landings at Tongatapu)

Year	Passengers	Number of Ships	In-Passengers	Flights
1958	1,715	3	64	n.a.
1959	2,600	5	45	8
1960	n.a.	7	189	23
1961	2,866	4	308	35
1962	3,677	6	524	66
1963	4,353	6	668	75
1964	5,626	10	992	117
1965	6,398	8	1,174	144
1966	14,581	20	1,460	146
1967	14,240	14	2,883	231
1968	11,111	12	3,465	182
1969	18,111	19	4,326	230
1970	21,025	24	4,001	324
1971	23,500	32	4,000	314
1972	27,259	29	4,599	358
1973	31,502	48	6,356	403
1974	36,308	43	6,403	397
1975	44,968	n.a.	6,770	n.a.

Sources: Kingdom of Tonga Premier's Report. 1958 +; Kingdom of Tonga (1970) DEVEL-
OPMENT PLAN 1970-1975; P. D. Wallis 1971; A. Buchanan 1975. [n.a. = Not
Available.]

The Director of the Tongan Visitors Bureau (TVB) wrote in 1973 that foreign exchange receipts generated through tourism amounted to approximately us$2,154,000, making tourism the second largest generator of foreign exchange after copra (us$3,052,000). In 1974 it was estimated that tourist revenue increased to approximately us$3,270,000, and that projected tourist-generated revenue could possibly amount to as much as us$15,300,000 by 1980. Tourism is definitely increasing in Tonga.

The Government of Tonga is interested in developing tourism for the apparent economic benefits. The TVB was created in 1971 to work towards that goal, and it is the TVB's function to disseminate information to promote tourism. A survey of tourist "likes" and "dissatisfactions" taken by the TVB indicated that many visitors felt that most Tongans did not know enough of their own culture and history (or at least the aspects of touristic interest), so the TVB published a pamphlet for local distribution to remedy this particular complaint. The government has also built small airstrips to encourage tourist travel to outlying islands and has allocated substantial sums of money for hotel expansion and construction. With the help of overseas (primarily Australian) backing, new hotels have been recently constructed on Tongatapu and Vava'u. Japanese companies have also expressed an interest in joint investment with the Tongan government, in facilities that would serve the public and *especially* entice the now almost nonexistent Japanese traveler to Tonga. With Japan in mind, the Tongan monarch traveled to Japan, exchange clubs have been established, Tongans have been encouraged to visit Japan. Late in 1976 the Japan/Tonga Friendship Fellowship opened a US$35,000 resort clubhouse in Tonga, in an effort to develop growing contacts and increase guests to Tonga. His Majesty also visited Hawaii in late 1976 to assess the role of tourism, as well as the role of Tongans in tourism at the Polynesian Cultural Center (see chapter 14).

Tourism, however, increases the economic problems—especially the need for additional imported foodstuffs. Air passengers, for whom facilities are largely being constructed, have to be fed, and although many enjoy the local fruits and bread (made from the imported flour), few would be content for long on the relatively bland Tongan diet of yams, taro, and fruit. Tongans are, in effect, competing with the tourists for the imported foods. The ever-increasing quantities of food that must be imported to feed the growing number of tourists contributes to the steadily rising CPI. A similar situation prevails in Fiji, as Ward (1976, p. 171) notes:

> Some [Fiji] hotels, in the interest of greater economy and convenience, only provide a strictly limited choice of meals and the sort of meals which tourists expect to receive in their home countries, e.g. of the steak-hamburger-mixed grill variety. Many hotels argue that this is all the tourist wants although the best hotels do provide more extensive menus. The majority [of hotels, however] do provide the food which is produced and consumed by the local inhabitants and this compounds the problem of buying requirements from domestic producers.

Ward also states that despite the availability of many local foodstuffs tourists might consume, hotels in Fiji prefer to purchase their requirements overseas because, it has been argued, "they can only then be assured of continuity in supplies and of a consistent high standard of quality."

Tourism has grown rapidly in Tonga, but it could evaporate just as quickly. Tongans occasionally have experienced situations when the anticipated tourists failed to arrive. In 1972, at least forty tour groups cancelled their planned air visits to Tongatapu because the tour operators could not be assured of making airline connections from the Kingdom to other points on the itinerary.

Because of mounting fuel and labor costs, long-haul cruises such as those that stop at Tonga are not as profitable as the short-haul, fast turn-around cruises that operate weekly or biweekly in the Caribbean (Waters and Patterson 1976). As a result, in the foreseeable future cruises stopping at Tonga might decrease as much as 50 percent in a single year, with a projected annual loss of revenue of us$600,000. This would seriously affect the handicraft manufacturers and other businessmen in the King-dom. Losses of anticipated revenue generated through tourism should serve to reinforce the potential disaster for Tongans if their economy is tied too closely to tourism.

It must also be noted that while short-term cruise passengers consume little of the imported foodstuffs, the airline guests (whose stay ranges from five to eleven days) must be fed for the duration of their visit. The host/guest competition for food and natural resources will further contri-bute to the upward inflationary curve.

What Price Tourism?

Tongans are increasingly becoming the victims of their own tourism. They are exceedingly happy when cruise ships dock with a thousand passengers (and several hundred crew members), and pump thousands of dollars into the economy in an eight-hour period, but Tongans are even happier at dusk when the ships depart. The physical impact of a thousand tourists on one town situated on a relatively tiny island is tremendous, especially when most of the tourists are bussed around to "see" all the sights of the island. The tourist literature has brought the visitors here "to observe the traditional Tongan way of life in the *natives' own habitat*" and the shore excursions promise that you will "see the daily work routine of men and women—gardening, weaving baskets, cooking, washing and their many other activities. This village walking tour offers you an excellent opportunity to photograph the Tongan people as they really are" (Itinerary for the International Institute, 24 June 1974). Tongans cannot tolerate being regarded as members of a "cultural zoo" and are not "on display" for wealthy visitors. Under these circumstances, there are exceedingly few opportunities for a true host/guest relationship to de-velop.

Tourists have usually heard something about Tonga long before they arrive. Many guests remember the late Queen of Tonga's memorable ride in an open carriage during a rainfall when Her Majesty Queen Salote Tupou III attended the coronation of Her Majesty Queen Elizabeth II in London in 1953. Tourists, therefore, already "know" something about

Tonga, and they want to "see" Tonga; but all too often cruise passengers get only a look at a "phony-folk-culture" in action—a Disneyland of the Pacific, so to speak.

The air guests, fewer in number (but staying longer), may have a somewhat different experience. They have the opportunity to enjoy the recreational facilities of a tropical island—swimming, fishing, and snorkeling—and they may also have the opportunity to see more of the island at a gradual pace, to meet some of the truly hospitable Tongans on a person-to-person basis, and to share a truly cross-cultural educational experience. However, the actual experiences of the tourist can be less than this ideal.

Forster (1964, pp. 217–22) pointed out that one of the fascinating aspects of the tourist process in the Pacific is the deliberate creation of a "phony-folk-culture," which the indigenous inhabitants develop to provide "authentic native culture" to the tourists. For example, a popular tourist "attraction" is a display of dances in Tonga: the program may contain almost a dozen Fijian, Tahitian, Hawaiian, or New Zealand dances performed by the Tongan dancers but show only one or two Tongan dances. The fact is granted that a Tahitian *tamure* has a tremendous amount of visual impact, and a Fijian fire dance is dramatic, but Tongan dances have a beauty and symmetry of their own that should be performed for the visitors to Tonga.

It is this alteration of their basic culture that has prompted Tongans to consider legislating the tourist industry. They seek to ensure the active preservation of the traditional Tongan way of life and culture by integrating traditional patterns into mass tourism and not making traditional culture a contemporary "phony-folk-culture."

Other tangible and observable social problems have developed in the Kingdom as a result of the tourist influx: some Tongan children now beg from tourists at the major tourist attractions; prostitution and homosexuality appear to be increasing (not necessarily for the tourists but for the crew members of the cruise ships); tourists are harassed as they walk through city streets and villages; and price-gouging, especially for transportation, is a common complaint.

The substantial amount of quickly-generated cash derived from cruise ship passengers (for an "authentic" Polynesian feast, shore excursions around the island, and the purchase of handicrafts), when placed into circulation in the port towns, can be the occasion for a party. Drinking may commence even before the ship has weighed anchor and drunkenness appears to be a major source of crime. Tongans still enjoy their traditional *kava* drink, but as I have stated elsewhere, when individuals begin to consume more alcohol than *kava*, in violation of their Christian ethic, it is an indication that the basic fabric of their culture and society has shifted. In recent years Tongans have been evicted from their own hotels for drunkenness (and for being badly dressed) in order to "protect the image of the Kingdom in the eyes of the tourist." Housebreaking, theft, and unlawful entry are prevalent crimes, and in 1973, for example, there were 427 convictions for theft.

Conclusions

Deep-seated economic problems induced by a growing population have almost engulfed the tiny islands of Tonga. The glitter of tourist money seemingly promises a substantial portion of much-needed economic help, but would it bring more "troubled times"? The current substantial cruise business might be considered relatively benign in that visitors are short-term, and they arrive and depart at a preappointed hour. Comparatively little capital or space is required to cater to their needs, aside from docking areas and taxis or busses. Further, the money cruise passengers spend is largely for local services (transportation, amusement, and for handicrafts as souvenirs) and directly benefits individuals. The threatened demise of the cruise industry, to be replaced with an increasing number of air travelers, may be potentially more disruptive to the economy and to the culture. To accommodate air visitors, hotels and resort facilities must be financed and built, and they occupy land—already in short supply, giving to it by virtue of location a changed economic value. No longer "bush" or "town," now it is "recreational" land. Given the small size of Nuku'alofa as well as Tongatapu, one must imagine the impact if one thousand guests were continually present, day *and* night, demanding that their needs be catered—including on Sunday when Tongans traditionally do not work. And although air travel is currently nascent, with a limited number of annual visitors, the advent of mass travel could "Waikiki" the beaches, and inundate local culture as has already happened in Hawaii.

The Prime Minister of Tonga (His Majesty's brother) has repeatedly stressed that Tongan culture can withstand the impact of modern tourism development. I, too, am certain that Tongans will survive; however, will they still be Tongans? Or will they become yet another example of a people who have been forced to abandon their traditions (or at least remove them "back stage" away from prying eyes) to prevent their becoming the "quaint customs" of ethnic tourism?

The anthropological analysis of economic process [here, tourism] differs from the statistical methods employed by economic planners in that the former assesses the impact upon culture and the social milieu rather than being restricted to balance-of-trade or the CPI. There is an ethnohistoric component to culture change—from then to now—just as there is a cross-cultural component—from there to here—that must be studied. Tongans must become aware of the changes that have occurred as a result of non-Tongan influences; they must also study the effects of tourism elsewhere in the Pacific islands. From these two sources, they should design for the future. The 1970–75 development plan stated that tourism if properly controlled could make a positive contribution to the economy. Possibly the wording of a new development plan should read that tourism *must be* properly controlled if it is to make a positive contribution to the economy, the Tongan hosts, and the non-Tongan guests.

California State University, Chico

6

Towards a Theoretical Analysis of Tourism: Economic Dualism and Cultural Involution in Bali

PHILIP FRICK MCKEAN

Tourism in Bali

Prior to World War II, Dutch ships brought passengers to Bali for a five-day tour of the island made famous in Europe when orchestras from Bali performed at the Paris Colonial Exposition in 1932. Artists, ethnographers, and other visitors spread the image of the exquisite aesthetic attainments of the Balinese. Following the Indonesian Revolution in 1945, President Sukarno used Bali as a retreat, and often entertained foreign dignitaries at his palatial home there. However, poor roads, small airfields, shallow harbors, and a permeating instability of both economic and political institutions in Indonesia inhibited tourism until 1969, when a more liberal government supported construction of a modern jet airport. Since then, visitors have increased from forty thousand to over one hundred thousand annually. Hotel facilities have been built along the coast at Sanur and Kuta, tour agencies and art shops have opened roads, electric systems, and other major investments in the infra-structure have been made, and a Master Plan for land use and development was commissioned by the World Bank. Mass tourism is now a social reality affecting the island in multiple ways.

The Theoretical Problem

A common theme in the anthropological study of tourism is the considerable cultural change wrought by the coming of tourists. Normal assumptions include that (1) changes are brought about by the intrusion of an external, usually superordinate sociocultural system, into a weaker, receiving culture; (2) changes are generally destructive to the indigenous tradition; (3) the changes will lead to a homogeneous culture as ethnic or local identity is subsumed under the aegis of a technologically-advanced industrial system, a national and multinational bureaucracy, a consumer-oriented economy, and jet-age life-style. Few analyses exist of alternative mechanisms available to indigenous populations to resist change, or to retain and even revitalize their social fabric and customs within the changed conditions wrought by the tourist industry. If this approach has not been considered by anthropologists, other writers have completely overlooked the possibility and typically turned up their noses in disdain at tourists and their effect on the host area. Concern that obnoxious, insensitive tourists will despoil Bali is widespread, especially among foreign intelligentsia, as the following passage indicates (Hanna 1972, pp. 2, 5, 6):

> Tourism, whether or not of a purely cultural variety, is now the boom industry in Bali; but jumbo-jet flights of joy seekers may blight the very enchantments that even the less cultured economy-class package-tour patrons are led by their hard-sell agents to breathlessly anticipate. . . . During the Sukarno years the island had unhappy experiences from tampering with the artistic traditions. Today's distortions, which are just as deliberate, are as artistically if not as politically sinister. . . . This, then, is the 'Waikiki-anization' of Bali. . . . Even the less sensitive tourists are starting to deplore it, and the more thoughtful Balinese are bracing themselves to withstand the worst.

This pessimistic hand-wringing for the return of the "good old days" is founded on the assumption that the Balinese will be willy-nilly, passive receptors of a total package of "modernization." Further, these critics have ignored the varied surrogates that enable groups to respond to both internal and external stimuli. Presuming that monolithic and uniform results will occur, these observers fail to appreciate the differential, selective changes that may occur within a cultural tradition. Although socioeconomic change is taking place in Bali, I argue that it goes hand-in-hand with the conservation of the traditional culture. My field data supports the hypothesis that tourism may in fact strengthen the process of conserving, reforming, and recreating certain traditions. The effects of tourism are examined in terms of two contrasting theoretical constructs—economic dualism and cultural involution—to assess the validity of the hypothesis.

Economic Dualism

In the simplest theoretical analysis, I posit two extremes: (1) a "tourist world" in which total sociocultural change occurs in the area affected by tourism and the host area becomes modelled after the patterns of the visiting groups; *or* (2) a "native world" in which no change occurs, and life-as-usual-prior-to-contact goes on. These are extremes on a continuum, and each should be viewed as an "ideal type."

If separation between the two "worlds" is emphasized, the apparent continuity or persistence of each must be explained in terms of a system that enables transactions to take place, but which binds them so that they are essentially autonomous and noninterfering. The Dutch economist J. H. Boeke noticed a separation between two sectors of the Indonesian economy—the capitalist and the peasant—and reasoned that there must be profound causes for the "dualism." Boeke felt that the peasant was not particularly "rational" in his economic behavior, and that he was less interested in saving and investing than in traditional goals such as gaining status, performing rituals, and building solidarity with neighbors. Capitalists, on the other hand, strive to exploit scarce resources and make profits, thereby responding "rationally" to the economic forces of supply and demand.

Boeke's theories of economics are based on a series of evolutionary phases, with capitalism at its climax in both its "eastern" as well as "western" guises. A unilineal and monolithic quality pervades his analysis (1953, p. 14):

> In each phase (pre-capitalistic through late capitalistic) society may be said to be uniform, homogeneous; it evolves as a whole, in all its expressions, whether spiritual or material, cultural or economic; there is harmony and coherence between the different social phenomena; one spiritual conception pervades all.

Modern Balinese, however, have *not* become exclusively "capitalist" persons, in antithesis to the "pre-capitalistic" persons posited by Boeke (1953, pp. 12 ff.). Nor have they, as Boeke asserts for the Southern Asian Chinese or Indian minorities, "been absorbed by, and become dependent on, the fully developed western capitalism" (1953, p. 15). Through a selective process, the Balinese have found ways to increase their cash flow without becoming "capitalists" nor following totally the socioeconomic trends that Boeke predicts. Boeke also develops several corollaries to describe the advent of capitalism, including these essentials: "a sharp distinction between business and household, and the continuous harrowing of the latter; the commodity-character of all products; a steadily growing division of labor, with its counterparts: organization and planning, in contracts and in corporations" (1953, p. 13). In contrast, Balinese organizations that promote and arrange tourism primarily function through family and neighborhood ties.

Boeke uses several specific traits to characterize "eastern forms of industry," which are listed below, and examined in terms of my data for their appropriateness to characterize tourism on Bali:

> 1. Aversion to capital; i.e. conscious dislike of investing capital and of the risks attending this. (1953, pp. 101–5)

Many hamlet cooperatives have worked strenuously to acquire the necessary capital to upgrade their orchestras, to obtain costumes, and rebuild the meeting halls used as performance centers—based on the risky expectation that they would be able to attract paying tourists on a regular basis. They have, in effect, invested in their cultural traditions, and planned for repayment, with accrued interest that could be both monetarily and culturally.

2. Only slight interest in finish and accuracy. (1953, pp. 101–5)

One who has viewed a *legong* dance in Peliatan, a mask carved by Ida Bagus Gelodog, or a statue carved by Ida Bagus Tilem, or examined the construction of decorations at a Balinese cremation, is likely to disagree with the preceding statement. The evidence in Bali, at least with reference to the best workmanship, does not support Boeke's assertion. However, the "tourist junk art" assuredly does lack "finish and accuracy."

3. Lack of business qualities. No attempt is made to compute the profitableness of a business or to find the most economical system of utilizing labor. (1953, pp. 101–5)

This generalized statement is not difficult to counter. For example, a royal family who owns the Pemetjutan Palace in Den Pasar maintains careful record of profit and loss. This family operates a variety of income producing schemes: promotion of paintings, a gift shop, and a weekly dramatic performance catering to the tourist market.

4. Failure to come up to even the minimum requirements of standard and sample. (1953, pp. 101–5)

While some handicrafts may fall under this judgment (weaving and carving, which are produced in large numbers by poorly trained workers), it is inaccurate as a whole, for the detail in architecture, temple ornamentation, costuming, and dance are evaluated critically. Balinese carefully distinguish between high and low standards in their traditional culture. Even in the products available to tourists, it is not true that there is a lack of "quality control." Sanctions may be imposed by an island-wide consultative body of artists and government officials (LISTIBIYA) and by a Conservatory for the Arts (KOBAR). Informal sanctions from villagers (laughter, for example) prevail on those who carve or dance poorly and have also served to maintain high quality among many of the artists and craftsmen in Bali. There are, of course, "sweat shop" production centers catering to the assumed lower standards of the mass tourist market.

Boeke asserts a unilateral development of economics, and further projects it into the life-styles, laws, and beliefs pervasive in a society. He views the "pre-capitalistic" societies of the East, especially Indonesia, as losing out to Western-oriented "late capitalism." The dialectic is a false one in Bali, for adaptive alternatives exist to link the local economy to the

Plate 1. *Legong* dancers shown at a temple gate. Although adapted from indigenous religious celebrations, even tourist performances require extensive training and fine costumes. (Batubulan, Bali)

international one without destruction of the former. Nor does the economic development accompanying tourism necessarily lead to "late
capitalism" in Bali. No mutually exclusive choice is enforced between the
multiple roles available to Balinese. The traditional roles have not been
entirely replaced or substituted with those found in the capitalistic West.
In significant ways, the advent of the tourist industry has meant an
addition of roles: the coming of tourists to Bali has strengthened the
"folk," "ethnic," or "local" survival of Balinese, rather than leading them
into the homogeneity of the industrialized world. Their traditional roles as
dancers, musicians, artists, or carvers are now alternative and additional
sources of livelihood for individuals and whole communities. By no
means has the traditional ethos perished, and a complex selective process
is operative. Some social units have gained greater cohesion while
simultaneously profiting from the tourist industry (a group performing
dances, for example). Other social units (such as residential groups) have
been necessarily modified. The nuclear family has become more important, especially in the residence compounds for employees provided by
the Hotel Bali Beach and other tourist establishments. For this segment,
the extended family is still supported, visited, and remembered, but at
a distance. Only a few mobile, career-oriented young persons forsake it
entirely.

Economic dualism as posited by Boeke is a theory with limited
explanatory validity. The many economic interactions between Balinese
and tourists bind the two groups in a common field.

Cultural Involution

A continuous syncretic process has occurred in Bali through which
elements of the traditions are mixed so that it is practically impossible to
distinguish them, yet it is possible to see adumbrations of each in the
current blend. More of the ancient *Bali aga* traditions persist in the rural,
mountain villages, and more of the modern occur in Denpasar's urban
sprawl, but in both contexts it is not unusual to see a blend that is at first
blush almost ludicrous. A young woman, for example, appropriately
costumed for the festival in which she is to dance, may arrive at the
village temple perched on the back of a Japanese 250cc. motorbike,
driven by a male friend dressed in jeans and denim jacket. Later, he may
appear in the festival acting the part of Prime Minister Gadja Mada in a
legendary opera about the Madjapahit Empire. Both of them will
participate in the rituals, which include the sacrifice of a live chick or
duckling, the possibility of entering a trance, and offerings of rice, fruit,
and flowers to the divine powers. Before dawn, as the celebration comes
to an end, they will return home on the motorbike to sleep a little before

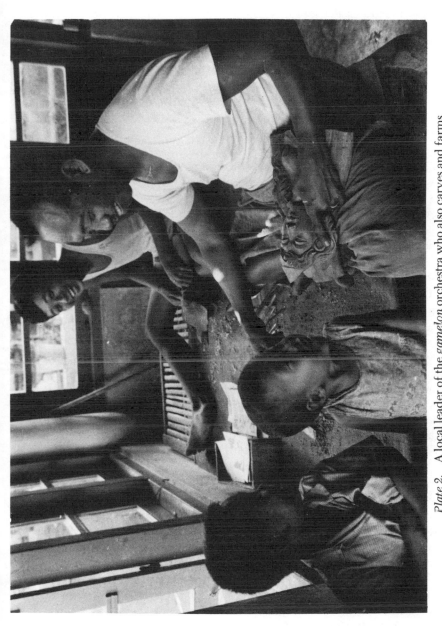

Plate 2.   A local leader of the *gamelon* orchestra who also carves and farms, shown with some of his children. (Sesetan, Bali)

attending classes in medicine or economics at the University. This example illustrates the gamut of historical influences that have created "Balinese culture." The process of synthesis is not unique to Bali, as Redfield has written (1955, p. 25):

> We have studied changes as processes; we see something happening to a native society or culture and we hope to discover significant generalizations. So long as things keep happening it is still a native society or cultural system that we see undergoing change. But when the effects of the outside influences become stabilized we begin to see a new and expanded total system in which part is of native origin and part is of Euroamerican origin.

That an "expanded total system" is coming into being in Bali is obvious. Knowing more of its configurations reward future researchers, and the present study attempts to describe and analyze only that portion of the system touching on tourism. Yet, mass tourism is a crucial aspect of the "expanded total system," for reasons of economics, social order, and aesthetics.

An ironic theme permeates this analysis: modernization in Bali is occurring; tourism introduces new ideas and is a major source of funds. Yet, the tourists expect the perpetuation of ancient traditions, especially in the performing and plastic arts, and would not visit in such numbers if Bali were to become a thoroughly modern island. Both conservatism and economic necessity encourage the Balinese to maintain their skills as carvers, musicians, and dancers in order to have the funds for modernization.

This process is "cultural involution," following the language of Geertz who introduced the notion of "agricultural involution" (1963a). Like Boeke, Geertz emphasizes the traditionalism of the Indonesian peasantry on the "inner islands" of Java and Bali; however, he attributes it not to ancient, indeed static sociocultural patterns, but to the impact of colonialism. Under that aegis, the productivity of the land was increased to absorb a rapidly growing population, and the resultant ornate, intricate social and subsistence systems are explained as "the overdriving of an established form in such a way that it becomes rigid through an inward over-elaboration of detail." (1963a, p. 82). Geertz (1963b, pp. 106–20) studied in the town of Tabanan to the west of Denpasar. He found a variety of voluntary organizations (*sekahas*) all organized by the princely families; members were recapping tires, manufacturing ice and soft drinks, trading in coffee and pigs, running new bus routes and stores. He suggested that the noble *Ksatria* families were attempting to retain their power through economic activity since their political prestige had waned:

> Drawing upon the "duck-like" collectivism of the Balinese village and upon their own oligarchic traditions, some of Tabanan's more dynamic aristocrats

have initiated a fundamental reorganization of the town's whole economic system. But now that the . . . groups have emerged into the strangely land-scaped and ill-defined zone where neither the forms of ancient custom nor those of the modern West offer reliable guides to action, they are gradually coming to discover that these readjusted older patterns are insufficient to complete the task for which they set themselves: . . . Tabanan's [firms] fail to rationalize. (Geertz 1963b, p. 140)

Geertz believes that the princely mentality will not serve the thrust toward development and that the professional manager must come to the fore if there is to be complete modernization. Earlier he noted that the dangers in the Tabanan system were already evident: too many persons were employed for the work to be done, inefficiency was compounded by multiple claims on profits, so there was little capital reinvested by the princes, giving the businesses the quality of a "relief project" (1963b, p. 123). Yet, these criticisms of the development potential in Tabanan may be viewed more positively. If the enterprises do not fail completely, but manage to provide a living for the multitude of employees, then the princes have accomplished at least a part of what they set out to do, that is, maintain power.

More centrally, the liabilities accompanying these changes may become assets if the assumption that Bali needs to go down the path towards an "industrial society" is challenged (Geertz 1963b, p. 140).

If, in the absence of local resources, future "modern society" in Bali could not be supported by the production of petrochemicals or machine tools, then it appears that economic prosperity might be based on cultural production—the establishment of a truly "post-industrial" service industry, which is at least in part what tourism fosters. The entertainment, education, and care of international visitors would then pay the Balinese to do what they have learned to do so well for their own satisfaction—perform their arts and religion, their crafts and ceremonials.

The economic "rationalization" would favor retention of the existent social ties, which connect villagers in overlapping planes (Geertz 1959). The fact is that Balinese are traditionally tied or bound (kaiket in Balinese, or terikat in Indonesian) to a wide variety of groups—irrigation societies (subak), residential hamlet organizations (bandjar), temple groupings (pura), voluntary associations such as musical and dramatic clubs (sekaha), and patrilineal clans (dadia) (Lansing 1973). Adaptation with minimal dislocation to the Balinese would then be possible were these traditional social bonds retained to some extent, and in a process of involution not unfamiliar to the Balinese, reaffirmed and gradually rearranged to include their aspirations for more education, better health care, and a share of the technological wealth that accompanies hopes of development in Bali as well as throughout Indonesia. It is these linkages, or more precisely what these ties enable the Balinese to make with them, that will attract, educate, and entertain the tourists.

Hypothetically, a transition to "post-industrial society" in Bali would involve the more ancient social organization; however, another dimension emerges, which has implications for social order and cultural creativity beyond Bali. In contrast to the anomic and uprooted quality of modern urban life, which so many analysts have held to be endemic, in these Balinese efforts may lie a clue to future development of human bonds and loyalties, group responsibilities, and productivity, which might make all human life more humane. However, will temple ceremonies, religious observances, their attendant music, dances, and offerings become a kind of "floor show" for the guests as well as the Balinese? Could they ultimately become a hypocritical "fake culture," created by the secularizing tendencies of tourism, converting *homo religiosus* into *homo economicus*? If the Balinese (and we could extend this supposition to any group) can thus be "bought," so that economic gain is the sole value, then an argument encouraging tourism in Bali will be false prophecy, bad social science, and a plague for the Balinese. I do not foresee this happening as long as Balinese are bound to other Balinese by ties of religious ritual, cosmic orientation, and ancestral loyalty (cf. Boon 1974, p. 24). An analysis of the production of art illustrates Balinese involution. The maintenance of self-respect through "presentation of culture" may be one of the primary factors in continued Balinese existence as a unique cultural entity. In earlier times, "presentation of culture" was demonstrated to other Balinese, to the spirit realm, and to alien neighbors in Java who posed a political as well as a religious threat to the Balinese.

Graburn has described other societies in which the production of art for outsiders has heightened self-identity and self-value, and has encouraged appreciation of indigenous craft and creativity. Analyzing the carving of Canadian and Alaskan Eskimos, the Maori, and the Kamba of Kenya, Graburn (1969, p. 467) has suggested that a "special economic relationship" may develop wherein a small-scale society uses its special skills to its advantage, surpassing the efforts of the larger society: "The Eskimos know that the white man cannot or will not carve soapstone as well as they can. The same might be said of Navajo jewelry and Maori woodcarving."

He has proposed a typology of the "portable arts" for cross-cultural analysis (1) *functional fine arts*, which have great contemporary cultural and social significance to the people themselves, comparable to Balinese offerings and temple carvings; (2) *commercial fine arts*, made for sale to a specialized audience of patrons or connoisseurs, analogous to tapestries hung in Balinese palaces or ornamental carvings decorating the homes of the wealthy; (3) *souvenir arts*, made for sale to a wider audience, which in

Bali include inexpensive carvings, paintings, masks, cloths, and jewelry; and (4) *assimilated fine arts*, including those attempts to copy or use the traditional arts of the outsiders by whom they are being influenced. The abstract paintings by the young painters of Ubud—who use "western" colors and canvases, as well as styles to paint Balinese landscapes, fighting cocks, and portraits—or weavers who make tablecloths with Balinese designs on imported looms reflect this category. Graburn acknowledges that the typology poses some problems of classification, as with the Canadian Eskimo soapstone carvings, which range from "commercial fine art" costing thousands of dollars to the inexpensive, mediocre, hurriedly-done works of less careful craftsmen, which is "souvenir art." A comparable range also occurs in Bali. Graburn (1969, pp. 465–66) discusses the phenomenon of "airport art":

> One fairly obvious feature of the many cases discussed is the recurrent tendency toward simplification, increase in volume, standardization and eventually mass production on an assembly line basis. Such trends almost inevitably preclude the maintenance of functional fine arts, and lead through commercial arts to souvenir art. The volume may rise and the economic support afforded may increase temporarily; however, in such cases the produce must repond to the market and the whole venture becomes subject to the fast changing whims and taste of a mass culture. However, if the majority of the producers are really responsive to the market they will probably adapt and find other products which sell, as long as their own aesthetic impulses are held in abeyance.

In Bali the rush toward standardization and simplification of the souvenir arts exists without the total loss of either functional fine arts or commercial fine arts, because indigenous institutions continue to demand high quality craftsmanship as appropriate offerings for the "divine world." Balinese could ignore this mandate only at personal and corporate peril. In Balinese ethos, to offer inferior gifts to the divine powers, and incur their displeasure, would be silly and shortsighted. It is one thing to sell inferior goods to tourists who do not know or care about artistic expertise, but to shortchange the infinitely superior taste of the spirit realm would be foolhardy indeed. Thus, Balinese craftsmen remain responsive to the marketplace in their willingness to alter the themes of their carvings from *wayang* (shadow puppet) figures to animal figures— and even to busts of Sophia Loren and Raquel Welch—and also responsive to the "market" of the "divine world" whose tastes and expectations are believed to remain infinitely more exquisite. Graburn (1969, pp. 459–66) reported that in other non-Balinese cases, craftsmanship has suffered a loss in quality, because the quality of the spiritual realm evidently suffered from degradation, and the spiritual "audience" was no longer significantly viable. This is not true in Bali, at least not yet.

While the sacred realm authenticates and legitimates Balinese craft, dance, and drama, these aesthetic creations simultaneously receive economic encouragement from tourists. This involution illuminates the peculiar characteristics of classic tradition and modernity which combine to strengthen the Balinese cultural productivity and self-identity.

Field data suggests that Balinese cultural traditions may be preserved by involution. This contrasts with the assertion by both anthropologists and tourists that culture is a static entity, self-contained and isolated, that will wither like a fragile flower when exposed to chilling exterior influences. Graburn's thesis that artistic production may integrate and express the special identity of a minority group is applicable to the Balinese situation. Anthropologists need to develop hypotheses about the conservation of culture in the midst of economic and social changes wrought by the international tourist industry, as well as consider the theoretical significance of anthropological studies of tourism in general.

Conclusion: Bali and Tourism

The reciprocal effect of tourists on contemporary Balinese is profound, and certain to develop in unexpected ways in the future, no matter how visionary analysts may try to be. Nevertheless, I will conclude with some observations about what may be expected in the coming years, based on research experience.

The trend in Bali towards increasing economic dependence on tourism reflects the growing worldwide interconnection between nations. Bali is no longer an insulated, self-sufficient, socioeconomic unit, but is dependent on the world economic cycles, especially those of the developed industrial nations that permit citizens to travel at will. Bali may boom for a period of time, but if economic cycles follow historic precedents, there will be times of world economy slumps, which would distinctly affect contemporary Bali. The "luxury" of tourism may be an early casualty in a general economic depression. Those Balinese dependent on tourism would suffer a loss of income, and need alternate sources of income or "welfare" or "relief." The persistent and ancient ties of kin, neighborhood, and temple obligations might provide sanctuary for the unemployed or underemployed. Reactivated or enlarged traditional social groups could care for members in need, but only if individual family members now supported by tourism maintained their traditional obligations and roles during their halcyon days. If these ties were still extant, Balinese might then weather the economic storms (Lansing 1973). Insofar as the Balinese understand that tourism may not be a totally dependable source of income, this very uncertainty and fluidity of the industry is likely to encourage the conservation of the social bonds, if for no other reason than a kind of familial social insurance.

Bali is a prime example of ethnic tourism, or as it is termed on the island "cultural tourism." The tourists have become patrons for particular cultural or ethnic expressions, such as the confrontation of the witch (*rangda*) and the dragon (*barong*), the so-called monkey dance (*ketjak*), and a wide range of wood carvings (cf. McKean 1977). Certain of these activities have become far more widespread in the past decade, and a kind of revitalization of folk arts is found in many villages. For example, school children are taught the *ketjak* dance and music in the elementary grades, and carving has also become a part of the curriculum. The identity of young Balinese is formed, in part, by the recognition that their skills are of value to visitors as well as to local audiences. If they carve or dance or perform in a drama sufficiently well, their abilities may become a source of profit to them and their families, and no small source of personal pride and satisfaction. I talked with several young dancers who recited "famous people and places" who had witnessed their performances, from Robert Kennedy to the Beatles. Memories of tours to Europe, Australia, or North America will be savored and shared. So the younger Balinese find their identity as Balinese to be sharply framed by the mirror that tourism holds up to them, and has led many of them to celebrate their own traditions with continued vitality.

Plate 3. Tourists attending a performance of the Balinese *Barong*. (Batubalan, Bali)

Certainly there are dangers for the Balinese in embracing tourism, and as in Toraja, the misuse of scarce resources, increased stratification with the "rich getting richer," or environmental and ritual erosion may be so damaging to the indigenous way of life that tourism could eventually be evaluated by both social scientists and local villager as a profound and disastrous blight. The results will depend to considerable degree on actions within the political structures.

The government will necessarily have a great deal to say about the benefits and liabilities that tourism brings to Bali or Toraja. The national government incorporated the growth of tourist facilities as part of the First Five Year Development Plan, and sustains it into the Second Five Year Plan (1974–79). Officials are naturally concerned with increasing the flow of foreign currency in to Indonesia, and view tourism as a new and important source of funds. But the provincial and local political structures in Bali have attempted to counter the national pressures on them. They have sought to zone certain areas as "off-limits" to tourist development; they have insisted that the new hotels be erected no higher than the palm trees; they have organized artists and master teachers to review the quality of tourist performances and prevent ill-trained troups from performing; and they have prohibited the sale of tickets to certain cultural activities, such as cremations. They have sought to enforce the national prohibition against alienating land, so that hotels may purchase leases for extended periods, but not the unlimited rights to it. Balinese efforts to have the Hindu religion legitimated under the national Ministry of Religion have met with considerable success, and there is now a national organization, the Parisada Hindu Dharma, with headquarters in Bali.

Safeguards need to be initiated if thoughtless or exploitative tourism, from multinational corporations to Jakarta-based speculators, is not to dominate in Bali. The provincial authorities will need to be vigilant in enforcing existent laws and proposing new legislation on behalf of villagers. Hamlet-level leaders should be better trained and held responsible to both local and regional authorities for the actions of hosts in their treatment of guests. Inspection teams could be appointed by the government to make regular and thorough reports on the processes of cultural change and the impact of tourism; such teams might be composed of prominent international and national scholars, artists, journalists, and professional and working persons who would speak on behalf of the powerless, indicating new problems due to tourism. Such "internal policing" of tourism would be in the self-interest of both the Balinese and the Indonesian government; otherise the extraordinary cultural riches of Bali might become so debased that they would no longer be of interest to travelers or valued by villagers themselves.

Underlying tourism is a quest or an odyssey to see, and perhaps to understand, the whole inhabited earth, the *oikumene*. Tourism can be viewed as not an entirely banal pleasure-seeking or escapism (MacCannell 1976), but as a profound, widely-shared human desire to know "others," with the reciprocal possibility that we may come to know ourselves. As social scientists we need to acknowledge the phenomena inherent in contemporary tourism, and closely study locales with different histories, ecologies, indigenous traditions, and socioeconomic structures to assess the range of tourist-native interactions in a variety of situations. We need to test the theoretical analysis suggested here, that tourism may selectively strengthen local traditions and societies, and then re-examine conditions in Bali, with particular attention to social bonds and cultural performances, cultural involution, and aesthetic-economic interactions. Anthropologists may thus contribute to the expanding appreciation of the tourists and the toured, not only in Bali but throughout the world.

Hampshire College

7

Tourism in Toraja
(Sulawesi, Indonesia)

ERIC CRYSTAL

Indonesia is the largest of the Southeast Asian states, but prior to World War II, tourism was largely confined to Dutch colonials and to occasional elite travelers who principally visited the island of Bali, noted for its ceremonial pageantry. The regime of the late President Sukarno (1945-66), with its anti-Western, often xenophobic policies, effectively discouraged tourism. Under the aegis of the "new Order" that came to power in 1966, tourism accelerated more rapidly in Indonesia that in any neighboring Pacific area country. Annual visits increased from a total of 20,000 in 1966 to 86,000 in 1968, and to 129,000 in 1970, primarily because of the changed political climate. Indicative of the new thrust towards development planning, the Director General of Tourism proclaimed the government's intent to move the "invisible export" [tourism] from its then eighth to third position as an earner of foreign exchange. The first Five Year Plan, implemented in April 1969 stressed tourist development in relatively accessible Java, north Sumatra, and the prime tourist target, Bali. Both foreign investment and tourism were encouraged consonant with the view that much-needed national development could be achieved only with massive infusions of Western capital. A Second Five Year Plan (1974) sought to actively promote tourism and to expand promotional activities to outer island areas including Sulawesi.

Sulawesi (formerly Celebes) is a spider-shaped island, lying east of Borneo (Figure 1). The island population of nine million is unevenly distributed, with some six million inhabitants residing in the southwestern peninsular province of Sulawesi Selatan. This province is further divided into twenty-three Regencies, roughly equivalent to U.S. counties, of which all but one contain predominantly Muslim populations of Bugis/ Makassar farmers and coastal traders. The inland Tana Toraja Regency lies at the northern extremity of the province, the population of 320,000 is minimally Muslim (5 percent), about 35 percent Christian, with the balance of the inhabitants adhering to their ancestral faith.

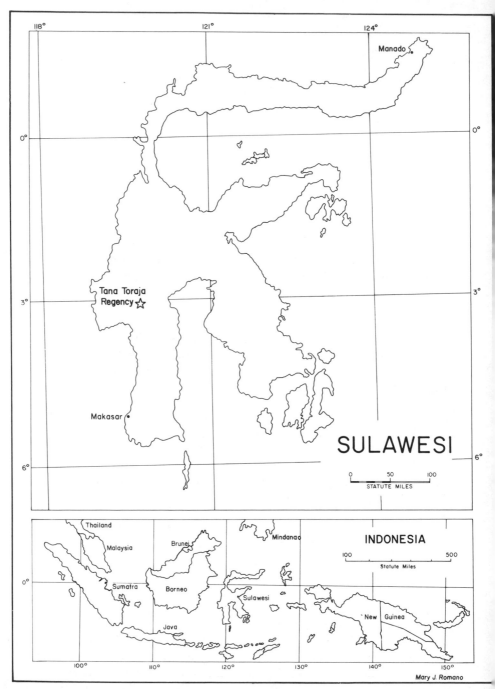

Figure 1. Map of Indonesia

Aluk To Dolo (ceremonies of the ancestors), the traditional religion, includes elaborate rituals that routinely draw hundreds and often thousands of adherents together. Economic planners, seeking ways to attract the tourists to more remote areas, envisaged that these ceremonies would be of touristic interest comparable to the religious rituals of Hindu Bali, and would generate increased visitors and more cash flow. Towards that goal, in March 1973, the Toraja Regency government hosted a local conference on tourist development that was attended by entrepreneurs, civil servants, and religious functionaries of traditionalist, Christian, and Muslim faiths. Government agencies aired plans to make of Tana Toraja an important national tourist center, and solicited the cooperation of local leadership.

The air/sea gateway for travelers to Sulawesi is the capital, Ujung Pandang (formerly Makassar). However, in 1974 the average of six hundred tourists per month who visited the city strained the available accommodations designated as "international calibre." Tourist travel to highland Tana Toraja was once inhibited by a twelve-hour jeep trip, but recent road improvements reduced the drive to six hours by chartered car or bus. However, the elapsed travel time necessitates an average stay of two nights, and hotel accommodations suitable for overseas visitors are very limited in number. Reservations of existent facilities as much as six months in advance has forced the refusal of many impromptu booking requests in recent years. August is the peak month for tourism, with more than twice as many visitors arriving than at any other time.

Despite the long drive and minimal facilities, in 1971 (the first year in which tourist statistics were compiled), 58 overseas tourists visited the Toraja region (Figure 2). I analyzed data for the first eight months of 1974, and found that 1,376 tourists registered at hotels and pensions in the principal Toraja towns, Makale and Rantepao. Continental Europeans predomianted, including 484 French, 144 Swiss, and 124 West Germans

Figure 2
Overseas Visitors to Indonesia 1971-75

Year	Visitors to Indonesia	Visitors to South Sulawesi	Percentage of Sulawesi Visitors to National Total
1971	178,781	58	.03
1972	221,195	427	.19
1973	270,303	422	.15
1974	313,452	1,908	.60
1975	366,000	6,008	1.64

Source: Idacipta, P.T. *Master Plan for South Sulawesi Tourist Development.* 1976 2:63.

compared to only 135 Americans and 56 Japanese. Given then existent travel trends, the numbers of Americans and Japanese are expected to increase as Toraja becomes better known. Regional, provincial, and local Regency funds have already been allocated for road and site access improvement and for the promotion of the Toraja region in government and private publications.

This case study assesses the impact of nascent tourism upon a small and fragile society, the Toraja, using a basic data base of 1974 with a brief postscript to highlight the changes from 1974 to 1976. In particular, it focuses on those aspects of traditional culture which draw visitors to a semi-isolated locale, the economic/political climate that encourages the advent of tourism, and the real and potential consequences of organized tourism upon ceremonial and secular aspects of Toraja life.

Toraja Culture

The approximate 192,000 Toraja who practice the traditional faith are bound together by a common language, an extensive network of family and kin, shared customs, and a mutual involvement in an elaborate ritual system founded upon the tenets of their ancient beliefs (Crystal 1976). Ceremonies of death periodically draw hundreds and often thousands together from scattered mountain homesteads. The most frequent Toraja rituals are funerals of one to seven nights duration that follow rigidly prescribed scenarios consonant with the status and economic resources of the family of the deceased. The largest death rituals involve the construction of substantial ceremonial grounds, include the sacrifice of scores of pigs and water buffalo, and present a full panoply of song, dance, and procession that center much of Toraja social life. The funerary traditions of these people are so deeply rooted, and so inextricably bound to indigenous conceptions of status, that even Christian converts adhere closely to the form if not the symbolic content of the great death rituals. Toraja funerals require a great deal of the energy and resources of the village community each year. Failure to reciprocate a debt of meat incurred during the ritual slaughtering of pigs and bovines is a cause for extreme embarrassment and loss of standing in local society. No effort is spared, including the pawning of irrigated rice land, to make good on obligations to neighbors and relatives.

The advent of the Dutch colonial administration in 1906 established health and educational institutions, transport links, and government administration. Far from being pristine, primitive isolates remotely secure in highland eyries, the people of Tana Toraja today are bound to external markets through their production of *arabica* coffee, participate in the national political process, and enjoy a mission-sponsored educational

Plate 1. Toraja funeral ground. In the forefront is a Lakkian catafalque housing the body.

Plate 2. Bearing sacrificial pigs to a funeral ceremony.

system unequalled elsewhere in the hinterlands of Sulawesi. Rather than attenuating indigenous ritual, access to external markets and to salaried positions for the relatively large number of educated Toraja has actually enhanced the scale of local funerary practice. Combined with spectacular population growth over the past seventy years (allegedly a six-fold increase) the modernization process has in fact occasioned larger and ever more sumptuous death ceremonies. Competition for social status is the rationale underlying the ongoing investment of time and resources in such ceremonies—a stimulus that has been accentuated by the rise of an indigenous, Christian-oriented middle rank group nurtured by local mission stations as a counter elite to the traditionalist and mainly conservative nobility. Each Toraja death ceremony is ethnically cohesive, yet it expresses the competition for position and standing among individuals and family groups, and masks a demanding ethic of reciprocity.

Social life in Tana Toraja is marked by a constant round of funerary comings and goings. Death and funeral are temporally separated. Large funerals commence months, often years, after the passing of the deceased. The body is washed, wrapped in layers of homespun shroud, and reserved in the house until such time as economic resources can be marshalled to stage the seven-night ceremony. When the funeral finally occurs, grief has been largely assuaged by the passage of time. The mourning taboos regulating food and clothing are confined to select kinsmen or their surrogates. For most participants in the death ritual, a lavish funeral renews reciprocal relationships through animal sacrifice and meat exchange, and allows for the expression of remorse at the passing of a prominent person. The honor shown the deceased is directly proportionate to the attendance, vigor, and splendor of his funeral.

Although less frequent rituals, such as those of agricultural renewal and trance, perhaps more cogently reflect the fundamentals of indigenous religious belief, the inevitability of death and the manner of its celebration in Tana Toraja render funeral rites a more or less regular feature of Toraja social life. Since rice is harvested once annually and the cultivation of alternate garden crops is not particularly intensive, much time and energy remain for the elaboration of ritual and status concerns. Save for four or five months of intensive irrigated rice cultivation (January–May), the balance of the year may at any time witness large death rituals—often easily accessible to foreign travelers and always appreciated with great interest by visitors to the region.

Political Environment

Until recently, however, commitment to death ritual was somewhat diminished in modernizing, elite circles, tempered by a consciousness of

Plate 3.   Traditional circle dances transpire at most Toraja rituals. Here, villagers dance the *Ondo* at Ma'bugi' ritual.

tension between customary village law and modern Indonesian values. Reflective of a generalized tentativeness and embarrassment toward village culture, this attitude mirrored the stance of foreign missionaries and indigenous evangelists who regarded traditional Toraja culture as fundamentally contradictory to the spirit of the modern (interpreted as monotheistic Western) world. Despite almost universal participation in reciprocal exchange in the funerary context, increasing numbers of local inhabitants subject to external influence shared the view that ritual activity must be constricted; consequently, the process of modernization inevitably presaged the disappearance of indigenous religious ceremony.

The most influential Christian organization in the Toraja region is the Gereja Toraja (Toraja Church), closely linked to the Gereformeerden Zendingsbond in The Netherlands. In the view of foreign and indigenous evangelists, the persistence of the autochthonous Aluk To Dolo religion presents a continuing challenge to the efficacy of local missionary activity. To the north, in other upland locales much more isolated than Tana Toraja, groups of highlanders have for decades universally embraced the Christian faith, abandoning *en masse* traditional religion. Yet, in Tana Toraja the best efforts of an expatriate Christian missionary force— numbering in 1971 eight Protestant ministers and fifteen Catholic priests—had yet to tip the balance in favor of a Christian plurality. Resistance remained strong in many quarters. Identification with the new faith brought with it access to education (almost all primary and most secondary schools in Tana Toraja are church affiliated) and entrée to modern Indonesian culture. A direct correlation exists between the image of modernity and conversion to Christianity (or Islam).

For most of the thirty-year history of the Republic of Indonesia, participation in the political process in Tana Toraja was predicated on both adherence to a monotheistic faith and affiliation with the dominant political party. Despite the constellation of Christian modernist and Aluk traditionalist factions, contradictions within the Christian ethos have persisted to the present. The strength of the Toraja Church may be measured in relation to its willingness to compromise with indigenous ceremonial tradition. Sects such as the Seventh Day Adventists—marked in Toraja eyes by their vegetarian ethic and absolute prohibition on consuming the meat of ritually slaughtered animals—have in their wide divergence from traditional practice succeeded in gaining very few converts (and these mostly from the lowest strata of society desiring to opt out entirely from the burdens of reciprocal exchange). The Toraja Church, with nearly 100,000 members, has validated participation in native ritual by its members as long as they abjure any role in Aluk sacrificial process as opposed to the reciprocal exchange of goods. Furthermore, Toraja Church funerals often parallel Aluk rites, with New

Testament readings and sermons transpiring in an environment of bamboo ceremonial structures, tethered water buffalo, and slung pigs awaiting dispatch at specific times during the week-long ritual. Urban Toraja as well as rural rice farmers remain locked securely within the system of ritualized reciprocity, and often abandon their urban office desks to attend rural rituals where their own livestock are scheduled to be slaughtered.

A significant change in elite views concerning indigenous ritual has been effected in Tana Toraja in recent years. To some extent this change is merely a reflection of altered political postures at the national level. Parkindo, the party of Indonesian Protestants, had for two decades dominated the local legislature, controlling some 75 percent of the seats. Since 1969 the rapid efflorescence of the new and pervasive tourist ethic has dramatically influenced Toraja self-image as well as development planning. Following the Indonesian national elections of July 1971, the strength of established political parties has steadily diminished under pressure from Golkar (the alliance of "functional groups" that now dominates Indonesian political life as the state party). Just as parties such as the Islamic Partai Mulimin Indonesia and the Soekarnoist Partai Nasionalis Indonesia have in recent years been eclipsed in regions formerly secured under their control, so also has Parkindo now lost its former preeminence in Tana Toraja, reflecting but a shadow of its former power in the regional Toraja legislative council. Displacing Parkindo with its sectarian modernism was the local Golkar faction. Consciously secular in orientation, the government party has enlisted support from Christian, Muslim, and Aluk To Dolo communities; in fact, Aluk adherents currently outnumber Parkindo representatives in the local Dewan Perwakilan Rakyat II (Regional People's Representative Council). The official Toraja government view regarding indigenous tradition has radically changed in the years since Golkar swept to unprecedented victories throughout Indonesia. Where once fundamentalist rigidity banned gambling as sinful, now lotteries and cockfights are held under government auspices with tax monies accruing to development funds. Similarly, the Aluk To Dolo religion has been granted legitimacy by the Ministry of Religion. Aluk officials have been asked to participate as equals with Catholic priests, Protestant ministers, and Muslim notables at the formal celebration of national holidays and during the administration of oaths to court witnesses and newly elected government representatives.

The Tourist Ethic

Inclusion of traditionalist adherents of the Toraja religion in the governmental sphere constitutes a significant departure from previous Toraja political practice. Coupled with the reversion to a traditional market system and linked to the validation of the indigenous faith by the central government, the changes that commenced with the 1971 election signalled a profound attitudinal shift by the local elite towards their own cultural heritage. Closely associated with the above political developments was the rise to prominence of a tourist ethic, the realization that development prospects for Tana Toraja were unusually promising in the tourist field. The promotion and maintenance of the unique ritual system that attracted the attention of early foreign visitors to Tana Toraja became a goal of traditionalist villagers and urban modernizers alike. Thus a congruence of political, economic, and cultural factors tangibly reoriented attitudes toward traditional culture. Where once local leaders had sought to mask their involvement in indigenous ritual, had minimized the number of Aluk practitioners, had constructed new homes in nontraditional style, and, at least in the urban milieu, had manifested negative views concerning the foundations of Toraja culture, these perspectives began to change in light of the newly perceived relationship between tourism and development. Death ceremonies especially came to be reassessed in light of regional economic planning potential and national priorities. For the first time in many years the previously ignored Toraja region began to be featured in provincial capital newspapers, with favorable comments about indigenous ritual practice.

From an anthropological perspective, the short-term consequences of nascent tourism in Tana Toraja must be evaluated positively. *Aluk To Dolo* religious practice has received official recognition from government, and its adherents now participate in the legislative process. A formerly negative embarrassment concerning local culture has been transformed into positive encouragement of ritual practice by members of the modern elite. Significant changes in the political sphere over the last several years have been reflected in a dramatic alteration of self-image in the Toraja region. One important short-term result of the above is that Christian evangelical threats to the continued existence of the ancestral faith have been checked, as the power of the church and its political allies have abruptly diminished. In part, the effects of tourism in Toraja parallel those in Bali (McKean, chapter 6).

The long term consequences of tourist influx present a somewhat less sanguine image of the future. Tana Toraja is semi-isolated, relatively overpopulated, and presents limited opportunity for the expansion of land under cultivation. Theoretically, the growth of tourist income will provide funds that may trickle down to the village level and enhance living standards generally, but practical results of accelerated tourism may be far different. It appears that those most likely to benefit from the tourist trade are the outside entrepreneurs who send tour groups to Tana

Toraja, and the few local merchants and hoteliers who accommodate tourists in the Toraja region. What benefits accrue to traditionalist Aluk villagers who are the mainstay of the ceremonial system? For instance, in 1969/70 some eleven million rupiah (us$27,500) were expended on the construction of a hotel facility by the government. Ostensibly this building was to function as a military hostel for high level delegations inspecting the hinterlands. In fact, the structure represented the first government-sponsored tourist accommodation in the region. Tastefully designed according to indigenous motifs and situated in a rural area overlooking the Sa'dan river, this large hotel cost money that, from the perspective of local requisites, might better have been used to eradicate endemic malaria, improve grain and vegetable seeds, or purchase fertilizers.

In 1971, the provincial press announced several major death ceremonies. One article proclaimed that facilities were being arranged for two hundred tourists; another suggested that food would be provided for overseas guests. Subsequently, an international English-language publication carried an Indonesian government-sponsored advertisement enticing tourists to Tana Toraja, now newly dubbed the "land of the heavenly kings." Such stories, aside from ethnographic inaccuracy, tend to create unreal expectations on the part of future visitors and provide a basis for exploitation of Toraja villagers in their new role of international "hosts." Dating to the era of Dutch colonial administration, occasional foreign visitors to Toraja funerals have been offered, free of charge, sleeping space and sumptuous meals prepared from the sacrificial animals. Of little consequence in the years past, this practice in an era of organized tourism now threatens to deprive village participants of their principal source of meat. Every gram of animal protein offered to tourists reduces the supply available to villagers, whose consumption of high grade protein is already limited to ritual contexts. Similarly, at large funeral feasts, both shelter and potable water are normally in short supply. To provide these essentials free of charge to an increasing number of tourist "guests," because the government seeks to stimulate tourism, becomes an economic burden upon simple peasants. In one known instance, a member of the deceased's family attempted to sell tickets of entry to the ceremonial grounds. Outraged kinsmen quickly thwarted the effort because tradition demands that all who wish to join in the rites of mourning must be welcomed without qualification. In another case, organizers of a major ceremony altered the normal course of the ritual to create for the several score foreign tourists a more dramatic and shorter spectacle. Conflict between traditionalist and modernist factions halted the ceremony until government officials stepped in and supported the innovators.

In an area of nascent tourism, problems in the host-guest relationship

Plate 4. Tourist photographers: an early (1971) French tour group at a large funeral at Tondon village, Tana Toraja. The structures are temporary residences for the mourners.

seem certain to occur. Government officials recently embarked on a misdirected tourist development scheme at Lemo, which is a prime attraction because of a large burial cave complex. The road to the site was greatly improved, and in accord with the local notion that good lavatory facilities are a constant preoccupation of Westerners, toilets were constructed although Lemo is less than twenty minutes from the customary tourist hotel. Great care was taken to whitewash the plaster walls with the brightest paint, to roof the new structure with gleaming galvanized iron, and to incise the lavatory doors with traditional patterns. Unfortunately this building was incongruously situated precisely in the line of sight from the parking area, and destroyed the once pristine vista of burial caves and funeral statues directly visible from the road. Of more consequence is the desecration of the striking ancient burial locale at Londa. Here a pristine assemblage of ancient carved burial vessels has been marred by the drawing of initials on wooden sarcophagi and painting of names on limestone-faced walls. Perpetrated in the 1960s by Indonesian visitors attending a national Christian youth group conference, this locale stands today as an ugly reminder of the malevolent potential of unregulated tourism.

Conclusions

The culture of Tana Toraja is a living example of autochthonous Southeast Asian architectural, craft, and religious tradition. Integrated politically into modern Indonesia, this rather isolated locale figured minimally in the national development planning until a new government began to promote international tourism by tapping the cultural resources of the population. As of the data base of November 1974, the relatively small scale growth of commercial tours to the Toraja Regency have had little negative impact and may even, in some cases, have supported a renewed interest in local ritual and artistic tradition, as McKean (chapter 6) has suggested is also true in Bali.

However, the possible long-term effects of a steady, if not massive, tourist influx must be considered. Almost as if he were writing specifically about Toraja, Nuñez (1963, p. 352) advises, "In the newly developing countries of today's world, when the larger society (particularly the formal apparatus of the state) takes special interest in previously overlooked rural communities, for whatever reason—tourism, nativist or nationalist—the anthropologist should be alert to the consequences." Predictions concerning the possible future effects of tourism must be tentative. Already, the tourist ethic in Sulawesi has drawn Tana Toraja into a position of unaccustomed prominence in provincial and national planning, compromising the highlanders' ancestral prerogative of ritual self-determination. Increasing tourism may necessarily lead to the commercialization of religious rites. If so, then Toraja ritual will become commoditized, and if one aspect of the ritual—the gift of food—is changed, can all other aspects of the complex customs associated with funerals remain untouched? As an alternative, the ritual process may be reorganized, turned into a "show" for the tourists with the potential of stripping the ceremonies of their integral meaning, as with the *Alarde* festival of Spain (Greenwood, chapter 8). To date the promotion and operation of tourism is external, and it appears that the primary benefits are also external.

There is every indication that tourism will become a constant and growing feature of Toraja life. Intelligent planning will be required if the deleterious effects of tourism such as the desecration of sites, sacrilege of ritual, and the victimization of traditionalist peasants are to be forestalled. Can the small Toraja region with its marked social, religious, and political factions maintain the delicate composite of cultural integrity, educational opportunity, and economic development that presently hold considerable promise? Will the tourist impact ultimately serve as a positive incentive for economic development, or become a negative stimulus to the dissolution of a fragile highland culture? No longer proud masters of their destiny and possibly soon doomed to become exhibitors of "quaint customs" for tourist eyes, the future of Toraja will depend to a great extent upon the foresight and capabilities of national, provincial, and regency officials.

Postscript

During 1976 I returned to Tana Toraja for brief visits in May and June, and for a six-week sojourn in August and September as consultant to BBC Documentary Films. The rapid development of tourism was startling, with a three-fold growth between my data base of 1974 and 1976 (Figure 2). When I initiated the field work in 1971, tourists were a curiosity, but by 1976 tourists from Europe and North America had become a firmly fixed feature of the Toraja social landscape. *Asia Travel Trade* (February 1977, p. 23) estimates that 10,000 foreign tourists visited Sulawesi in 1975 and that the numbers increased to 12,000 in 1976. The official statistics cited in Figure 2 are derived from reports submitted by local hotels. However, my informal queries of many 1976 visitors revealed they had not been asked to complete any registration forms and thus their presence was unrecorded. During August and September, I observed that hotels in Tana Toraja were filled to capacity with mainly European tourists. Some evenings the 150 seats in the two prime Chinese restaurants in Rantepao were occupied entirely by foreign visitors. Therefore, I believe the official statistics are too conservative, and that the *Asia Travel Trade* estimates are more realistic.

One unforeseen development in 1976 was the degree to which French enterprise had entered and now dominates the Toraja tourist market. Travelers originating in Paris, on Singapore-bound charter flights, made two-week trips around Indonesia including visits to Jakarta, central Java, Bali and Tana Toraja (total price about us$1,000). Chartered buses met them at the Province airfield as they arrived from Bali by plane, and drove them directly to Tana Toraja over 285 kilometers of newly-improved, all-weather road. Five French nationals, stationed in Tana Toraja during the months of July through September, escorted the visitors and arranged local transportation. Duties of the expatriate guides also included arranging walking tours through the Toraja countryside and scheduling overnight sojourns in "picturesque" mountain villages where they could enjoy "local color."

The influx of tourists to Tana Toraja (at least 90 percent of all tourism in South Sulawesi Province flows to this area) has created new economic opportunities but also increased cultural and administrative dilemmas that have not been squarely confronted. Tana Toraja has experienced a boom in hotel construction, an inflation of land values in potential construction sites, and a rush to improve access roads to prime physical attractions. Accommodations available to visitors range from small us$1.50 per night guest houses to the international calibre Toraja Cottages (daily rate, us$30.00 double occupancy) opened early in 1976. Most of the nineteen hotels are owned and operated by native Torajas, and most facilities retain Torajan motifs in architectural style and decor. The magnitude and rapidity of the shift from nascent to charter tourism was totally unexpected, and administrative officials were ill-prepared to cope. Local governmental policy has quietly restricted hotel development to the environs of the Makale-Rantepao axis road, and also to date has dissuaded capital from beyond the borders of Tana Toraja to invest in the tourist infrastructure within the region. In view of the national policy to encourage tourism, and the "ripple" effect that tourism generates, the prospect that the industry will remain under tenuous local control is dim.

Tana Toraja may be unique, and worthy of on-going careful study, because of the dramatic change within two years. The area has passed directly from the obscurity of elite, ethnic tourism to become a target for cultural, charter tourism without passing through any of the intermediary stages (see Introduction). It is too soon to fully assess the touristic impact, but some trends are evident. The local Torajas are bewildered, and uncertain as to the choices open to them, or their outcome: (1) If they open their villages, and their ceremonies, to tourism for the sake of economic gain, they are victimized by the compromise of cultural integrity; (2) If they exclude the tourists, they are victimized by the inflation accompanying the influx, and enterprising neighbors reap the profits. Cultural conservatism does not "pay." During the tourist season of 1976 it was evident that rituals were being commercialized as "spectacles" for the foreigners, including being rescheduled at the request of foreign guides. Further, the disappearance of antiquities into the souvenir market indicated another potential cultural loss. My cautious optimism based on the 1974 data is strained, and further field research is needed. If, as anthropologists, we have the capacity to guide, our skills should be applied here and now lest this fragile mountain community, which has only its cultural traditions to attract tourism, loses both its heritage *and* the tourists.

Center for Southeast Asian Studies
University of California, Berkeley

Part III

Tourism in European Resorts

Europe—the continent that produced Greece, Rome, the Renaissance and the Industrial Revolution—has historically been host to more tourism than any other area. Even today most tourists in Europe are Europeans, vacationing away from home in some other country. In addition, Europe is an important historical-cultural destination for overseas visitors and especially for individuals whose forebears departed Europe a generation or more ago to colonize elsewhere, and who now still feel a sense of bond or identity with an ancestral homeland.

Mass tourism is pervasive throughout most of the continent, and the industry is well-organized and economically very important to many countries. However, the attraction of tourists to any given center is highly competitive, and governments have been active and influential in stimulating tourism. Despite good intentions to generate outside income, the promotional techniques have not always been beneficial as Davydd Greenwood shows in chapter 8 that government efforts, using "local color" as a "come on," proved disruptive to the target community. Rayna Reiter in chapter 9 delineates the role of a political leader who initiated tourism for potential personal gain to the detriment of more traditional industries and social cohesion. In chapter 10, Oriol Pi-Sunyer provides an insightful analysis of the effects of mass tourism in changing interpersonal relations between European hosts and guests.

8

Culture by the Pound:
An Anthropological Perspective
on Tourism as
Cultural Commoditization[1]

DAVYDD J. GREENWOOD

Tourism is now more than the travelers' game. A few years ago, we could lament the lack of serious research on tourism, but now, like the tourists themselves, social researchers are flocking to tourist centers. This is necessary since tourism is the largest scale movement of goods, services, and people that humanity has perhaps ever seen (Greenwood 1972). Economists and planners have been tracing the outlines of this industry and its peculiarities, and many anthropologists and sociologists have begun to chart the social effects of tourism on communities.

The literature generally points out that tourism provides a considerable stimulus to the local and national economy, but it also results in an increasingly unequal distribution of wealth. Tourism thus seems to exacerbate existing cleavages within the community. It is not, therefore, the development panacea that a few hasty planners proclaimed. This nascent critical literature is useful because it places tourism-related development in the analytical perspective from which a variety of different development strategies are being reviewed. The conclusion that tourism-related development tends to produce inequalities takes on added significance because it seems to parallel the inequalities produced by other development strategies, like enclave factories, capital formation schemes, and the "Green Revolution." This serves as a needed corrective to overly exuberant dreams of an El Dorado paved with tourism receipts.

Tourism is not a monolith. It is an exceedingly large-scale and diverse industry, operating in a variety of ways under differing circumstances. Necessarily this means that we must differentiate between types of tourism and the range of impacts tourism can have on local communities.

[1] I am indebted to Pilar Fernandez-Cañadas de Greenwood for helpful substantive and editorial criticisms.

This case study concentrates on the promotion of "local color" as a part of tourism merchandising and its impact on one community.[2] For clarity and to avoid any possible misunderstanding on this point, my analysis is not a general indictment of the tourist industry, but considers only the use of "local color" in tourism. The pros and cons of other aspects of tourism are weighed elsewhere in this volume and in the literature generally.

Social researchers and moralists often speak cynically of the uses and abuses of "local color" by the tourism industry. Spokesmen for local cultures decry the vilification of their traditions by tourism. Planners, too, feel vaguely uncomfortable about this but are quick to point out how little we understand the potential impact of these practices. Lacking well-documented research into the implications of the use of local color in tourism, it is not surprising that neither planners nor local people can decide just how to approach the problem. This study attempts, in brief compass, to analyze the commoditization of local culture in the case of Fuenterrabia, Guipúzcoa, in the Spanish Basque country.

Can Culture be Considered a Commodity?

Logically, anything that is for sale must have been produced by combining the factors of production (land, labor, or capital). This offers no problem when the subject is razor blades, transistor radios, or hotel accommodations. It is not so clear when buyers are attracted to a place by some feature of local culture, such as the running of the bulls in Pamplona, an appearance of the Virgin Mary, or an exotic festival.

Economists and planners dealing with tourism have papered over this difficulty either by considering local culture a "natural resource" (that is, as part of the land factor) or simply by viewing local culture as part of the "come-on" and focusing their attention entirely on the number of hotel beds and the flow of liquor, gasoline, and souvenir purchases. Such a perspective is not very helpful because in ethnic tourism settings, local culture itself is being treated as a commodity *sui generis*.

A fundamental characteristic of the capitalist system is that anything that can be priced can be bought and sold. It can be treated as a commodity. This offers no analytical problem when local people are paid to perform for tourists. Like the symphony orchestra of economics textbook fame, they are being reimbursed for performing a service consumed on the spot. It is not so clear when activities of the host culture are treated as part of the "come-on" without their consent and are invaded by tourists who do not reimburse them for their "service." In this case, their activities are taken advantage of for profit, but they do

---

[2] By "local color" I mean the promotion of a commoditized version of local culture as part of the "come-on," a widespread practice with little understood consequences.

not profit, culturally. The onlookers often alter the meaning of the activities being carried on by local people. Under these circumstances, local culture is in effect being expropriated, and local people are being exploited.

We already know from worldwide experience that local culture—be it New Guinea aboriginal art and rituals, Eskimo sculpture (Carpenter 1972, 1973), Balinese dancing, bullfights, voodoo ceremonies, gypsy dancing, or peasant markets—is altered and often destroyed by the treatment of it as a tourist attraction. It is made meaningless to the people who once believed in it by means of a process that can be understood anthropologically. I think we have the social science tools to understand the fragility of local culture and the humanist's responsibility to put these tools to use.

Anthropological Definitions of Culture and Public Ritual

To develop this view of local culture as a commodity, working definitions of culture and public ritual are needed. I will follow Clifford Geertz's views here. For Geertz, *culture* is an integrated system of meanings by means of which the nature of reality is established and maintained. His concept of culture emphasizes the authenticity and the moral tone it imparts to life experiences, as he calls attention to the fundamental importance of systems of meaning in human life. By implication, anything that falsifies, disorganizes, or challenges the participants' belief in the authenticity of their culture threatens it with collapse. *Public rituals* can be viewed as dramatic enactments, commentaries on, and summations of the meanings basic to a particular culture. They serve to reaffirm, further develop, and elaborate those aspects of reality that hold a particular group of people together in a common culture (Geertz 1957, 1966, 1972).

As can be seen, the anthropological view of culture is far different from the economists' and planners' views of culture as a "come-on," a "natural resource," or as a "service." The anthropological perspective enables us to understand why the commoditization of local culture in the tourism industry is so fundamentally destructive and why the sale of "culture by the pound," as it were, needs to be examined by everyone involved in tourism.

The *Alarde* of Fuenterrabia

To analyze the process of cultural commoditization, I will use the specific case of a major public ritual in Fuenterrabia: the *Alarde*. Fuenterrabia's *Alarde* is a public ritual *par excellance*. It involves almost all the men, women, and children in the town during the preparations for it and includes a staggering number of them in the actual enactment.

The *Alarde* is essentially a ritual recreation of Fuenterrabia's victory over the French in the siege of 1638 A.D. This town was important from the fifteenth to the nineteenth centuries as a walled citadel standing almost on the border between Spain and France, where the Spanish and French crowns contested the rights to control the territory in the northeast corner of Spain. As a result, Fuenterrabia was besieged an immense number of times. Most famous was the siege of 1638, which lasted sixty-nine days and which the town successfully withstood, leading to the rout of the French army. Following this victory the town was accorded a number of privileges by the Spanish crown and was given an important honorific title to add to its official name.

But the *Alarde* does much more than simply commemorate a battle. Fuenterrabia is made up of the citadel, a fishermen's ward, and five local wards, each with a corporate identity and responsibilities. The walled city and the six wards of the town each send a contingent of children who play Basque flutes and drums, and march, dressed in the white shirt and pants, red sandals, sash, and beret symbolizing the Basques. They also send a contingent of men armed with shotguns. From among their young women, each ward elects a *cantinera* (water carrier) who is supposed to be the best flower of young womanhood in the ward. She dresses in a military style uniform and carries a canteen. Various nonlocalized occupational groups are also represented. There is a contingent of *hacheros* (woodchoppers) dressed in sheepskin cloaks, with huge black beards and tall black fur hats. The mayor and the town council dress in military uniform and ride on horseback, leading the procession.

After an early Mass, the groups form in the square outside the citadel gates. Each contingent of children marches through the gates and up the two-block street to the plaza where the somber fortress of Charles the Fifth is located, to the cheers and smiles of hundreds of relatives who crowd the streets and the overhanging balconies. The martial music is played with great fervor. The continual passing of each group, all playing a different tune, and the endless drumming have a profound effect on the bystanders.

Then come the mayor and town councilmen on horseback, symbols of leadership, valor, and nobility. They pass amidst general cheers and then dismount and move to the balcony of the town hall, which overlooks the main street about halfway up to the plaza, to review the parade. Led by its *cantinera*, each ward's group of armed men then marches up the street and stops under the town hall balcony. After saluting, they fire a unison shotgun salvo with deafening effect. The trick is to fire as if only one huge gun has gone off, and the audience continually comments on how well or badly each ward does this. The men then march on to the plaza and form up there.

At the end of the parade, the mayor and town council rejoin the people, all now in the plaza. Together they fire a unison salvo that very nearly deafens all present. Everyone reloads and fires until he has run out of shells. With that the people begin to disperse. After rejoining their families, they walk down to the fishermen's ward for food and drink.

There are far too many elements in this ritual to permit a full commentary here. And, *Alardes* are not restricted to Fuenterrabia but are performed in many Basque and non-Basque towns. In each case, the details differ greatly (Caro Baroja, 1968).

A few basic points about Fuenterrabia *Alarde* should be made. The siege of Fuenterrabia was one in which wealthy and poor—men, women, and children, farmers, fishermen and merchants—withstood a ferocious attack together. The *Alarde* reproduces this solidarity by involving all occupational groups, men, women and children, in the activity. The guns, by ward and then together, speak with one unified voice of the solidarity between the inhabitants that allowed them to survive. It is a statement of collective valor and of the quality of all the people of Fuenterrabia. It is an affirmation of their existence and identity at a time when most of the people earn money outside Fuenterrabia. It is a closing of wounds of gossip and bad faith opened up during the year of town life. The mayor and town councilmen, often thought of as dishonest manipulators rather than as good men, are momentarily transformed into the embodiment of civic virtue and valor to the death. The fishermen and farmers, in much of their daily lives trying to free themselves of the rustic and working-class identity their trades give them, are for a moment the embodiment of the poor but free and noble Basques with whom they affirm an historical identity. Together these people, who most of the time are divided, vulnerable, and confused, are a single spirit capable of withstanding the onslaughts of the outside world as they once withstood the siege of 1638.

There is much more to it, but this suffices to provide the flavor of the event. What is most important is for whom the *Alarde* is performed. It is clearly not performed for outsiders; it is a ritual whose importance and meaning lies in the entire town's participation and in the intimacy with which its major symbols are understood by all the participants and onlookers (the latter often having spent months sewing costumes, directing marching practice, and teaching music to the children). *It is a performance for the participants*, not a show. It is an enactment of the "sacred history" of Fuenterrabia, a history by its very nature inaccessible to outsiders, even when equipped with a two-paragraph explanation courtesy of the Ministry of Information and Tourism. A few unrelated outsiders have always been present, especially members of the Spanish elite who have been summering in Fuenterrabia since the time of the monarchy (Greenwood 1972). They are welcome, for they share some durable tie with the community. The presence of people who have no enduring relation to the community is much less welcome.

The *Alarde* is more than merely an interesting symbol of unity. As I am endeavoring to show in historical research on the Basques, the unique concept of Basque "collective nobility" is deeply involved here. By tradition, all people born in Guipúzcoa of Guipuzcoano parents were declared by that fact alone to have *limpieza de sangre* (no Moorish or Jewish blood), something that happened nowhere outside the Basque country. It gave rise to a unique situation: the Basques could assert that a cobbler, a farmer, a fisherman, a mayor, and a count were all equally noble. Though they recognized the differences in wealth and power, they asserted a common human equality by virtue of *limpieza de sangre* (Greenwood 1977).

Although the importance of *limpieza* is now gone, the equalitarian values arising from the idea live on in a Spain of stark class differences. To my mind, part of the importance of the *Alarde* is that it is the only occasion in which these ideas of equality and common destiny are given general expression. In this respect, the performance of the *Alarde* is a statement of their historical identity as Basques as well as an enactment of a particular moment in their history. The ritual is thus very important.

But the *Alarde* has the misfortune of taking place during the tourist season. The local population of Fuenterrabia is swollen fourfold; innumerable tourists drive in and out of town during the day to visit the beach, to watch boat races, to eat, swim, and take pictures of farms, old houses, and the city walls. The *Alarde* is listed by the Spanish tourism ministry in a national festival calendar that is given wide circulation. Tourism developers, a group including local politicians and contractors plus large national companies that specialize in tourism-related construction, have added the *Alarde* to their list of advertisable features about Fuenterrabia. Posters and other publicity for the *Alarde* are circulated, as is anything else that makes the town attractive to the tourism consumer.

I do not wish to give the impression that the *Alarde* is singled out for this treatment. In fact, in the "come-on," the *Alarde* is relatively unimportant. It lasts only one day, and by comparison with tourist interest in the fortifications, the frequent boat races, and the other attractions of the town, the ritual is of only passing interest. The *Alarde* is simply part of the list of "local color" to attract tourist receipts; it is an offhand addition to the basic tourism package.

The Turning Point: The *Alarde* Goes Public

This offhanded treatment of the *Alarde* is not reflected in the effect its incorporation into the tourism package has had on the people of Fuenterrabia. Though the *Alarde* is still a going concern, it is in trouble. It has suddenly become difficult to get the people to show and participate in it.

The turning point occurred while I worked in Fuenterrabia during the summer of 1969. The town streets are narrow and all the balconies along the street belong to private houses. The plaza must be cleared of people to make room for the military formations. Thus, there is very little room for onlookers in the narrow streets of the old citadel.

In 1969, the Spanish Ministry of Tourism and Public Information finished remodeling the old fortress of Charles the Fifth in the plaza and opened it as a part of their well-known chain of tourist *paradores* (hotel, restaurant, bar combination). It was personally inaugurated by Generalisimo Franco, an event commemorated on national television. Even a facsimile copy of Padre Moret's eyewitness account of the siege was published to add a note of "culture" to the occasion (Moret 1763). With the boost of national publicity, the municipal government felt obligated to resolve the problem of the onlookers. Not only should the people in the *parador* see the *Alarde*, but so should everyone else who wanted to. They declared that the *Alarde* should be given *twice in the same day* to allow everyone to see it.

In spite of the fact that the *Alarde* has not, to my knowledge, been given twice, the effect of the council's action was stunning. In service of simple pecuniary motives, it defined the *Alarde* as a *public show to be performed for outsiders* who, because of their economic importance in the town, had the *right* to see it.

The Aftermath: The Collapse of Cultural Meanings

There was a great consternation among the people of Fuenterrabia and a vaulting sense of discomfort. Soon this became the mask of cynicism that prefaces their attitudes toward the motives behind all business ventures in Fuenterrabia. Little was said publicly about it. But two summers later, I found that the town was having a great deal of difficulty in getting the participants to appear for the *Alarde*. No one actively or ideologically resisted, but in an event that depends entirely on voluntary compliance, the general lack of interest created serious organizational problems. In the space of two years, what was a vital and exciting ritual had become an obligation to be avoided. Recently the municipal government was considering payments to people for their participation in the *Alarde*. I do not doubt that they ultimately will have to pay them, just as the gypsies are paid to dance and sing and the symphony orchestra is paid to make music. The ritual has become a performance for money. The meaning is gone.

Conclusions: Culture by the Pound

This is undoubtedly a small event in a small place that few people will ever hear of, but its implications seem to be significant. The "local color" used to attract tourists to Fuenterrabia came to include a major ritual that the people had performed for themselves. Its meaning depended on their understanding of the whole system of beliefs reaffirmed by it through dramatic reenactment and commentary. It was not a performance for pay, but an affirmation of their belief in their own culture. It was Fuenterrabia commenting on itself for its own purposes.

By ordaining that the *Alarde* be a public event to attract outsiders into the town to spend money, the municipal government made it one more of Fuenterrabia's assets in the competitive tourism market. But this decision directly violated the *meaning* of the ritual, definitively destroying its authenticity and its power for the people. They reacted with consternation and then with indifference. They can still perform the outward forms of the ritual for money, but they cannot subscribe to the meanings it once held because it is no longer being performed by them for themselves.

I do not think this is a rare case by any means. Worldwide, we are seeing the transformation of cultures into "local color," making peoples' cultures extensions of the modern mass media (Carpenter 1972, 1973). Culture is being packaged, priced, and sold like building lots, rights-of-way, fast food, and room service, as the tourism industry inexorably extends its grasp. For the monied tourist, the tourism industry promises that the world is his/hers to use. All the "natural resources," including cultural traditions, have their price, and if you have the money in hand, it is your right to see whatever you wish.

As an analytical perspective has finally begun to develop with regard to the socioeconomic effects of mass tourism, it has become obvious that the increasing maldistribution of wealth and resultant social stratification are widespread results of touristic development. Various remedies are proposed as an attempt to counteract these problems. While these problems are serious and must be remedied, I am terribly concerned that the question of cultural commoditization involved in ethnic tourism has been blithely ignored, except for anecdotal accounts. The massive alterations in the distribution of wealth and power that are brought about by tourism are paralleled by equally massive and perhaps equally destructive alterations in local culture.

The culture brokers have appropriated facets of a lifestyle into the tourism package to help sales in the competitive market. This sets in motion a process of its own for which no one, not even planners, seem to feel in the least responsible. Treating culture as a natural resource or a commodity over which tourists have rights is not simply perverse, it is a violation of the peoples' cultural rights. While some aspects of culture have wider ramifications than others, what must be remembered is that culture in its very essence is something that people believe in *implicitly*. By making it part of the tourism package, it is turned into an explicit and paid performance and no longer can be believed in the way it was before. Thus, commoditization of culture in effect robs people of the very meanings by which they organize their lives.

And because such a system of belief is implicit, the holders of it are hard pressed to understand what is happening to them. The people of Fuenterrabia only express confusion and concern about their *Alarde*; they know something is wrong and do not know exactly what it is or what to do about it. The *Alarde* is dying for them, and they are powerless to reverse the process. Making their culture a public performance took the municipal government a few minutes; with that act, a 350-year-old ritual died.

That is the final perversity. The commoditization of culture does not require the consent of the participants; it can be done by anyone. Once set in motion, the process seems irreversible and its very subtlety prevents the affected people from taking any clear-cut action to stop it. In the end, many of the venerated aspects of Basque culture are becoming commodities, like toothpaste, beer, and boat rides.

Perhaps this is the final logic of the capitalist development, of which tourism is an ideal example. The commoditization process does not stop with land, labor, and capital but ultimately includes the history, ethnic identity, and culture of the peoples of the world. Tourism simply packages the cultural realities of a people for sale along with their other resources. We know that no people anywhere can live without the meanings culture provides; thus tourism is forcing unprecedented cultural change on people already reeling from the blows of industrialization, urbanization, and inflation. The loss of meaning through cultural commoditization is a problem at least as serious as the unequal distribution of wealth that results from tourist development.

Epilogue

As this essay was going to press, I received word of the tragic consequences of the *Alarde* of 1976. The now "public" ritual became a major political event. In the context of the acute political tensions in the Basque country, the *Alarde* seemingly provides a means of political expression. Apparently the *Alarde* was celebrated this year amidst an atmosphere of considerable tension. Late in the evening in the fishermen's ward, a boisterous crowd confronted the police and a young worker from the nearby town of Irún was killed. The sense of shock and anger was intense and will probably play a role in the political future of Fuenterrabia. Perhaps the debasement of the *Alarde* set the scene for this event, and perhaps not. However, it is certain that, given the magnitude of the potential consequences, we cannot afford to merely guess at the political implications of cultural commoditization.

Cornell University

9

The Politics of Tourism
in a French Alpine Community

RAYNA RAPP REITER

Mass tourism has transformed economic and social relations at the regional, national, and international levels. Because the populations who live in the areas of tourist development usually stand in asymmetrical relation to the outside forces that are responsible for such development, there is a political aspect to the process as well. Political power may dominate in the redefinition and reallocation of local resources to be used in tourist development, and may also be important as local folk attempt to control aspects of planning and financing tourism. Local political structure may be transformed in an attempt to deal with powerholders both within and outside the area of tourist development. This case study examines the political implications of such development in a French Alpine village.

The Commune as Community

The commune of La Roche is a center for both summer and winter tourism, and is located at the northern limits of the Basses-Alpes about ten miles west of the Italian border at the western edge of the southern French Alps. La Roche is a dispersed alpine community whose population of just over 200 persons live in twelve hamlets ranging from 1,100 to 1,400 meters in altitude. Above the hamlets the commune extends up the western slope of a mountain, which peaks at 2,500 meters. The combination of meadows for grazing and steep slopes provides recreational resources for summer hikes and winter skiing.

Communards use the mountain resources quite differently than do the tourists. Mountain ecology influenced the location of homesteads up and down the steep slopes, wherever access to relatively flat fields and water could be found. To survive socially under rigorous climatic conditions, communards traditionally utilized links of kinship and hamlet organization in which work was seasonally pooled. Until well into the present

139

century, individual hamlets maintained their own paths and roads, a communal bake oven, and small-scale irrigation works. Hamlets usually housed a chapel; resident families participated in the celebration of a patron saint's day, and shared in feeding the local priests. Prior to the imposition of a state-supported educational system, several hamlets joined together to provide schooling (often Church administered) to their youth. Extended ties of kinship and commune membership linked households from different hamlets to undertake other tasks, such as large-scale road maintenance, communal summer herding, and exchange of labor in the harvest, as crops matured differentially with altitude.

The linkages among hamlets had secular and religious ritual aspects. A secular ritual, the *fête de couchon*, brought neighbors and kinfolk together to share in the work and the festivities organized around butchering each homestead's meat throughout the winter months. Formal religious ties also united the twelve hamlets that were grouped into two parishes, each of which, until very recently, had a parish priest. In each parish the priest strongly influenced education, the maintenance of voluntary organizations, and political decisions. Extensive and varied bonds of work, kinship, neighborhood, and religion created a familiarity with and acceptance of social organization through voluntary associations.

These linkages also conditioned a strongly communitarian ideology. The people of La Roche perceived themselves as a large family in which the need to *rendre service* (literally, render service) was obligatory among members, and which supported their secular and religious forms of social organization. As the local agricultural extension agent pointed out, "These people are quick to see their individual interests in forming groups." However, mountain ecology and economy mandated an inheritance system that was traditionally impartible, and consequently, landless heirs were forced to work on neighboring farms, or even leave the commune to find jobs. In contrast to the generally communitarian and familiar ideology, the role of the individual and his life-chances and expectations were markedly different. Each person was responsible for his success or failure beyond the limits of the household, and communards expected strong, hardworking individuals to survive. Thus, there was a dialectic to the interplay of communitarianism and social Darwinism with respect to individual success. The current political situation is now manipulated in terms of these divergent ideological frameworks.

Traditional Politics

Until recently, formal political organization at the commune level functioned only minimally. The position of mayor was considered honorific and was controlled by three of the wealthier families from the late nineteenth to the mid-twentieth century. As current residents now describe it, people were concerned only with maintenance of and access to local resources. In departmental and national elections, individuals voted as the priests suggested. This description overly simplifies the intricacies of a century of electoral politics but does suggest the level at which people made political decisions. Church influence was quite strong and one resident priest even served a term as mayor during the 1950s. The commune always supported Christian Democratic candidates whenever they appeared on the national slate.

The political support given to Church and other right-wing parties by the residents of La Roche must be placed in its regional and national context. The Department of the Basses-Alpes is considered part of the French Midi, which has been historically associated with left-wing republican politics (Vigier 1963; R. R. Reiter 1973). Although most of the Department consistently votes to the left, especially for Socialist Party candidates, La Roche (and a few other mountain communes) is consistently a Church and right-wing bastion in the sea of socialist voting. This electoral pattern is linked to social and economic differences between villages of the southern plains and plateaus. In the former, socialists and republicans have been active since the coup of Louis Napoleon, whereas the mountain areas, which were never organized by the republicans, maintained a Church-centered social structure of their own. This historic difference makes La Roche a right-wing wedge in a solidly socialist area.

Since World War II, economic and political differences between La Roche and the southern socialist communes have continued to widen. Unlike the southern communes, which were penetrated by railroads and wheat markets in the late nineteenth century, La Roche remained relatively isolated from massive marketing until very recently. Mules were the special "money crop"—an adaptation that accorded some people wide experience with a marketing system, but also enabled them to intensify their agropastoral economy without splitting up their common lands, as was the rule to the south (Vigier, 1963; R. R. Reiter, 1973). The mule trade disappeared during World War II and residents of La Roche gradually adopted a highly capitalized farming economy. First, cows replaced mules, then tractors and other agricultural machinery replaced work animals and human labor. Rapid capitalization required government subsidies, and La Roche was suddenly within the orbit of markets dominated by the emerging European Economic Community. The need for increased cash that accompanies mechanized farming caused depopulation and made outside sources of employment, especially for homesteads with marginal amounts of land and labor, a necessity. Simultaneously, individual households were more fully integrated with the nation with the introduction of an expanded secondary educational system, special agricultural finance programs, the availability of state welfare in the form of family subsidies, and old age pensions. In response to massive changes in the economy and social structure, new voluntary associations formed and included professional farm groups such as dairy co-ops, machinery co-ops, and agricultural extension services. Others dealt with the relations between tourism and agriculture. Farmers with both left and right tendencies became politically organized by national syndicates.

Politicalization of the Commune

Many of the services traditionally provided by hamlet organization and its familiar associational ties were ceded to the commune itself, as the administrative branch of the State. As a result, individual hamlets no longer operate their own irrigation systems, bake ovens, or road crews; the commune now administers waterworks, electricity, road service, and garbage disposal. Increasingly, taxes (which require a cash income) pay for these services, and participation in their upkeep and administration has correspondingly dropped out of local life. Hamlets and parishes were formerly functional units; now their roles have been assumed by the political entity of the commune serving as the governmental agency (R. B. Reiter 1974). The office of mayor has become very important as individuals must now apply there to obtain road repairs, to receive welfare stipends or to place a child in secondary school. Ties between homesteads have diminished with depopulation, and as individual families became more strongly linked with the communal and national government. It is within this changing context that the politics of tourism must be viewed.

Until the late 1950s, a few families rented out summer rooms to vacationers, but tourism played no important part in La Roche. The political career of Jean-Joseph Hernot, who has served as mayor since 1959, is directly associated with what he identifies as the "active phase of tourist development." Hernot, one of fourteen brothers, comes from a respected family in the commune. His family was identified with Catholic activism in the pre-World War II years, and all the Hernot sons are considered intelligent, industrious, and association-minded. They exemplify both communitarian and individualistic values of success and work together closely and effectively. Brothers who left the commune have established solid careers in business, religion, or education. Jean-Joseph rose through the ranks of the JAC (Catholic rural youth organization) and served a term as a national officer. This training developed his interest in politics, and in the Gaullist Party, which he eventually joined. He also acquired a sense of mission to save his depopulating native commune. As mayor, Hernot boldly set out to improve the commune's physical facilities by redeveloping the communal grazing area and improving roads, electricity and, water services. He initiated garbage collection and snow clearance. To underwrite the costs of these improvements, Hernot designed a program to attract tourists, and convinced his constituency that tourism would bring personal income and needed tax money to the commune.

Each local improvement became part of the tourist development plan. Several projects involved the sale of communal land. Vacation chalets were built on marginal communal parcels and initially rented, then sold to urbanites. Another piece of communal land was sold to develop a family vacation center operated by a nonprofit corporation whose membership includes several communards. Most recently, commune funds were used to build a ski slope, and a group of locals (including the mayor) have invested land and personal money into a profit-making corporation, which is developing the site at the base of the slope. Plans for the site include major hotels, restaurants, boutiques, and luxury services. Many of these facilities will be developed by outside capital brought into the commune through the mayor's personal contacts. The mayor asserts that the large-scale development is the only way to create the jobs and modernized milieu to save an area where agriculture is in crisis.

Tourist development in France is co-ordinated by several ministries, directly or indirectly controlled by the Gaullist Party. As a Party member in a socialist stronghold, Hernot is able to bypass Departmental agencies and directly solicit the Parisian ministries to obtain subsidies and loans for tourist development. He sits on many national and regional political and parapolitical boards that oversee developmental projects, and La Roche's share of subsidies has expanded commensurate with his own political career. From commune mayor, Hernot has become the cantonal counselor and has run three times in the elections for National Assemblyman. Departmental politics have denied him that seat all three times, but he continues to be the Gaullist Party's best regional candidate, and his chances of eventually winning a seat remain good. His national influence, linked tightly to tourist development, is growing.

In addition to his career as local political patron, Hernot has many other roles that affect the considerable support gained from residents of the area. Hernot is the region's largest employer. The construction firm he owns and manages with one of his brothers has expanded through the building of many tourist facilities in the area. It employs both seasonal and year-round help, including most of the worker-peasants and many of the ex-peasants of the area. They are suitably grateful for the income and for Hernot's personal attention to the well-being of their families and farms; consequently, they reciprocate with their votes. Hernot is thus in a position to deliver regional votes to Gaullist candidates.

Most of the new voluntary associations created since World War II to deal with agricultural modernization, tourism, and politics bear his imprint. As local initiator and continued participant, Hernot works closely with almost all of them. Any association that might lack his direct presence is sure to include his wife or one of his brothers among its membership. Hernot is a private investor in tourist development through his own landholding and construction interests, and is also the contact who has brought outside corporations to invest in the ski slope site. In addition, Hernot is a member of the board of directors of the local agricultural bank. While the bank is considered apolitical, it makes decisions about loans for tourist development that have political implications. In all these roles—mayor, counselor, employer, associational activist, private investor, and member of the board of directors of the bank—Hernot's weight is felt. And increasingly, it is his network of ties to the Gaullist Party that allows him to deliver the needed subsidies and services on which his many positions depend.

Tourism in La Roche

Hernot's enthusiasm for tourism is expressed to his constituency in great detail, and is always phrased in terms appealing to the communal family. He invokes traditional values to justify radical innovations and to cede to him the power to carry them out. Hernot has taken up an essentially administrative post and politicized it in new ways. Yet his discourse masks the politicization of the office of mayor by exhorting people to revive local life for the sake of their children and to think of their families in traditional terms rather than of his new politics.

Tourism in La Roche presents problems to the communards. The job market created by tourism is problematic. Those individuals who have full-time employment in construction, or the very few who have been wealthy enough to invest in the ski slope shops, are doing well; many others are not. Most of the part-time work in tourism is menial and ill-paid, such as lift operators at the slope and chambermaids and janitors in the hotels. These jobs are better suited for teenagers needing pocket money than for adults on marginal homesteads struggling to survive. When the latter send out labor, it is often at the expense of the family farm. Young farmers who want to expand their agricultural operations face additional economic problems. They are unable to buy fields at agricultural prices because the price of land has skyrocketed with tourist development. This rapid rise in land value has also affected the impartible inheritance system. Heirs who have migrated are now more likely to demand that their share of the estate be paid at the inflated prices, which may block the ongoing agricultural enterprise of the sibling who remained to farm the land.

The modernized social milieu that is supposed to accompany tourism and make the area more attractive to local youths has also mixed results. On the positive side, a few women who have come in to work as camp counselors have married local men and slowed depopulation. The cafe established at the ski slope has become a new social focus for some locals and has replaced the church as a place for Sunday sociability. On the negative side, many tourist-related jobs and contacts between communards and urban vacationers cast the former in roles of economic and cultural inferiority. Communards often complain of feeling rusticated in the face of city folk. Their local culture has been turned into folklore for outside consumption. In summer, their peak work season conflicts with the schedule, road use, and noise levels that tourists impose on the countryside.

The Politics of Tourism

While the majority of communards support the mayor, they worry about the increasing load of communal debt financing tourism. They are not entirely satisfied with his increasing commitment to personal and political profit, but they acknowledge that his governmental contacts have made him indispensable. Like a Melanesian big man, Hernot's reputation expands ever outward, but the total cost is increasingly felt by his local supporters. They understand his capacity to bring in political and economic resources in the forms of subsidies and loans for rural development and his ability to act as buffer between them and the State. But these resources also mean radically increased penetration of local economy and culture by outside investors and clients, and the residents of La Roche see themselves as dependents of both the mayor and these outsiders. In the last fifteen years, the commune has become less a unit of social solidarity in which all residents participate, and more a redefined commodity for the use of outsiders with superior status.

Not many communards oppose the mayor, but their ranks are growing. Whenever they voice their complaints, Hernot uses the communitarian ideology to argue down their grievances. He asserts that only a strong political leader can unite the various hamlets to direct the future of the communal family. He identifies all nonsupporters as shirkers who do not have the good of the commune at heart. They are labelled individualists, lacking the skills and courage needed for success; they are seen as exceptions to the communitarian spirit that Hernot mobilizes to justify tourism. His ability to manipulate the traditional symbol system nets Hernot considerable continued support.

Hernot sustained his position through one local political crisis. Two modernized farmers requested a permit to open an industrial piglet nursery in the commune. Hernot supported the request, but a coalition of summer residents and locals associated with tourist development blocked it, claiming that the nursery would foul the air and decrease the tourist attraction of the commune. Hernot weathered the storm surrounding the issue, but it seems evident that other conflicts will develop. The mayor is caught in the middle, trying to support both parts of his constituency: those who have invested in tourism under his guidance and farmers involved in the modernizing process he claims to desire.

The mayor, simultaneously, has the power of political office and control of voluntary associations, the economic power of employer, and the social power of local respect and ideology all on his side. He is well-placed to recruit his supporters from diverse bases. Those who oppose him have no similar focus for leadership or for organizational bases. Most traditional forms of organization have been phased out, as political power and administration have passed directly to the mayorship and, through it, to the State. His opponents share no common base for faction formation. Included among them are young farmers trying to expand, traditionalists who see no need for a modernized economy, and a few who maintain links to the Socialist Party. Hernot's opponents may increasingly turn to the Socialists, but the national program of that party offers no alternatives to tourist development. And there is a deep conflict entailed for communards who cast their votes for a traditionally anticlerical party. The changing nature of the Church coupled with the penetration of local life by outsiders who hold clear economic and cultural superiority over them may make it possible for them to eventually reconcile a Socialist vote. The French governmental structure is highly centralized, which makes it virtually impossible for dissidents to form a faction to replace the mayor except by allying themselves with a centralized party whose power (at the regional level, at least) equals his own. These factors make opposition to Hernot appear unlikely.

As long as tourism continues to be written into national planning, and the Common Market continues to juggle its subsidy policy for small-scale dairying, Hernot is likely to maintain and expand his growing national reputation. Under these circumstances, his political career at the local level will prevail. But the costs of tourist development and the mayor's personal ambitions are high for the communards. They find themselves increasingly tied to outside investments and subsidies that are politically allocated; they are becoming dependents of a personal political network and the Gaullist Party. In the process, most traditional forms of participation in economic and social organization have either been phased out or subsumed within the mayor's political network. Local folk are being reduced to acceptance of a national development scheme over which they have no control, and to which they articulate primarily as the mayor's clientele. Thus, tourism conditions more than changes in economic and cultural life in the local population; it reorganizes their political position and outlook as well.

New School for Social Research

10

Through Native Eyes:
Tourists and Tourism
in a Catalan Maritime Community

ORIOL PI-SUNYER

The majority of anthropological studies on tourism examine the social, cultural, or economic impact that tourists or the tourist industry have on host communities and/or regions, and omit consideration of this impact on the interpersonal level. Tourism may strongly influence the manner in which local people—the hosts—perceive outsiders and lead to the development of negative ethnic attitudes. The effect of mass tourism on the residents of Cap Lloc (a pseudonym), a community on the Catalan coast of northeast Spain, is marked by a growing lack of concern, loss of empathy, and even intolerance toward outsiders. This case study examines some aspects of the images hosts and guests may hold of each other, and describes some of the changes on interpersonal relationships due to mass tourism.

Tourism does not invariably lead to external economic control, the decay of local institutions, and negative attitudes toward outsiders. Some societies seem to flourish in a tourist milieu. The Swiss and Austrians apparently have adapted to tourism in a manner that is profitable and free from discontent and internal dislocations. For a very different environment Philip McKean (chapter 6) has interpreted tourism in Bali as a positive source of cultural reaffirmation. However, one may reasonably ask whether Balinese institutions would survive if the island had to cater to three tourists for every four residents—the ratio for Spain in 1972.

The 26 million tourists who visited Spain in 1972 did not, of course, all arrive at once, nor were they evenly distributed over the countryside. Around Cap Lloc and its environs, some six-thousand permanent population (plus a few thousand seasonal workers) "hosted" approximately seventy thousand tourists during 1972, mostly during the three summer months. This is an overwhelming burden of outsiders. Rose Macaulay (1949, p. 36) noted that in the summer of 1947 the Costa Brava was a string of unspoilt fishing villages preserved from the "cosmopolitan smartness" that vulgarized the French coast. Motoring from the French frontier to Barcelona, she encountered only three cars with "GB" (Great Britain) plates; had she returned in 1972, she would have found tens of thousands of cars with foreign license plates and would soon have lost count of automobiles of British registry. Mass tourism began to reach the Costa Brava in the early 1960s, and the rapidity of its subsequent development coupled with its gross size heightens the social impact. Although most villagers derived economic benefits from the influx, local people felt they had very little control over the changes. Seldom verbalized as such, tourism was conceptualized as a sort of "mixed blessing," and the literature suggests that this attitude was not unique to Cap Lloc.

Natives and Outsiders: A Historical Perspective

Since the late nineteenth century, village communities in northeastern Spain have hosted a limited number of tourists including Catalans of urban background (mostly from Barcelona), non-Catalan Spaniards (in particular Castilians), and foreigners (in the sense of being nationals of countries other than Spain). This section of Catalonia is part of the "Spanish marches," a region that for centuries felt the consequences of war and political conflict between France and Spain. The French frontier is nearby, and until the early nineteenth century, Cap Lloc was the site of a major Spanish military and naval base guarding the coast and protecting the hinterland from French incursions. Then, during the Napoleonic Wars, Cap Lloc and other adjacent villages were under French military and administrative control. Although not on the main artery across the eastern Pyrenees, the road to France was close enough to bring to Cap Lloc a quota of foreigners long before the boom in international tourism. In summary, the exposure of villagers on the Coast Brava to outsiders has been continuous for several centuries. During this time, the people of Cap Lloc subtly categorized distinctions between native, stranger, and foreigner, as a guide to interpersonal relations or as a means of specifying how one should deal with whom and when.

Catalans of all classes maintain great pride in their language, culture, and national heritage, but their traditional culture also places substantial emphasis on the concept that each individual is a person, to be evaluated in terms of his or her merits. Bonhomie is not a dominant trait in the Catalan national character; in fact, many observers consider the Catalan as somewhat dour and pragmatic. However, the Catalan has a sensitivity to good manners and a consciousness of the duties inherent in the role of host, and, conversely, expects the guest to know his reciprocal obligations. Costa Brava communities traditionally viewed outsiders as individuals in a true host-guest relationship, but large-scale tourism now necessitates the use of ethnic stereotypes.

Modern tourism is more than a mere quantitative jump in the incidence of travelers. The numerical scale is very important for it has a direct bearing on the degree of impact imposed on a local sociocultural system. The interactions of host and guest also differ in rural and urban environments. Cities generally contain foreign or ethnic minorities, and strangers and foreigners tend to blend in the overall anonymity. The presence of tourists in cities simply does not make the same kind of visual and social impact as in newly developed resort localities. In a small town such as Cap Lloc, it is difficult to escape the tourists. They are present in their numbers day and night, walking the streets; in stores, the post office, and bars; lying on the beaches or hiking through the woods. Every tourist has great visibility and proclaims his alienness through dress, speech, and manners.

Although tourism may be regarded as just another "industry," it differs from other transformations of the countryside in one very important respect: tourism is a service-oriented operation that may entail a great deal of face-to-face contact between hosts and guests. Mass tourism indirectly affects everyone in a small community, including other tourists who seek to get away from the "beaten path." In the past, the elite travelers who visited such out-of-the-way communities as Cap Lloc seemingly assumed that it was they who had to adjust to the given sociocultural milieus; local people were scarcely expected to meet the standards of the visitors. If their stay was to be prolonged, as the seasonal visitor, then they largely entered the native system of accommodation and transportation, and lived as a marginal native. But the seventy thousand tourists who inundated Cap Lloc in the summer of 1972 for the most part traveled in what Graburn (chapter 1) has called the "tourist bubble," and expected their wants and needs to be catered according to some unknown (and as yet, unstudied) "international" standard. Mass tourism is therefore qualitatively different in the degree of impact upon a local sociocultural system.

If not physically present at a given moment, tourists are ready topics for local conversation. Through local eyes, they appear well-off and privileged, except perhaps for the "hippie" types that pose problems of categorization. Most residents are aware that the average modern tourist is not a person of great wealth, but it is difficult to translate socioeconomic concepts ("modest means," "average standard of living," "rich") across cultural boundaries, especially in the case of summer visitors. What the native recognizes is that the tourist is leisured at the very time when he may have to work hardest. Further, as in the case of northern Europeans visiting the Mediterranean, somatic differences may be striking; the myth dies hard that, in some subtle way, blond hair, blue eyes, and a light complexion do not spell money. Finally, most tourists are city people, which brings into play some very ancient cleavages. The social discontinuities created by mass tourism are less a matter of cultural isolation than the sudden change from a historic, steady interaction with a limited number of outsiders to the massive influx of short-term tourists.

Hosts and Guests: Contacts and Interaction

The traditional Catalan values of individualism in the host-guest relationship are no longer feasible under the impact of mass tourism but the need to classify individuals—to differentiate between native, stranger and foreigner—as a guide to interpersonal relations persists. An ethnic typology, based on the summary of experiences with different nationalities and/or subcultures, has emerged as a workable way to distinguish various categories of tourists, what may be expected from them by way of behavior, and the appropriate Catalan response. In general, the ethnic stereotypes are negative in composition and leave little room for the role of individual personality. Villagers have little doubt that, all things considered, the Catalan character is superior to all others, not because other peoples lack admirable traits, but because the Catalan personality strikes a better balance. It might be claimed that this is more a function of Catalan ethnocentrism than of mass tourism, but I do not believe this to be true.

Villagers readily elicit fairly concrete descriptions of personality profiles distinctive of a variety of nationalities and ethnic groups. When the subjects are nationals of major European countries or of countries geographically close to Spain, the responses are fairly uniform. Disregarding Spanish ethnic groups, the sharpest delineations include the English, French, Germans, Italians, and Portuguese. Most villagers also voice concrete opinions about Americans and Russians, although I suspect the American image owes much to Hollywood and television, while the Russian image may be attributed to the emergence of the Soviet Union as a world power combined with some memories of the Russian role in the Spanish Civil War.

In general, these images combine positive and negative evaluations of behavioral patterns or personal qualities. For example, the English are perceived to have the good qualities of nice manners, honesty, and general integrity. One cannot escape the impression that a degree of culture lag is involved in some common evaluative statements such as "The English always pay"; "Their children are very obedient"; and "You can depend on an Englishman's word." This seems to hark back to an era when the pound sterling was worth considerably more than it is today and the English directing classes (the only ones that traveled) behaved abroad in a dignified and quiet manner. The negative elements in this characterization also have a certain quaintness. English people are described as cold and aloof, haughty, and very demanding. In complaining about an English customer who made a fuss over the quality of the tea served in a restaurant, a middle-aged waitress quipped in Catalan to the local customers, "They are never satisfied, perhaps they think they are in India." Not unrelated to this complex of attitudes is the still fairly standard usage of the term *lor* or *milor* ("lord," "my lord") when referring to an upper-class Englishman, although to my knowledge it is never applied as a term of address. The context would indicate that, in most instances, it implies an overbearing attitude on the part of the individual so designated.

English character thus combines good points (steadiness, integrity, etc.) with elements that are viewed less favorably (social distance, stiffness, etc.). The stereotype exists as a generalized evaluation applicable to mass tourism. However, given a reasonable length of contact between an individual foreigner and local people, the stereotypes are amenable to adjustment. Thus, in the case of an Englishman who lived for some months in the village—a retired army officer who dressed in what locals regarded as very "English" attire and carried himself with dignity—the general consensus was that English national character as manifest in this particular personality was an extremely agreeable combination. In the words of a local storekeeper,

Sr. —— is a real English gentleman. He has the English character, very correct. You can tell that he has a sense of discipline and order. No doubt this is the result of many years in the British army and before that having attended one of those expensive boarding schools they have in England. But he is not haughty and will always stop to say a word or two. He tries very hard to speak Spanish and has even picked up some Catalan. Yes, you could never mistake him for anything else but an Englishman, but he does not behave like a *lor*. In the past, most of the English who visited the village came from the same educated classes, although not all were as understanding. Today, we generally get a much more rowdy group, drinking at all hours and keeping people awake with their noisy singing.

The man in question never failed to doff his hat to the women of the neighborhood, smile at the children, and greet the men with a cheerful "Good day." The comment of the storekeeper reflects a certain deprecation of the current run of tourists as being less educated and less well-mannered than those typical of an earlier generation. I have heard this theme repeated many times, and to listen to some villagers, one is almost led to believe that visitors in the past, regardless of nationality, were all upper-class people. This was hardly the case, but it is another instance of elaborating cultural categories through a process of selecting some traits and ignoring others, so that hosts view most of the tourists that visit Cap Lloc in an essentially negative way.

Natives and Tourists: The Loss of Individuality

The Englishman described above does not fit the category of a typical tourist and it is just for this reason—for the purposes of contrast—that the case has been examined in some detail. He lived in the village long enough for his qualities as an individual to emerge above the flood of thousands of other foreigners who overnight or stay only a week or two. Many comparable examples could be cited of other outsiders, of different nationalities, who have similarly established their right to be considered as individuals and not just as stereotypes. In a culture where individual qualities are deemed so important, the loss of individuality is akin to the loss of an important human attribute. For practical purposes, most tourists are treated as something less, or at least something different, than ordinary folk.

This touristic separation from normal humankind involves two variables; length of residence and the matter of numbers. The longer a foreigner resides in the village, the more likely it is that he or she will be treated as an individual with a distinct personality, a set of more or less predictable habits and recognized interests. However, as increased numbers of outsiders reside for longer periods in the village, it becomes progressively harder for residents to differentiate between them on personalistic criteria.

Proportionate to the growth of mass tourism, traditional stereotypes are applied to all foreigners, without the corrective factors that were normally applicable when guests were relatively few. These changed patterns of perception and interaction mean that strangers are viewed in an ever more negative light. Traditional stereotypes are also applied virtually automatically, and with increasing emphasis on those attributes of ethnic group identification deemed most negative by villagers. Samples of local conversation suggest that *all* French people are pushy and bad-mannered, *all* Germans are stingy, and *all* Italians are untrustworthy. These stereotypes suggest the generalization that tourists as a group are unworthy of friendly consideration.

If the above interpretation is correct, it facilitates—even legitimates—modes of interaction designed to capitalize on the ignorance of the average tourist. The rules of social intercourse among villagers are simply waived or bent when the other party is a tourist. Everyone in the community knows that for many goods and services there are two price structures: one for hosts and the other for guests. This double standard is expressed in statements such as, "Anything is good enough for tourists" (poor accommodations, bad food, etc.), and even in a differential application of legal sanctions. For example, the local police usually give parking tickets only to motorists from outside the community, and especially to those driving cars with foreign license plates.

In summary, the tourist is a stranger or foreigner, and is now perceived as devoid of his essential individuality and human qualities. He or she is "faceless" and interchangeable with any other tourist. Stereotypes of national character are reinforced and the gulf between natives and outsiders is accentuated.

It is difficult to escape the conclusion that tourists, now the mainstay of the local economy, are disliked. Given the reality of mass tourism, residents no longer view an influx of temporary "guests" as positive. At the risk of oversimplification, the dominant attitude is indifference and dislike. Outright hatred of tourists is rare. Tourists, like the weather, have become a fact of life, and the average villager feels that there is little that he can do to change the status quo.

The situation is paradoxical. One of the characteristics of contemporary life is the persistence of ethnic identities in an age of mass communication wherein shared values and expectations crosscut different class and ethnic groupings. Contacts between villagers and outsiders have never been greater, but the barriers to understanding have probably never been higher. However, on closer examination, the paradox is resolved because the tourist universe and the universe of the village are two separate realities coexisting in the same physical space. The people of Cap Lloc have simply adapted to the tourist presence by withdrawing from the tourist many of these qualities that the traditional culture insists are part of the general partrimony of humankind. This process of dehumanization involves a dulling of the sensitivities and occurs whenever people refuse to "get involved" or when the world appears too large or too complex to warrant consideration for others. The experience of Spanish workers hired to work in more developed Western European countries is comparable, as these migrants are seldom integrated into the local societies. In part, they encounter prejudice abroad, but they are also disinclined to participate or become involved with the new life-style. One worker commented on his two years in Germany, "I never think of my stay in Germany as forming part of my real life. You know, it was like doing military service." Psychologically, this worker never left Spain, and is analogous to many tourists who never truly leave "home." Cap Lloc villagers remain in place and respond to tourists by erecting virtually insurmountable barriers to genuine human relations.

The host culture has learned their lesson well. If tourism commoditicizes culture, natives categorize strangers as a resource or a nuisance rather than as people. The wheel has turned full circle, at least conceptually.

University of Massachusetts

Part IV

Tourism in Complex Societies

Humans everywhere seek status symbols to reaffirm their identity, and some Western tourists count countries as evidence of their widened experience. For others, the ownership of boats and second homes as forms of recreation are important. John Peck and Alice Lepie in chapter 11 examine the impact of dominantly American tourism upon three American communities and suggest a typology of power, payoff, and tradeoff to assess the differential effects of recreational tourism.

Souvenirs, derived from the Latin *subvenire*, "to come to mind," are an important symbolic adjunct to the tourist industry, providing the tourist with something tangible to take home while simultaneously providing local employment in an arts and crafts industry. The dramatic renascence and increased production of Southwest Indian crafts (Deitch, chapter 12) has been accompanied by an equal upturn in both quality and style, in sharp contrast to the "trinkets" that fill many curio stands elsewhere. However, as Laurence Loeb describes in chapter 13, the available supply of genuine antiques cannot meet the demands of expanded tourism, and in Iran a new industry has emerged specializing in the production of quality "fake art."

The Polynesian Cultural Center (Stanton, chapter 14) is an innovative tourist attraction that has attained great financial success in its thirteen years of operation, but for those who might seek to emulate it elsewhere there is a clear warning: the model culture has succeeded in Hawaii because of the large available audience engendered by mass and charter tourism but might not be a success were it to be undertaken as the primary attraction to an area.

11

Tourism and Development in Three North Carolina Coastal Towns[1]

JOHN GREGORY PECK
and
ALICE SHEAR LEPIE

As part of a regional planning project, in 1973 we undertook a study of the impact of recreational tourism on three coastal communities of North Carolina. A preliminary reconnaissance trip indicated the need to develop a framework or model around which we could quickly organize the data, given the complexities of the topic and the stipulated time-lines. As the model (Figure 1) emerged, we recognized that it was a potential methodology that could be used to establish a typology of touristic development. Our hypothesis was that both the rate (magnitude and speed) of development and the amount of community involvement and control (power) over the change would affect the amount and distribution of payoffs and tradeoffs associated with increased tourism. We further suspected that of the two, power would be the more crucial factor.

Tourism is subdivided in terms of three criteria of central importance to the indigenous people: (1) Power, (2) Payoffs and (3) Tradeoffs. "Power" includes the ownership of the land that is developed, the source of the financing, the input from local people, and the relation of local traditions to the development projects. "Payoffs" includes benefits to the host culture from tourism, and potential changes in social mobility within the existing social order. "Tradeoffs" primarily involves the social impact, which changes the nature of the communities, such as the consequences of a shift from agriculture and fishing to commerce; a change from three-generation extended families to two-generation nuclear families; and the

[1] The research on which this case study is based was partially sponsored by NOAA Office of Sea Grant, under Grant No. 04-3-158-40, and the State of North Carolina, Department of Administration. The U.S. Government is authorized to reproduce and distribute reprints for governmental purposes notwithstanding any copyright that may appear hereon.

Figure 1
Typology of Touristic Development

Rate of Change	Power Basis	Payoffs and Tradeoffs—Effects on Life-Style of Community
Rapid Growth	"Bedroom" communities Summer residents Specialized commerce (Outside financing)	Rapid change of local norms New power structure and economy
Slow Growth	Individual developments Local Ownership Expanding local commerce (Local financing)	Slow change of norms Stable power structure Expanding local economy

Transient Development	Pass-throughs
	Weekenders
	Seasonal Entrepreneurs
	(Local financing)
		Stable norms
		Individual mobility within
		   power structure and
		   economy
		Little overall change in
		   local economy

impact of a wider range of norms and mores on the existing methods of social control. These criteria suggested that dynamic tourism is divisible into three parts: *Rapid Growth, Slow Growth* and *Transient Development.*

Rapid growth occurs when corporations purchase and develop large tracts of raw land to the subdivision lot stage. The lots are then sold to a nonlocal urban market either as an investment or as a site for vacation or retirement homes. Within this context most of the profit realized from sale of the land flows out of the community; much of the labor utilized in the developmental building process comes from outside the local area; and many of the services developed to meet the needs of the new community are provided by outsiders as part of the developer's package.

Slow growth is primarily controlled by local landowners, and involves a substantially smaller number of newcomers and new homes. Development is locally incremental, proportionate to the stability or *status quo* of the population, and is comparatively unplanned. The occasional newcomers who buy into established businesses or open new enterprises become integrated into the traditional power structures of the communities.

Transient development refers to primarily a weekend and "special event" tourist trade that supplies seasonal income for local native entre-

Figure 2
North Carolina

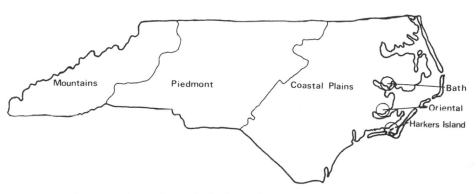

preneurs but requires relatively little cash investment to provide facilities or accommodations for the tourists.

To test the hypothesis we chose three coastal communities (Figure 2), each representing a different style of development yet sharing a number of features with the other two. Each community was small and geographically discrete, and populations ranged from 350 to 1,600 people. None of the communities had full-time municipal employees, and local leadership was largely a combination of voluntary service groups and elected part-time officials. Each community was situated on an inland waterway (oceanfront property now is either almost completely developed or held by State or Federal agencies) and had a mixed economic base of either local commerce and fishing or local commerce and farming. All three communities shared the process of change and nascent development.

The three target communities were expected to roughly approximate the three styles of tourism development in the typology. Oriental would reflect the rapid growth pattern because of several moderate to large-size real estate developments on its outskirts; Bath would resemble the slow growth aspect of the model because of the relatively stable land ownership patterns and the absence of large tourist developments; Harkers Island would represent the transient state of tourist development based on its position as a potential gateway port to the Cape Lookout National Seashore.

Field Methods

As "outsiders," the customary role of participant-observer proved useful. Residence in local households validated the field worker's presence in the communities and afforded an intimate view of family life. In the routine daily cycle, daytime hours were normally spent in the community with a spectrum of townspeople of varied occupations and ages. Late afternoons were devoted to the household and socialization during the evening meal. Evenings were spent at church or other civic or voluntary association meetings.

One of the more useful, productive field techniques was an "essay contest" in the schools on Harkers Island. With administrative cooperation, the contest was conducted among fifth and sixth grade children for the best essay on "How tourists affect my community and my Island." Although prizes were awarded to the three best literary essays in each school, our anthropological interest was in the content of *all* essays. Other field methods included extensive interviews and review of historical data. From the wealth of material, three distinct community types emerged, each sharing many aspects with their counterparts yet maintaining their own individuality.

The Region

North Carolina is divisible into three general topographic areas. The Blue Ridge Mountains in the west contain some of the highest peaks in eastern United States, and western North Carolina has relatively little industrial development, many small towns and hamlets, and a predominately rural, white population. The dominantly agricultural Piedmont section of North Carolina is an area of gently rolling hills containing most of the state's population and industry and most of the north-south arterial highways. East of the Piedmont lies the Coastal Plains of North Carolina: a 100 to 200-mile strip of flat, sandy soil stretching to the Atlantic Ocean.

Coastal North Carolina has a rich history. For over three thousand years, American Indians maintained maritime settlements and hunted, fished, and feasted upon the abundant shellfish taken from the estuaries and coastal shoals. During the early period of Colonial development, pirates sought the protection of the Outer Banks and the many estuarine and river systems served as safe harbors between their forays, and even today local folklore is rich with stories of Black Beard's buried treasure. Later, with the advent of three-masted clipper ships and the whaling industry, whaling stations and fishing villages were established along the Outer Banks. Their only means of communication with the rest of the world was by water. Fishing, ship building, lumbering, and to a lesser extent plantation agriculture became the coastal zone's primary sources of revenue, but the communications and commercial channels remained by water.

An abundance of navigable waterways has been both a boon and a bane for North Carolina's Coastal Plains. The area is bisected from north to south by the Inland Waterway (a series of shallow estuaries connected by canals), protected from the fury of the Atlantic Ocean by North Carolina's Outer Banks. On an east-west axis, the area is intersected by a number of great river systems, including the Neuse and the Pamlico. These rivers, often several miles wide as they approach the sea, provide the necessary nutrients for bountiful harvests of fish and shellfish. A series of human habitations similar to isolated peninsulas grew up where ground communication and transportation between settlements is often many times the straight-line distance between points. Bridges across the major rivers are relatively few, and the interior areas of the peninsulas were, until recent times, almost impenetrable swamps.

Major changes in the Coastal Plains have occurred in the twentieth century. Despite relatively little in-migration since the Civil War, a series of major storms along the Outer Banks forced the abandonment of many fishing villages and their subsequent relocation within the protected waters of the estuarine and river systems. Massive corporate tree farming has replaced the harvesting of the virgin timber. Within the last decade, giant corporate farms began to assert a dominant position in the agriculture of eastern North Carolina, as well as open-pit mining of phosphate ores and large-scale draining and clearing of former swamp areas.

The coastal area had experienced significant changes since World War II: a rising population, increased affluence, the extension of improved highways to the coastal area, and a large market for "second" homes and recreation areas associated with the tourist industry. Coastal communities that over the last century had had relatively little contact with the outside world began to expand—first with new summer residents and tourists, later with retirees and "newcomers" who came to service the needs of the expanding communities.

North Carolina is rich in natural resources, and her coastal area is unrivaled for sheer beauty anywhere on this continent. Her greatest wealth, however, lies in the peoples of North Carolina. Inherent in this study is an analysis of the life-style, the "gut feelings" of North Carolineans and Down Easterners. Ahead lie choices involving values important to their life style, between various kinds of tourist development, industrialization, and agri-business.

The Community of Oriental

Oriental is a rivertown situated near the mouth of the Neuse River where it empties into Pamlico Sound. Oriental is not an old town by coastal North Carolina standards. Prior to the Civil War, the Pamlico Bay area was divided into large plantations, and eighteenth-century homes can still be found around the town.

According to local legend Uncle Lou Midyette (pronounced mid-jet) sought a safe harbor from a storm around 1870, when he "clem a tree" and was enchanted with the area. He envisioned a bustling town and encouraged others to settle there by selling his land cheaply. This booster attitude continues today.

Many businesses in Oriental are composite two-generation, family-owned, and family-run. Typical are a construction firm owned by a county commissioner, his two sons, and their head carpenter; a gasoline station and a hardware-grocery owned by a local father and son; and a combination grill and beauty shop, housed in an old filling station. The grill is operated by the parents of the girl who runs the beauty shop.

The Oriental Marina, Restaurant, and Motel is run by a local widow, and her large bay-view restaurant has a regional reputation for its seafood. The local Rotary Club holds its dinner meetings here. On busy summer weekends the area around the motel stirs with activity as summer camps open and Oriental holds its annual sailing regatta.

Nearby is North Carolina's most modern crab processing plant. To its left is an oak-lined residential street, with large homes once built for lumber company executives or as hotels. Ten years ago they were in disrepair, but now many of them have been restored by summer residents. Beyond these riverfront mansions is the town's public park and fishing pier, a popular place for Black residents and White tourists to spend a congenial evening, each commenting on the other's catch.

The established political and economic order in Oriental has traditionally been maintained by white male and female permanent residents, forty years of age and older, who own and operate the majority of local essential businesses as well as the most profitable tourist establishments. Despite the decline in lumbering and tourism in the 1940s and '50s, these people have long-term cultural and economic commitments to the town.

In the face of a declining adult population, this core group filled multiple roles in various religious, political, and social organizations to provide continuity in the essential functioning of the community. They are now leaders who can "get things done" at local and County levels, and from whom newcomers, rich and poor alike, must seek informal sanctions and official validations that are necessary to live and work in Oriental.

This host group views Oriental's growth as a revitalization of a once-dying town, and work actively and well with newcomers through the Rotary Club, the volunteer fire department, and other local institutions. They deem the influx of population as furnishing much-needed helping hands, rather than as a new group of outsiders competing for power and prestige. In their eyes, the solidarity of the town and its traditions is enhanced rather than threatened by the developing tourism.

Within the last ten years, Oriental has become an "in" place for a growing group of sailboat enthusiasts from Raleigh, the capital of North Carolina, who are enamored with what they perceived to be an "old New England Fishing Village" atmosphere and quality of life. These summer sailors are mostly professionals—doctors, lawyers, professors, and legislators—who, from early March to late October, drive with their families the two hundred miles from Raleigh on weekends to work and live on their boats or to fix up their "summer cottages," often renovated and repainted old homes left over from Oriental's prosperous lumbering past. They are usually affluent, in their forties, and they actively encourage others like themselves to buy summer homes as they become available. However, they are not involved in the rapid expansion of the retiree community and the "second home" real estate developments.

In addition to summer residents, many retirees and a growing group of college-educated, young entrepreneurs have settled in Oriental. Each group claims a strong sense of loyalty and love for the town and for its quality of life and have been integrated into the local scene through participation in service businesses and service organizations.

Completion of a Planned Unit Development resort project will attract more retirees as Oriental is within commuting distance of Cherry Point Marine Air Station, whose medical and post exchange facilities are of major value to retired military personnel. Most of these new residents are widely travelled, with administrative experience. They are accustomed to being busy, and see themselves as important and tend to integrate easily into service organizations such as the Rotary Club, where they predominate.

The retirees in Oriental typify a phenomena found in all three of the communities studied. Many of the retiree couples consist of native-born eastern North Carolina women who went away to a university, then married and lived elsewhere, only to later return to their native area. Their in-migration tends to import husbands with a higher level of skills than the community norm. Occasional local resentment is aroused however, when these people wish to change the town "too much" or are insensitive to traditional lines of authority.

The college-educated young entrepreneurs are a relatively new phenomena in Eastern North Carolina and in Oriental. For several decades the area exported its college-educated youth as farming became increasingly mechanized and a shrinking population base offered progressively fewer job opportunities. Adventurous and aggressive youths found few rewards here and sought their futures in the North and in the bigger cities of the South.

This traditional pattern appears to be modifying, as a result of changing life goals and value systems among the young. Many of the young couples now settling in Oriental come from the eastern part of the state, but few have direct kinship ties in Oriental. They have been attracted by the quiet, small-town way of life and the newfound opportunity to make a good living in the new businesses generated by the summer sailors and the new retirees. These young people primarily integrate into the community through service clubs and churches, and in time can be expected to play their role in the local political arena.

The increased population and infusion of tourist dollars has improved the economy but heightened an awareness of differential income. Individuals on fixed or limited income, seldom directly affected by tourism but caught in an inflationary squeeze, sense a relatively great deprivation as the income and status of newcomers increase. Some residents are distressed by Oriental's growth and tend to view their declining purchasing power as a disruption caused by progress. They do not want more money; they only want to keep what they have.

Those on a limited or low income also say that they are being victimized by local merchants who have raised their prices to a level accommodating the more well-to-do newcomers. They feel that a progressive town is regressive by taxing them disproportionately for services that will not benefit them. They see no need for city water when they already have a well and pump and are resentful when tax revenues are used to provide Sea Vista—the new retirement community—with city services rather than repairing their own roads.

In addition, they see their neighborhood being invaded by weekend sailors with differing behavioral norms. The weekender's consumption of alcohol is felt by many to be immoral. They experience stress in their family when they must cope with the difference in child rearing practices between themselves and the weekenders. Frequently they complain that vacationing children are allowed to run wild throughout town and that teenaged "hippies" hang out around town and "make love in the park."

Socioeconomic change in Oriental is subject to other counter trends. Many lots in the new development may be bought by outsiders for investment purposes and not built on. Other purchasers, in an era of tight money, may not be able to complete their payment schedule or to build. These empty lots and sections could remain mosquito-infested marshes, and, except for pockets of retirees and second home owners, it might become a neighborhood without people.

Oriental's growth, paralleling that of the national economy, seems to be slowing. Perhaps this will afford the community a period in which to integrate the differing goals of people who have settled and prevent it from being solely a Rapid Growth community, primarily benefitting outside investors. Newcomers are entering into Oriental's political process, and this seems the most promising road to community integration.

The Community of Bath

Bath, the oldest incorporated town in North Carolina, is a hamlet of only 350 people located on the north bank of the Pamlico River near its entrance into Pamlico Sound. The surrounding land is flat and empty, with stands of tall loblolly pine alternating with fields of corn, tobacco, and soybeans and areas of uncleared swamp land. The community has minimal stores and services. Most shopping is done in Belhaven or Washington, a fifteen-mile distance to the east or west, respectively.

Bath is a National Historical Landmark, with an air-conditioned visitor center offering the tourist a free movie on Bath's history, and where tickets may be purchased to tour the two renovated homes and other landmarks.

Tourists are hardly visible to the town residents. The restored homes are at opposite ends of a long, two-block street and sightseers are encouraged to *drive* the distance between the two houses. Even though the number of tourists is relatively small, the driving tends to reduce the interaction between the residents and the tourists.

Tourism in Bath serves local residents more than outside visitors. The visitor center and the renovated historical landmarks, built with locally-raised funds, are properly to be admired by outsiders but are fully appreciated only by local residents. The antique shops advertise items for sale to outsiders, but sell more to local county residents. Local history is primarily for local rather than outside consumption and is a main focus of Bath's Colonial Book Club, the Historical Society, and daily conversation. By local assessment, tourists seldom stay more than two or three hours, but town-folk will endure.

Life in Bath is kinship-based. The small resident population includes families and kin who own much of the farmland around the town. Hence, there is a sense of belonging to a kin group, to the land and its richness, to the river, to the traditions and ways that have been a part of this eastern North Carolina area since well before the Civil War.

Although a great deal of the timberland surrounding Bath is owned either by the phosphate mining companies or by a large wood-pulp and timber company, the traditional wealth is based in agriculture. The crops are tobacco and corn, and in recent years, soybeans. The younger people, the sons and daughters, live on the rural family farms, while the older people have moved into town. There they live a quiet, comfortable, generally affluent life filled with childhood friends and a routine of never-too-busy to visit. One of the comments frequently made about those who now work for the phosphate mines is that "they never seem to have time to neighbor."

While making money is a goal for the retail and service businesses in Bath, retaining an unhurried atmosphere is more important. The gift shops and the visitor center are places where locals—friends and relatives—can pass the time of day, relay a message, or stay to have a soda. The women who work in the stores feel free to bring their younger children to play while they work, or to supervise them from the shop. A gas station ostensibly run for "through trade" gets very little of it; the two adjacent garages are used for the storage of old and miscellaneous junked automobile parts. The man who pumps gas is on a pension and takes little if any salary. His reward is to be useful, and to be able to sit and talk with the other retired men who gather in front of the station.

Outsiders whose destination is Bath are usually professionals from Greenville or Kinston who either have a vacation sailboat at the marina or a summer cottage in a section out from town, along the Pamlico River. They purchase little in Bath except groceries or occasional bits of hardware and gasoline. Store prices sometimes vary depending on whether or not one is a local or an outsider. Rarely do the outsiders (sailing enthusiasts) and residents, who prefer motor boats if they can afford them, interact.

Bath, which has changed little in the last half century, will probably expand dramatically in the near future. Adjacent are some of the richest phosphate deposits in the United States. A world-wide fertilizer shortage has prompted companies with extensive mineral options in the area to begin or expand their strip-mining operations, which will create hundreds of new jobs. In the absence of an adequate local labor supply, the new employees will have to be imported.

Bath offers many attractions to the new residents. The school system is deemed better than average in the county; the town is installing a deep-well, central water supply system and plans a municipal sewer system. In addition, large tracts of open land adjacent to the city are potentially available for large scale housing subdivisions.

The future development of Bath will, in large measure, depend upon the continued expansion of phosphate mining in the area and upon the method of bridging the Pamlico River. The existent mines are located across the river, with limited access provided by a ferry service operated by the State of North Carolina on an hourly basis. The alternative to the four-mile ferry trip requires approximately fifty miles of driving west to Washington then east to Aurora, North Carolina. If access to the phosphate strip mines can be significantly improved, then Bath will grow and consequently will shift from the present Slow Growth phase to that of Rapid Growth.

Harkers Island

Harkers Island lies off the Carolina Coast about twenty miles east of Morehead City, and is linked to the mainland by a mile-long bridge and causeway. Until the 1930s, access was limited to private boats or the mail ferry.

Isolation once permeated the island, and old-timers remember when one could walk the entire length of this island freely, with the bay at one side and a dense buffer of forest on the other. In that era hunting and fishing were at will, anytime and anywhere on the island. Since construction of the two-lane, four-mile long highway three decades ago, most of the former rabbit, coon, and deer-hunting areas have been cleared for vacation home sites, and fishing sites are regulated.

Local entrepreneurs along the island road solicit some of the tourist trade by combining a seasonal business such as a restaurant, sports, or gift shop, or seafood stand with an essential, year-round island service such as a grocery, gasoline station, or repair shop. Shops are frequently run by one parent with the assistance of the children once they are out of school. Local retailers prefer "pass-through" customers because they pay with cash, whereas islanders expect credit. While there is a seasonal rise in business, tourist dollars do not continue to circulate in the community. With the exception of seafood caught by the islanders, all supplies must be brought from the mainland by middlemen.

Harkers Island has a stable, exclusively white population of 1,600. Residents trace their origin to Diamond City, an eighteenth Century whaling town on Shackleford Banks, on the edge of the Atlantic Ocean, that was finally abandoned in the 1900s after a series of disastrous hurricanes. The present settlement was subsequently relocated landward on Harkers Island. Elements of the former whaling tradition persist in the construction of "flaired bow" boats for which the island is famous. Craftsmanship is still revered; the keel of the fine wooden boats is customarily hand carved by the owner of the shipyard. Orders even come from Europe because Harkers Island is one of the few remaining sources of custom-made, wooden motor yachts.

Islanders still look fondly across the bay to their "banks" and love to hear the old people's stories about life there. A favorite trip for island families is to boat across the bay to the family's primitive squatter cabin, to spend a weekend swimming and gathering food from the sea. It is a peaceful time, away from modern conveniences and pressures, and they return home wistfully wishing there was a way they could bring back the old way of life.

The islander's concept of land ownership conflicts with that of the vacation home owners. The island is loved as a whole by the natives, and access to all its parts—beaches and open land alike—is considered an islander's birthright. Although land may be sold to outsiders, islanders still expect to be able to pull up their boats anywhere along the bay, and children are supposed to be able to walk and play everywhere. But outsider's bulkheads and "No Trespassing" signs block that inherent right.

Frustrated outsiders, imbued with their legal rights, have taken islanders to court and even threatened to shoot at children who step across their lot line.

An indication of the hostility between islanders and outsiders is the vandalism of "outsiders'" vacation homes by local teenagers. By contrast, island fishermen also may have things stolen from their boats, but they usually find out who stole the items and then are able to put out the word that they would like the articles returned.

The concept of ownership also extends to the area between the banks and the island. Local fishermen resent the vacationing outsiders who aggressively stake out the best fishing spots. In addition, island fishermen see their work made harder by the sports fisherman who follows the commercial boats, steals from their nets, or unthinkingly tears their nets by running his motorboat over them. Commercial fishermen feel it unjust that sports fishermen are allowed to cut into the limited supply of fish upon which the commercial fisherman depends for his livelihood.

Natives see their island as a finite area that is gradually being taken over by outsiders through inflating land prices. Traditionally, three-generation extended families owned the land, but because of higher land prices many people now doubt that their children or grandchildren will be able to afford to stay on the island. In selling their land, they have also sold the joy of watching their grandchildren grow up.

Outsiders are almost never integrated into the community. An inward-focused world-view persists where "foreigners" are defined as any nonkin person living outside the island. To be truly accepted requires a church membership and the capacity to trace kin back to the fifteen or so families that came over from the Banks. Few summer people learn to understand the seemingly Elizabethan dialect the Islanders speak. Even if they do become accustomed to the speech, the largely urban, middle class tourist runs up against a rigidly fundamentalist closed society that coolly protects itself against the patronizing "quaint" or "backwards" label they get from outsiders. Consequently, vacation lots are bought by outsiders who rarely stay for more than a week because they begin to feel isolated. To entertain themselves they encourage groups of friends either to come down and party with them or to buy adjoining lots.

A strong sense of loss and resentment permeates when islanders talk about the tourists. Islanders believe they are economically caught in a losing battle. Stories are told of people who sold bay property lots for more money than they had ever seen, only to discover that their land had been sold for less than its replacement value. They feel that the outside encroachment lessens the quality of life on the island.

Religion is very important to the islanders. Touring revivalists are still able to draw the biggest crowds of any event on the island. God's Will involves every aspect of the individual's life, and the intimate and comforting closeness they feel to Jesus reveals, for them, the direction their lives should take. For the more fundamentalist churchgoer, it is a joyous, liberating kind of religion that involves the whole body in its worship. For all island church members, religion is an involving association that encompasses their family, kin, and closest friends.

For the great majority, the Sabbath is a restful day devoted to church attendance, a big noon meal, and to visiting family. But weekend outsiders do not conform to this expected behavior, and resentment is deep towards streets congested with a steady stream of big cars pulling large fiberglass motorboats, or when spirited gospel singing is drowned out by the weekender's power lawnmower or a boisterous party.

In the face of the tourist invasion, Islanders are resigned to the attitude that there is little that can be done to modify the almost apocalyptic process they envision. Passivity in the face of God's Will is an interpretation that Fundamentalist religion encourages. Attention to the soul and that of the family is the most constructive course to ease dissatisfaction.

In addition to the religious introversion, Harkers Island has no truly functioning local political or governmental mechanisms. As a result, the community is poorly equipped to cope with the outside world, and with the internal problems of integrating rapid changes, when concerted group action or "political clout" is needed. Few members in the community are experienced in dealing with outside political entities. The future is problematic for Harkers Island. While today's tourism is still "transient," it has already been able to change the land use of the island, if not yet its social norms. More significantly, due to the lack of political strength and cohesiveness, the future development of tourism may be decided by people, conditions, and forces well outside the kinship, religious, and social networks of the Islander community. Thus Harkers Island reflects the Transient Development stage in its early phases.

Conclusions

The three-fold model of tourism proved a useful device to distinguish between the three communities and the level of tourism associated with them. The nature of tourism in any given community is the product of complex, interrelated economic and political factors, as well as particular geographic and recreational features that attract "outsiders." The model also suggests that the *rate* of culture change induced by tourism affects the integration of the community, as well as the *magnitude* of the change. The nature of change associated with tourism must also be correlated with the *source of regulatory power*—that is, whether the host culture or an external force is the prime element. Power, both economic and political, emerged as the central differentiating factor in the impact of tourism. A strong local power base tended to direct the development toward compatibility with the local community and tended to foster integration of newcomers into the established network. Tourism may be assessed as an acculturation process with cyclical tendencies. In those situations where the acculturating groups have roughly equal power, a minimum of community disruption and disintegration will occur.

North Carolina State University

12

The Impact of Tourism upon the Arts and Crafts of the Indians of the Southwestern United States

LEWIS I. DEITCH

The role of tourism in altering segments of a traditional culture has not fully been examined. This study examines the impact of tourism upon the arts and crafts of the Indians of the American Southwest. Diffusion has been one of the major mechanisms of cultural change, but in assessing the role of diffusion the anthropologist has most often looked at the impact of trade, migration, war, and missionary contact. The tourist has been ignored as a potential source of new ideas that could alter or disrupt segments of a traditional culture.

The peoples of the Southwest have been exposed to European culture since the Spanish settled the Rio Grande Valley of New Mexico in the early 1600s. Their arts have experienced periodic infusions of new ideas, materials, and techniques. Art forms have flourished and waned. However, in the twentieth century (particularly since World War II) tourism generated many changes. Never before has there been such an abundance of Indian rugs, pottery, jewelry, *kachinas*, and baskets, nor have prices been so high. Other art forms, such as paintings, are also rapidly developing. Throughout the nation, people are aware of the native arts of the Southwest, and many are eager to possess something Indian. For the first time since white contact, the Indian has a commodity that is sought by members of Western society.

This study examines the phenomenal growth of the Indian arts and crafts market brought about by their exposure to the rest of the nation through tourism and other factors, such as the national awakening to the importance of preserving those roots of the total American heritage that were a decade ago in danger of vanishing, and the Indian's self-awareness resulting from the Civil Rights movement, which has further engendered a pride in his traditions.

A Brief Historic Sketch

The concept of aesthetics exists in most societies, and such activities express an artistic sense of value and provide a measure of self-satisfaction. Among the Indians of the southwestern United States, arts and crafts have been integral to their culture for centuries. The present forms reflect an evolutionary process that has been heightened in the twentieth century by the creation of a commercial market of significant importance.

The sedentary cultures of the Pueblos trace their origins to pre-Columbian farmers who left a rich heritage in crop domestication, house construction, tool-making, and ceremony. At the time of Spanish contact, the Pueblo people were already well versed in the arts of pottery, baskets, cotton cloth, shell jewelry, and *kachina* figures. Other sedentary peoples also had developed the arts of pottery and basketry. Among the Papago, Walapai, and Ute, basket-making had reached a fine level of craftsmanship. The seminomadic ancestors of the contemporary Navajo and Apache (the Athapascans) were newcomers to the Southwest at the time of Spanish contact, and appear to have lacked the artistic sophistication of the Pueblo dwellers.

The Navajo appear to have been quick to learn new concepts. By the start of the eighteenth century they were weaving garments—a trait learned from contact with the Pueblos. During this same period, the Spanish introduction of sheep into the Rio Grande Valley led the Navajo and Pueblo to incorporate livestock into their economies and to the art of weaving in wool. The Navajo, however, more readily took to the domestication of sheep and goats as a major livelihood, and thus the weaving of wool garments and rugs became a more integral part of their aesthetic expression than it did among the Pueblo peoples. The Navajo weavers experimented with designs and color, and began to use new commercial woollens such as bayeta and Saxony. By the mid-nineteenth century, Navajo skill in weaving reached a level of excellence seen by surviving museum specimens. Among the Pueblo people, weaving was a male-dominated activity associated with religious ceremonies. In Navajo society the women became the weavers as ownership of livestock was vested in the matrilineal family.

During the mid-nineteenth century, another art form, silverwork, diffused into the Southwest from Mexicans of the Rio Grande Valley. The Navajo first derived silver jewelry in trade for horses, but by 1860 they were manufacturing their own silver ornaments. From the Navajo, the trait spread among the Zuni and Hopi. The Rio Grande pueblos also developed silverwork from direct contact with the Spanish. The earliest Indian jewelry consisted of only silver. The use of turquoise, coral, and shell developed toward the end of the nineteenth century, and turquoise became the most valued stone. Turquoise has been used in the Southwest for centuries, primarily strung into necklaces. It has in many cases strong significance in ritual and ceremonial life, especially among the Pueblo peoples.

At first the Indians imitated Spanish styles, but as with weaving, new designs appeared including the so-called "squash blossom," which many tourists consider "typically Indian." The design is a Navajo interpretation of the popular Spanish pomegranate worn as ornamentation during the mid-nineteenth century. Silversmithing has remained a male-dominated art form, as was also true among Spanish craftsmen.

Among the sedentary tribes of the Southwest, decoration varied widely both spatially and temporally. Prior to the coming of the Spanish, pottery was essentially utilitarian and for storage. With the introduction of metal pots, the manufacture and quality of Indian pottery declined until the early years of the twentieth century when tourism brought about a resurgence of the art.

Early Twentieth-Century Impact

For most Indians in the United States, the coming of the white man spelled certain doom for traditional ways. The railroad, for example, heightened the pressure upon the Plains Indians and was a major contributor to the end of their way of life. So, too, in the Southwest, the Indian was threatened. However, since significant settlement did not occur until the 1880s, and the major influx commenced after the turn of this century, these Indians were spared much of the cultural devastation that disrupted other groups. Furthermore, in the 1920s the government began to reverse earlier policies aimed at assimilation.

The Southwest has long held a degree of fascination for Americans; its majestic canyons, vast and colorful vistas, and unique desert flora appealed to the frontier spirit of the American personality (Turner 1920). The blend of Hispano and Indian cultures further exemplified this romance. Most of the early twentieth-century visitors or settlers were drawn here because of medical advice from the Public Health Office and private physicians that the arid climate offered amenities for respiratory illness. White businessmen found that catering to these newcomers was profitable, and the first stage in the development of a resort industry commenced. Fortunately, the historic flavor of the Southwest manifested itself in an architectural revival of Spanish and Indian styles, and by 1930 these designs were widespread in use for private homes, public buildings, and hotels. Sante Fe, New Mexico, enacted legislation prohibiting all but Hispanic-Indian construction and generated an awareness of and an interest in the people from whom the architecture was borrowed. The growing white communities needed recreation, and rodeos and fiestas were expanded and Indian ceremonies took on new meaning as rituals for outside enjoyment. The colorful pagentry of the "Wild West," the Spanish, and the Indians all stimulated tourists to come to the Southwest.

The Fred Harvey Company and the Sante Fe Railroad pioneered tourism and were very instrumental in fostering the Southwestern image. Begun as a curio business in 1899, the Fred Harvey Company later erected a chain of hotels along the Sante Fe route to facilitate stopovers and at adjacent scenic locations easily ascessible from the railroad. With the exception of the rustic Grand Canyon lodges, all their hotels promoted the rich Spanish and Indian flavor, and included shops stocked with Mexican and Indian arts and crafts, staffed by native peoples. To the visitor this was the epitome of the Southwest, and nearly everyone bought something to take home. The trend continued and local residents also adorned their homes with handicrafts representative of the traditional cultures upon whose history the new image was being based. The Santa Fe Railroad constructed most of their stations in Spanish style and permitted Indians to sell their wares on the platform, thus further stimulating a market for such goods. Until the decline of passenger service in the 1960s, the stop of a train at Albuquerque was a colorful occasion as dozens of Indians lined the platform selling beads, jewelry, small pottery pieces, and other tourist-oriented curios. Often this was a traveler's first introduction to the romanticism of the region. It was fortuitous that the early twentieth-century settlers and health-seekers became interested in the indigenous cultures and historic traditions of the Southwest, and that the prime entrepreneur recognized their marketability as a tourist attraction. Otherwise, the decline of Indian arts and crafts would have paralleled other elements of their culture, as was true in other parts of the United States where White settlers paid little or no attention to the existing culture or to their aesthetics.

To best understand the early twentieth-century impact, each major art form is examined separately:

1. *Navajo Rugs.* During the nineteenth century, the trading post introduced aniline dyes, and Navajo weaving reached a dynamic level of brilliant color and design. The advent of the railroad brought an availability of colored, commercial yarns (Germantowns) that were used from the 1880s until the early 1900s. Many of these rugs represented excellent craftsmanship, both in design and in the quality of the weaving. But with increasing tourist interest, many traders encouraged rapid production,

and as a result many rugs of the early twentieth century were inferior. Also during this period, many Navajo weavers turned away from the aniline dyes and began to use natural wool including dark browns and blacks.

Fred Harvey encouraged weavers to produce fine quality rugs and wall hangings that would appeal to tourists, with designs reflective of the nineteenth-century Navajo traditions, and to experiment with new designs. Thanks to his mercantile outlets, he could afford to pay higher prices and also absorb expanded production. Thus he prevented many of the earlier Navajo weaving traditions from being lost. Another entrepreneur, Don Lorenzo Hubbell urged weavers to produce rugs based upon predrawn designs he provided. Hubbell must be credited with helping to produce many fine rugs in the classic tradition as well as introducing the Navajo of the Ganado area to a deep red dye that has since become known as Ganado red (today a valued rug style). The quality of craftsmanship and design in Navajo rug weaving points to a latent sense of aesthetics added by weaving to the culture of a people who had previously been nomadic and had not possessed the technology through which their artistic values could be expressed. The Navajo simultaneously developed a new mythology to accompany rug weaving, and believe the art was handed down by Spider Woman. In honor of her, any rug with a border to the design must possess a slight flaw in the border (a spirit line), lest the weaver's soul be bound up in the rug. On the practical side, the Navajo woman gained new status and earned substantial income to keep pace in a world of ever increasing economic desires.

Throughout the Navajo area, trading posts competed with each other to capture the rug market and thereby fostered local weaving. By the 1930s, it was possible to recognize regional patterns, and a rug was known by the name of the trading post near which it was woven. Many new styles emerged, of which the major ones are grouped as follows:

a. Yei Rugs: Rugs portraying yei-bichai or ceremonial dancers, using a combination of natural wools and aniline dyes.

b. Vegetable dyes: Rugs that combine old geometric designs with the use of wools that have been dyed naturally.

c. Storm patterns: Woven mainly in the southwestern portion of the reservation, these rugs are characterized by sharp black and white contrasts with jagged lines that resemble lightning.

d. Two Gray Hills: Rugs of very fine quality (over one hundred weft threads to the inch) woven of carded natural colors into intricate geometric designs. By the 1930s these were the most sought-after rugs by those who wanted quality weaving.

Until the 1960s, prices were comparatively low, and the weaver often received only a few cents per hour for her labor. Although traders often marked up prices to allow for considerable profit, most rugs could be purchased for less than us$25. Even considering the value of the dollar prior to World War II, Navajo weaving was not expensive, and local Whites used the rugs as floor coverings. Although no accurate counts were ever made, the number of rugs produced per year was considerably less than today, and because of other modernizing influences many young Navajo girls were not interested in learning the arts of the loom. Thus the future of weaving among the Navajo showed definite signs of eventual decline. The post-war years, however, were to change that prospect.

2. *Jewelry*. The buying tastes of American tourists suggest that they often want "trinkets" as souvenirs, especially something that, unlike rugs or pottery, is a personal adornment. Its visibility says "I've been there," and Indian jewelry fits that category. Much of the jewelry was originally made for the Indian market, used as a display of wealth among Navajo people and as a medium of pawn among the Navajo and Pueblo people when spare cash was needed.

The tourist trade motivated the production of a wider range of jewelry styles including necklaces, rings, bracelets, concho belts, and bola ties. Silversmithing became a full-time profitable occupation for many men. During the early twentieth-century period, distinctive regional jewelry styles emerged as a result of individual creativity and the urging or suggestion of various traders. The main styles were:

a. Hammered silver: The original Indian jewelry made from silver dollars or Mexican pesos later gave way to designs hammered from sheet silver.

b. Sandcasting: This form of silver working is the most difficult to master and has not been widely adopted. A sandcast piece is formed in a mold usually of finely ground volcanic pumice.

c. Overlay: a design is cut out of one piece of silver, which is then joined to a second piece by means of sweating (heating). By oxidation, the cut out area is discolored to produce a tarnished appearance. Overlay is best associated with Hopi silver and was encouraged in 1938 by the Museum of Northern Arizona as a means of duplicating in silver the geometric patterns of Hopi pottery.

d. Silver and Turquoise: Turquoise was set into sandcast pieces and on occasion into overlay. However, the best uses of turquoise were achieved by setting the stones into prepared casements (referred to as channel work) or by careful mosaic inlay. The Zuni became the experts of such finely delicate turquoise, shell, and coral work, although other groups used the same materials.

3. *Pottery*. The cultural flourish of classical pottery occurred among the Pueblo peoples prior to 1300 A.D., and also among the Hohokam of the lower deserts. Exposure to the Spanish and later to the Americans led to a

decline in pottery making among the Pueblos, Pima, and Maricopa as trade goods replaced the traditional storage and cooking pots. The increase in tourism during the early twentieth century created demand for small pottery pieces, but many of the older designs had been forgotten. Among numerous tribes, such as the Hopi, archaeologists and museums helped reintroduce traditional designs that where thought lost. A classic example of the revival of lost designs occurred during the 1920s, when noted archaeologist J. W. Fewkes was excavating at skyatki near the Hopi First Mesa. One of the Hopi workers encouraged his wife to copy the designs. Fanny Nampeyo became one of the revivalists, and her pottery is today classic and exceptionally valuable (Sikorski 1968). Tourism thus restored a craft that had nearly disappeared, the one major difference being the decrease in the size of the pieces from those of former utilitarian value to those of saleable value.

4. *Basketry*. Basketry is one of the oldest art forms of the Southwest, and its manufacture has continued for ceremonial use while other art forms decline. Tourism during the early twentieth century appears to have had no effect upon basket manufacturing.

5. *Bead Making*. Like basketry, bead making is an ancient craft that has persisted among some tribes. Shell and coral beads were easily sold to early tourists and thus the art continued.

6. *Kachinas*. Among the Pueblo people, small *kachinas* carved as a symbolic likeness of the spirits that play an important role in their worldview served as a medium of instruction for the young. For the tourist, the *kachina* figures had great appeal. It is lightweight (carved of cottonwood root), and the variety of "grotesque" figures seemed to imply a connotation of "savage" and of "Indian" in the minds of the tourists. Since *kachinas* are sacred, touristic demands for the figures necessitated a change in their style, one that lacked the full symbolism and was more brilliantly painted using inexpensive tempera. Genuine *kachinas* were and still are available, but since the 1940s even they have been painted in poster colors. Kachinas are and always have been produced by men as they represent the sacred spirits with whom only initiated males have intimate association.

The New Awakening

During the depression years of the 1930s, tourism to the Southwest decreased, but the number of migrants traveling highway U.S. 66 to California rapidly increased. Military bases and aircraft plants built during the war years brought a new influx. Traffic through the area by rail and auto increased, and although people were concerned about the war, the market for Indian goods grew during the 1940s.

In the postwar decades of 1950 and 1960, with greater national affluence and increasing expenditures on highway construction, Americans took to the road. The national parks and resort areas became major foci of attention, and the Southwest became one of the favored locales. Advertising and publicity of the desert climate, the scenic attractions, and the romance of the Indian and Hispanic past paid off. The resident population rapidly grew with the expansion of the aircraft and electronics industries and the continued importance of military bases.

In 1960, most Indian handcrafts were priced well within the reach of the average American tourist or collector, most of whom did not consider them true art or valuable. They were curios of the Southwest, and even to most local residents they were decor elements that represented the flavor and romanticism that the Southwest had created as its image to the nation.

A combination of factors and events has changed the picture. Today Southwestern Indian arts and crafts are valuable. With prices spiraling, most quality objects are beyond the reach of the average tourist or collector. Production, price, and quality have all simultaneously increased. Although some old-time residents lament about the "good old days" of fine rugs and jewelry, the fact clearly remains that the classical rugs of the nineteenth century, and the old sandcast or inlaid jewelry, or the earlier pottery pieces, are artistically no match for the precision and quality of today's crafts. At the same time, the market is being flooded with much poorly-made art: imitation turquoise, silver plate, and commercial yarn rugs. Some of the merchandise is of foreign manufacture or made by Indians in assembly-line fashion by shops selling their products as "genuine" Indian-made. For example, rugs of Navajo design woven on shuttle looms in Mexico can be found in the Southwest. Normally they are sold as copies, but less reputable dealers may not be so honest and sell them as genuine Navajo rugs.

The Indian attitude toward handicrafts has changed rapidly. Until the present "boom" in the Indian art market, these crafts were both a means of expressing the artistic values of each Indian culture as well as a way of providing extra revenue.

The Indian has always resented the exploitation of the crafts market, which tended to put him "in the blanket" as he once stood on a railway platform proffering his wares to the tourist who often cared little about its symbolism but bargained for something "Indian," bought from a *real* Indian. That subservient role has totally disappeared. Although some Indian entrepreneurs still set up sidewalk stalls around the plaza in "old Town" in Albuquerque or at the Flagstaff Pow Wow, today they firmly hold to their price and little or no bargaining occurs.

The factors responsible for the rapid rise in the 1970s in the popularity of Indian crafts, in the accompanying price increases, and in the change in the Indians' attitude include:

1. *The Civil Rights Movement.* The success of the civil rights movement, especially among Blacks, stimulated many of the tribal leaders in the Southwest to appraise the social and economic position of their people. In light of rising wages nationally, one obvious area of exploitation was in the sale or trade of rugs, jewelry, pottery, and other art objects. Tribal guilds were established as a means of assuring the direct sale of crafts and a better price for the artist; however, not all handicrafts are sold to tribal guilds. Much still enters the open market, and today most Indian craftsmen know the value of their work and demand higher prices for their labor. A pride in being Indian, and a desire to preserve and foster Indian traditions during the 1960s, have profoundly influenced the Indian artist who is now more concerned with tradition and fine craftsmanship than at anytime in the past.

Traditional sex roles still persist with few exceptions. Pottery making, basketry, and rug weaving are traditionally women's crafts while painting, jewelry, and *kachina* making are men's activities, with Pueblo men weaving cotton sashes and garments. Much of the work takes place in the home, but some of the more noted artisans perform at exhibitions and have furthered their own careers by such appearances. A strong sense of competition has entered into the production of fine pieces for exhibition at tribal, county, and state fairs as well as at museum shows, and the prize ribbons are greatly valued by more aggressive individuals. However, the majority of the craftsmen are only part-time artists, people who engage in handicrafts as a supplemental activity. Thus the majority of the Indian artists are unknown to the buyer.

2. *The Increase in the Southwestern Population.* By the 1960s, the Southwest contained over three million residents, a gain of several hundred percent over the 1900 figure and a gain of over 150 percent above 1940. This was mainly an urban gain fostered by economic opportunity and retirement. Consequently, the home market for Indian art was enlarged and the wearing of at least a piece of Indian silver became almost a Southwestern tradition.

3. *The Increase in Tourism.* By the 1960s, most of the Southwest was accessible by road, and increasing numbers of retirees, winter vacationers, and "snowbirds" (temporarily leisured farmers from the wheat states of the U.S. and Canada) flocked to the Southwest for recreational tourism. The open spaces of the Southwest, the many parks and monuments, and the appeal of the western frontier image—including an ethnic interest concerning Indian culture and life—have involved the area in mass tourism. A significant trend of the 1970s is the increased number of international visitors, notably Europeans and Japanese for whom the Grand Canyon and the Indians are a specific, preplanned target. Individual tourists also discovered the diversity and quality of Indian culture and art. Sales increased, stimulating production increases, and stimulating

further Indian awareness among the tribes. As the merchandise diffused around the country and the world, interest was generated even among those who had not been to the Southwest.

4. *The "Americana" Trend.* During the late 1960s, partly as a result of foreign entanglements, pollution, and governmental mistrust, many young Americans began to look back to early Americana. Natural foods, communal living, and collecting of antiques, artifacts, and other bits of Americana became widespread. Indian crafts, especially jewelry, fell into this category, thus further increasing demand and helping to raise prices.

5. *Investment.* Economic uncertainties prompted many investors to seriously consider solid objects such as fine paintings, ivory, and Indian art as sources for capital gain. Financial journals encouraged such collecting as sound investment, which motivated smaller collectors to invest, and this in turn further raised prices.

In addition to their increased value, changes in the art forms have also occurred:

1. *Navajo Rugs.* Today the emphasis is on fine-quality rugs using natural wool and vegetable dyes. Two Gray Hills, Tec Noc Pos, Chinle, Crystal, and Wide Ruins rugs are in greatest demand. Small saddle blankets and coarse weave rugs are less commonly seen. The average size of most rugs today is four feet by six feet. Yei rugs are more popular and their quality in weave and color has greatly improved. Few good quality rugs can be purchased for under us$100, and bargains are rare. Navajo weavers recognize the value of their skill, and tribal guild shops as well as traders pay well for fine-quality work. Large, well woven rugs such as Two Gray Hills sell for prices as high as us$4,000.

2. *Jewelry.* Silversmithing is diversified, and in addition to the traditional items now includes silver platters, hollow ware, flatware, and decorative cigarette boxes. Designs have been expanded to include animal and bird motifs such as the popular roadrunner. Navajo craftsmen imitate Zuni, Zuni copy Hopi, and even a sophisticated buyer is less certain of tribal origins. Turquoise quality has deteriorated because of the cost of high-grade stones, and the soaring cost of silver results in small rings, thin bracelets, and lighter-weight necklaces. Mass distribution through chain stores means that many silversmiths work under contract with specific outlets in mind. Prices range from under us$10 for small rings to over us $5,000 for fine squash blossom necklaces using premium quality spider web or Bisbee turquoise. Some craftsmen, mainly Hopi, have produced small amounts of gold and turquoise jewelry.

3. *Pottery.* Pottery continues to be made by the traditional methods of coiling, then firing in earth kilns; styles also remain traditional. The Hopi mesas—Acoma, San Ildefonso, and Santa Clara—are the major pueblo potters. The Maricopa and Pima also produce pottery. Most recently

there has been a resurgence of undecorated Navajo pottery. As with the other major art forms, prices depend upon quality. A small Hopi pot may cost as little as US$15 whereas the Acoma pottery (usually larger in size) starts at US$75. The black San Ildefonso pottery may range up to US$1,000 or more for choice pieces, especially if signed by "Maria," the most noted of Pueblo potters.

4. *Basketry*. The traditional pattern of baskets remains unchanged. The Hopi and Papago literally dominate the market, but because of the tedious hours of labor they now turn out a greater number of small baskets. Apache water baskets have been scarce for years, but with the demand for genuine crafts regardless of their aesthetic appeal, even Apache baskets bring up to US$100. Good quality Hopi wedding plaques may sell for as much as US$1,000.

5. *Bead Making*. Turquoise, shell, and coral beads are still found, but they are overshadowed by the silver jewelry.

6. *Kachinas*. Today the Hopi are almost the exclusive makers of *kachinas*, and are still willing to manufacture fine-quality genuine *kachinas*. The most popular kachinas depict a degree of motion, in contrast to the more traditional fixed stances. Kachinas are expensive with quality work priced from US$30 for a small doll (under ten inches) up to US$200–300 for an eighteen-inch doll.

7. *New Art Forms*. In the postwar years, two new crafts have developed: painting and sand painting. Stemming from the use of water color and tempera paints at school, many adult Indians have developed a distinctive style. Most of the paintings have a formal but graceful quality reminiscent of Chinese or Japanese art. Animals and birds are common themes; one Navajo artist is famous for depicting a large wild mustang or "spirit horse." Sand paintings are the most recent art form and are similar in style to the true sand paintings created as part of the Navajo curative ceremonies. A true sand painting must be destroyed before dark, or its powerful magic may become harmful. No traditional Navajo would dare reproduce permanently such a painting on a resin surface, but some paintings are marketed that have many of the basic attributes of the curative creations.

Prospect

At present the outlook for Southwestern Indian art is good, as quality remains high and public interest appears to be steadily gaining. Tribal shops and trading posts on the reservations do an active business. Urban stores have expanded beyond the areal cities and now include Indian specialty shops in many towns throughout the nation. Indian wares are also displayed for sale in many discount-type chain stores.

This assessment of the Indian crafts of the Southwest suggests that massive in-migration and mass tourism have not been disruptive. Rather, the contact with Anglo society offered extended markets that served to heighten artistic productivity and to revive old traditions. It might be argued that in contrast to the "trinketization" of crafts in other milieus— e.g., plastic totem poles or printed textiles that simulate hand block prints—the very nature of the materials with which Indians work, and the designs that are integral to their culture, are not easily transferred to the "fake art" that clutters touristic markets elsewhere. Cheap pot metal adorned with fake stones abounds but is patently not Indian, and the difference is clearly evident even to a novice.

Further, the revival of Southwestern handwork has served to strengthen Indian identity, pride in heritage, and perhaps most importantly, local income as an alternative to out-migration to jobs or joblessness in an urban setting.

Northern Arizona University

13

Creating Antiques for Fun And Profit: Encounters between Iranian Jewish Merchants and Touring Coreligionists

LAURENCE D. LOEB

Antiques collecting as a form of ethnic art is a tangential tourist activity, usually confined to knowledgeable and well-to-do travellers and to geographically-restricted areas with ancient traditions, such as Iran. Increased tourism heightens demand for a limited, dwindling product and may lead to the creation of spurious antiques. In Iran, tourism is an important industry for Persian Jews who own many of the upper-category hotels and at least one of the active and highly-regarded travel agencies, specializing in handling foreign visitors. This involvement as well as the antique trade, including the "fake art" made and marketed to tourists, has positive values supportive of an ethnic minority struggling to survive as a distinct entity in an unfavorable clime.

Of Iran's total population of 26,676,000 (1968), the Jewish population approximated 80,000, of whom 50,000 lived in the capital city, Teheran, with lesser numbers in the tourist centers of Shiraz (8,500) and Isfahan (3,500), and the remainder scattered in provincial cities. Nowhere do the Jews represent more than 3 percent of the total resident population. In 1968, fewer than 250,000 tourists visited Iran. Jewish tourists were most certainly less than 5 percent of the total and possibly as little as 2 percent. Nevertheless, their presence has had an effect disproportionate to their relative numbers on both native Jews in the tourist industry and, indirectly, on Iranian Jewry in general. Evaluated here are the effects of interaction between a limited segment of the Iranian tourist trade and a likewise restricted portion of the Iranian population having contact with them.

Isolation of Persian Jewry

During the 8th century B.C.E., Jews were forcibly settled in the mountains of Kurdistan by conquering Assyrians. By the sixth century B.C.E., there is good evidence of Jewish settlement in western Iran where they have lived for more than twenty-five hundred years. The social conditions of this Diaspora have varied considerably over time. Long periods of persecution, forced conversion, harassment, exploitation, and segregation from non-Jewish neighbors have alternated with short periods of comparative tranquility. The general insecurity of this milieu was capped by nearly three hundred years of severe repression ending only in 1925. Jews were often denied the right to participate in the primary subsistence activities of the region, agriculture and pastoralism, and thus gravitated to urban settlement and marginal subsistence means including shopkeeping (Loeb 1970). The past fifty years, which have been quiet by contrast, have afforded Jews an opportunity for social, economic, and intellectual development unparalleled in this millenium.

For nearly a thousand years, the Jews of Iran were largely isolated from their coreligionists, with catastrophic consequences for their cultural development. Literacy declined, familiarity with the Jewish Great Tradition was reduced, and major creative innovations were minimal. Beginning in the 1870s, contact was reestablished with Jews in Palestine and Europe, and after World War II interaction between these communities intensified considerably.

The first outside contacts were primarily missionary visits by Jews from Baghdad and Jerusalem for the purpose of collecting charitable contributions and propagating Jewish learning. These missionaries described in vivid detail the misery, poverty, and ignorance of Iranian Jewry. After 1900 representatives of Jewish social agencies including Alliance Israélite Universelle, the Jewish Agency, the American Joint Distribution Committee, and Otsar Hatorah (an orthodox religious education foundation) had considerable impact on the lives of Iranian Jews in Teheran and in the provincial cities. While the social concern and relief efforts of these institutions were most welcome by indigenous Jews, the arrogance and assumed superiority of these Western Jews were highly resented, though such sentiments were rarely verbalized. Until the early 1960s most Iranian Jews had minimal contact with foreign Jews outside the confines of these agencies.

Except for emigrants to Israel, who rarely returned home, few Iranian Jews went abroad before the 1960s. At that time, wealthy and middle-income Jews began to visit Israel, and numbers of college students were sent abroad, especially to England and the United States.

Tourism in Iran

In the 1960s, Iran became an important tourist site, attracting an increasing number of Jewish tourists from Europe, the United States, and, on occasion, Israel. Many American and European Jewish tourists were willing to spend considerable sums for the exceptionally fine art and artifacts crafted in Iran. Stories circulated about illuminated Hebrew manuscripts, rare Megillah scrolls, and prized amulets. Tourists actively sought authentic "Jewish" art and ritual objects; the more quaint, the better!

For generations, one of the most common occupations among Jews (almost exclusively identified with them) was itinerant peddling. Many Jews extensively peddled "second-hand" goods and were expert in evaluating carpets, silver, copper, mosaics, painted objects, manuscripts, and trinkets. Gold and silversmithing were also plied by many Jews because Islamic law prohibits the sale of gold or silver by Muslims at a greater value than their metal is worth. Because there could be no profit to a Muslim in working or dealing in gold or silver, these professions were largely taken over by Jews and Christians. These various, traditional Jewish occupations have given rise to skilled, shrewd managers of the best located gift/antique shops in the major tourist centers, Teheran and Isfahan.

Jewish entrepreneurship in the tourist trade is pervasive and supports the worldwide observation that ethnic minorities are frequently associated with this industry. In Iran, tourism has had considerable impact on the economic well-being of those participating directly in the trade of tourist goods, and has created a new "home" industry with a spin-off of petty, secondary entrepreneurship. Tourism has also been a source of acculturative ideas from the West, a wellspring of socioeconomic contacts all over the world, and an opportunity for personal interaction with far-flung coreligionists for the first time in centuries.

Persian Ethnic Art

Jewish tourists coming to Iran are bedazzled, as are all tourists, by the variety and superior quality of Iranian artisanship. They are equally impressed by the monuments to Persia's past glory and bewildered by the strange customs of the local populace. Most touring Jews crave something familiar within this environment and thus actively seek contact with local coreligionists and their institutions, especially the synagogue.

It is a noteworthy pattern of Western Jewish tourist culture that Jews, who are totally disinterested in Jewish life at home, become avid anthropologists abroad. Their overseas observations become anecdotal "back home," and they strive (in the "show-and-tell" manner) to take back items of material culture having historical, social, and religious import. If the goods are aesthetically pleasing, so much the better.

Since the turn of the century, traveling Jewish scholars have obtained prized manuscripts and artifacts on their infrequent sojourns through Iran. The more astute Jewish merchants catering to foreign tourists had already noted this predilection amongst their touring coreligionists. By the early 1960s, Jewish merchants had delved into communal resources, finding quantities of talismans and amulets, some handwritten manuscripts (including a few poorly-illuminated ones), printed cloth, and silver and copper objects of dubious ritual significance. To further enhance their status with touring coreligionists and to attract them away from non-Jewish competitors in the antique trade, merchants put up easily understood symbols of commonality. Most popular of these is a sign reading: *barukh habba*, Hebrew for "welcome." Although active wooing of Jewish clientele might have the potential of discouraging non-Jewish tourists, the latter are unmoved by such symbols, and probably do not understand them.

In fact, the "aware" non-Jew sometimes picked up the wrong set of signals. On one occasion, my wife and I observed a fascinating exchange that took place early one evening in a non-Jewish tourist shop in Isfahan. A group of Iraqi tourists were considering the purchase of mosaic boxes, when one of the more perceptive members of the group noted the hexagonal pattern of stars adorning the many boxes. Well-indoctrinated Muslims, they stormed out of the store protesting that the proprietors must be Jewish since the mosaic was full of Zionist symbols!

By 1967, the once inexpensive, authentic Jewish artifacts had become scarce and the price correspondingly high. More and more Jewish tourists were coming to Iran, and ever fewer authentic Jewish culture items were available for marketing. Further, demand for these items was increasing abroad as kinsmen of the original Iranian Jewish shopkeepers opened stores in Jerusalem, Paris, London, and New York.

Spurious Antiques

In the 1960s, traders in Iranian Jewish artifacts began to commission the manufacture of appropriate items for the Jewish tourist trade. My "scientific" interest in this industry and tourism generally began with a request from the cultural attaché at the American consulate in Isfahan. A reputable art museum in New York had purchased, for several hundred dollars, a Hebrew-character astrolabe (for fortune telling) of considerable antiquity. Since it appeared to be the first one of its kind purchased by an American museum, they required some verification as to its age, source, and authenticity.

Shirazi Jewish informants, who had been dealing in astrolabes for over fifty years, denied ever having seen or even heard of this device with Hebrew characters, which aroused both my suspicion and curiosity. The signature in Hebrew identifying the craftsman as 'Eli, according to the museum, was in fact that of 'Ali (a common Muslim name). A variety of evidence indicated that Isfahan was the source of the "antique," and a quick trip there confirmed my doubts. Already acquainted with the antique dealers of Isfahan, my primary suspect readily confessed to having commissioned the manufacture of these "antiques," approximately one hundred of which were then available for distribution. I purchased a smaller version of the museum astrolabe for US$10, as the workmanship proved to be quite good and the aging excellent.

The manufacture of fake "Jewish art" for the tourist market exploits a wide variety of crafts. "Authentic" antiques include: 1) ceramic tiles and plaques styled in a crude imitation of Western-styled paintings of Moses and Aaron; 2) round metal plates (mostly tin-washed copper) with Hebrew-text borders and appropriate images; 3) Kashan carpets—mostly stylized portraits of Moses and Aaron, with a few more sophisticated forms combining a variety of Jewish symbols; 4) crudely carved wooden arks and altars in sharply contrasting pastels; 5) illuminated manuscripts; 6) painted miniatures and portraits; 7) astrolabes with zodiac signs and Hebrew lettering; and 8) simple amulets and silver containers for *mzuza* (ritual scrolls). In general, the craftsmanship of these articles is universally crude, the painting sloppy, and the Hebrew calligraphy often inaccurate and erroneous.

Authentic antique Jewish craft was, by contrast, well constructed, carefully crafted, and Hebraically accurate, although the artisanship was somewhat below the level attained by master craftsmen designing secular items. Insofar as I can determine, most of the items mentioned above, with the exception of the illuminated manuscripts and amulets, did not exist in the traditional past. In fact, very few artifacts used by Persian Jews were decorated in a specifically and uniquely Jewish manner, with the exception of some *glims* (woven carpets) and paisley cloths with Hebrew-lettered borders, used in synagogues and homes for ritual purposes, and *tora* casings of wood, velvet, and silver. Some vases, perfume or rosewater flasks, silver cups, and oil lamps used for ritual purposes may have been specially decorated, but informants could not recall having seen them. Despite these obvious shortcomings, most Jewish tourists can easily obtain ostensibly authentic items of Persian Jewish culture. The Iranian Jewish "antique" shops in Israel, New York, and Europe are filled with such artifacts. The really crude artifacts are easily identified as fakes, but good work has fooled the experts. The artisans are without peer when it comes to antiquing.

An extensive feature article in an English-language Iranian newspaper in 1968 reported the experience of a young Persian Jewish merchant who set up shop in downtown New York. He reputedly sold an ostensibly antique "portrait" of a nineteenth-century Persian Jew to an apparently gullible New Yorker for several hundred dollars. The customer returned several days later with the painting under his arm and informed the merchant—after having the painting appraised—that the painting was not as old as had been represented. The sheepish merchant reached into his pocket, intending to refund the buyer's money. But the buyer hurriedly continued that the painting was well over two hundred years old and valued at many times the purchase price. As the happy customer left clutching his "bargain" the proprietor chuckled to himself over the duping of the experts. He had had the work commissioned only several years earlier.

Iranian Jewish antique sellers are as wiley and shrewd as their counterparts elsewhere, and they have undoubtedly "cleaned-up" financially from touring coreligionists, but duplicity is a two-way street. In one case, a glib French Jew, posing as a major importer of art objects and antiques, used a falsified testimonial from an important French Jewish leader as an introduction to the Isfahani antique trade. Having convinced them of his integrity, his reputation spread by word of mouth or letter of introduction throughout the country. He departed Iran, taking with him merchandise worth thousands of dollars, all on credit, and was never heard from again.

In this respect, the most astute Jewish merchants are quite vulnerable. They are constantly taken-in by apparently pious foreign Jews who are able to convince them of their sincerity and authenticity. Coreligionists can not be viewed as apt to swindle or exploit. On the contrary! Foreign Jews, having established some relationship with Persian shopkeepers, are often persuaded, with the help of a small gift, to smuggle artifacts to relatives abroad for resale. Some may be entrusted with samples as bait for large overseas orders. Usually such faith is rewarded, but sometimes the consequences are disastrous, as alluded to previously. This apparent naïvete is understandable, because major swindles of Iranian Jews by indigenous coreligionists were immediately publicized widely with harmful social and business consequences for the offender. The fact that this long arm of justice is not effective outside the country is totally foreign to the Iranian Jewish experience.

Typically, Jewish tourists are attracted to an antique shop by its location, display of goods (both quality and variety), and Hebrew ethnic symbols. The tourists are often as interested in finding an access to the local community and their way of life as they are in making a purchase. Interaction often begins as the entrepreneur expresses a guess (usually wild) as to the tourist's origin. He then attempts through questioning (usually in English or French) to evaluate the tourist's interests in merchandise, the seriousness of his intention to purchase something, and how much he might be able to convince him to spend. Frequently, as the conversation progresses about objects, their artistic merit, authenticity, and antiquity, the shopkeeper offers his customer tea and suggests he sit and make himself comfortable. If it appears that there is a good chance of the sale coming to fruition, the initial meeting and conversation may last half an hour or more. Later contacts may be even more extensive. Eventually, the shopkeeper may even host the tourist at his home—a minor triumph for the tourist, as such invitations are rare in cosmopolitan Teheran. If the tourist expresses an interest, the entrepreneur sometimes offers to guide his guest through the Jewish quarter and aid him in finding the local synagogues, especially for Sabbath worship.

An initial interest shown by the tourist in Jewish artifacts is often used by the shopkeeper to create interest in other items as well. Ritual items may thus induce tourists to buy more. With the seller having the added advantage of an appeal to piety, and common identity, the tourist may feel guilt because his purchases fall almost within the category of *zdaga* (pious charity), or a subtle, financial device to keep Iranian Jewry alive (cf. Khury 1968). Having been exposed to apparent poverty, piety, friendship, and sincerity in the proprietor, the tourist is ripe to be plucked.

While the tourist is obtaining many insights and "representative" artifacts from Iranian Jewry, to be brought home and shared with friends and acquaintances, the Iranian Jews also benefit in a number of ways from this contact. In many cases, the proprietor's best advertising is by word of mouth, and he is not loathe to sell some items at marginal profit if he suspects this will cement a long-term relationship with the tourist, a few of whom return or maintain contact by mail with the entrepreneurs.

Social Effects of Tourism

The antique dealer serves as an agent of social contact between Iranian and non-Iranian Jews. He often introduces foreign Jews to the community, or alternatively, serves in a buffer capacity to ferret out those who should be kept apart from the community. The activities of foreign Jewish teachers may have had an intense impact on Iranian Jewish acculturation to Great Tradition Judaism, but foreign Jewish tourists have also been an important source of knowledge of foreign Jewish secular life and customs.

The antique dealer benefits economically from tourism by acquisition of wealth, and socially from increased prestige through contact with foreigners. For many, successful entrepreneurship provides the means to move up from low to middle or high-middle rank within Iranian Jewish society.

The creating of "authentic Jewish antiques" for foreign Jewish tourists has forged close links between Iranian Jewry and their coreligionists from abroad. Both parties benefit from their encounters despite the underlying fraud in their business dealings. These outside contacts have been of considerable value to Iranian Jews as a means of perserving their identity in a modernizing Islamic state.

Tourism has radically altered the assessment of the values and culture of foreign Jews by at least part of Iranian Jewry. Culture shock, induced by tourists in the form of counterfraud and secularist rather than basically religious attitudes and behavior, as well as curiosity, charity, and concern shown humanistically (rather than arrogance and social administration), has forced some Iranian Jews to reevaluate their own behavior and world-view with respect to education, religion, philanthropy, and even business ethics. Tourism is thus a powerful force in the ongoing process of secular westernization and in the acculturation of the Jewish Great Tradition that Persian Jewry is presently experiencing.

University of Utah

14

The Polynesian Cultural Center:
A Multi-ethnic Model
of Seven Pacific Cultures

MAX E. STANTON

The Polynesian Cultural Center (PCC) is located in the community of Laie on the Northshore-Windward coast of the island of Oahu, forty miles (an hour's drive) from the prime Hawaiian tourist target of Waikiki. In the past ten years the PCC has emerged as the second most popular visitor attraction in the state (surpassed only by the U.S.S. *Arizona* Memorial at Pearl Harbor) with a paid gate attendance in excess of one million guests per year.

The "typical" visitor to the Center generally spends the better part of a vacation day at the facility, beginning with a chartered bus trip from Waikiki arriving at mid-day. Upon arrival, there are guides waiting to lead the tourist on a choice of a walking tour, or (at extra cost) a canoe or tram tour. Once the formal conducted tour is completed, the visitor is free to return to the various exhibits alone. At dusk, a buffet-type dinner is served, followed by a one and one-half hour music and dance review. After the evening show, the visitor then boards the bus and returns to Waikiki. The basic charge for the show, dinner, and village walking tour is us$17.50, to which the tour companies charge an additional us$10-$15 per passenger for transportation. Individuals can also rent automobiles or ride the city bus from Waikiki, reducing the transportation costs.

The PCC is privately owned and operated by the Church of Jesus Christ of Latterday Saints (LDS), commonly known as the Mormons. The Center was established in 1963 with a three-fold purpose: 1) to preserve the culture of the Polynesians; 2) to provide employment and work-scholarship support for the students attending the Brigham Young University–Hawaii Campus (the immediate neighbor of the PCC and founded as the Church College of Hawaii in 1955; the name changed in 1974); and 3) to provide direct financial aid to BYU–Hawaii.

For most PCC visitors, the state of Hawaii is their only contact with distant Polynesia, a vast Pacific triangle that encompasses many islands within its apexes of Hawaii, Easter Island, and New Zealand. The opportunity to take a vicarious trip through time and space to "Old Hawaii" and the rest of Polynesia has obvious appeal. A satisfactory fiction emerges wherein a guest can imagine for a brief time that the idyllic life of Polynesia and the "Noble Savage," described by Robert Louis Stevenson and James Michener, is a "reality." On numerous occasions, visitors have exhibited loud outbursts of exuberance because they have "seen real natives at work in their own grass huts." Most workers at the Center are accustomed to such rather naïve behavior and recognize that this type of reaction is intended to be complimentary. This image of ethnic reality is also projected in PCC promotional efforts. The student-workers also recognize that a full, less-superficial glimpse of their culture is impossible in the few hours guests spend at the facility. Thus, any portrayal of their cultural heritage that might be appreciated by the visitors is better than none at all. In this case study, the concept of a model culture is examined in terms of the expectations of the guests and the economic and social requisites imposed on hosts to create and sustain the model.

Plate 1. Visitors at the PCC view a demonstration of Fijian pottery making. (Photo by Noel McGrevy)

The Evolution of a Dream

Laie provides a social setting well suited for the establishment of an institution such as the Polynesian Cultural Center. For well over half a century, Latter-day Saints from Hawaii, Samoa, and the other Polynesian Islands have been gathering in the area because of the presence of the Mormon Temple in the community. In 1955, construction was begun on the Church of Hawaii (CCH). The work was facilitated by over 450 volunteer workers (called Labor Missionaries by the LDS Church) many of whom hailed from Samoa, Tonga, and New Zealand. After the completion of the construction, many of these Pacific Islanders remained in Laie as students of the college.

Because of the rather isolated location of Laie and also because of the socioeconomic background of the large majority of CCH students, various income-generating possibilities were explored for possible development into student-related employment. The most promising idea was a Polynesian dance troupe that traveled twice weekly into Honolulu to perform. The first performance was staged in 1959 and proved to be an immediate success.

Although the Polynesian group in its Honolulu location was successful, many problems emerged. It was a formidable logistical task to transport a full company of seventy-five performers, plus "back-stage" personnel, on a semiweekly round trip from Laie to Honolulu. Also, the time involved in such a venture was a serious drain on the productive study time of the students involved. It soon became apparent that the only logical solution to these problems would be the establishment of an adequate performing site in Laie. Following the usual deliberations and planning associated with any large-scale project, construction of the Polynesian Culture Center was initiated early in 1962, and the facility was opened to the public on 12 October 1963.

There was a great deal of apprehension concerning the ability of a tourist facility so far from the main tourist destination center in Waikiki to attract a large enough volume of visitors to be successful. It soon became evident, however, that the car-rental and tour bus companies saw the PCC as a perfect "lure" to get the visitors out of Waikiki and into their vehicles. From its first days of operation, the Center has witnessed an upward trend in its clientele, and a current major problem is how to adequately accommodate the daily volume of guests. The average daily attendance ranges from about fifteen hundred in the fall and winter months to nearly twenty-five hundred during the summer. During Christmas and Easter vacations, and such holidays as Memorial Day, the Fourth of July, and Labor Day, the Center entertains over five thousand visitors daily. With such a large number of persons at one time, it has become

Plate 2. A PCC reconstruction of a *Maota Tofa*, or sleeping quarters, of a Samoan high chief. (Photo by Noel McGrevy)

increasingly difficult to maintain the casual, relaxed atmosphere that the tourists expect.

The Functioning of a Model Culture

The Polynesian Cultural Center is a model culture that selectively attempts to portray the best of those tangible, believable aspects of Polynesian culture with which the tourist can identify. Because of the interplay of time imperatives, cultural preferences, and personal inclinations, all facets of Polynesian culture are not portrayed. Tourists are on vacation—they are seeking a change from the routine or ordinary and want to experience the "unusual." However, they generally lack the time and the depth of experience to understand the more complex and intricate aspects of Polynesian culture. The visitor can briefly participate in a simple dance in the Samoan village, look over the shoulder of a person making *Tapa* in the Tonga area, and is encouraged to take pictures of Polynesians in Polynesian settings. There simply is not enough time in a one-day visit to discuss the nature of the Polynesian extended family (*ramage*) with its complex variations in political, economic, and kinship elements; or to explain the economic aspects of the conscription of manual labor as a form of capital; or to explore many of the other deeper, more complex aspects of Polynesian culture. Nor does the Center see its mission as a forum for addressing the long-standing social and economic injustices found throughout the Pacific.

As a model and not the reality, the process of selecting the cultural elements to be shown admittedly creates a "fake culture," one which would not be found today anywhere in the various Polynesian Islands. The alert visitor needs only to recall the trip from Waikiki to Laie to realize that the Hawaiian Village represented at the Center is unlike anything seen from the bus window. In fact, one central theme pervading most of the presentations at the PCC is that this is *not* what typically exists today in the various Polynesian Island groups. The Center is basically an attempt to reconstruct life-styles that are vanishing or have disappeared in the wake of the vast flood of technological gadgetry of the twentieth century. The model caters to ethnic tourism, providing to the tourist asn opportunity to see in one afternoon what many of the indigenous residents of the various Polynesian societies themselves rarely, if ever, see. The visitor is, through the model-culture experience, able to gain a brief insight into a selective array of Polynesian cultures without the necessity of traveling throughout the Polynesian Triangle. Another PCC purpose is to keep alive (even revive) traditional art forms and practices, giving the guest a chance to view some limited historical aspects of a life-style as it once was.

It is a sobering assignment to coordinate the efforts of five hundred student-workers and three hundred full-time employees so that the end product will, at 10:00 A.M. each morning, greet the first visitor as "just another happy day in Polynesia." Behind the scenes, there are electricians, payroll clerks, mechanics, florists, public relations experts, anthropologists, and a host of other persons all working to make the operation run smoothly. If one were to visit the PCC two or three hours before opening time, the at times nearly frantic tempo of activity would be blatantly evident: "Paradise is two hours away so let's get working." It is exciting to be a part of the PCC and to realize the manifold tasks that precede the opening, so that those persons who are directly involved in face-to-face contact with the visitors are able to be at ease and sustain the illusion of spontaneity and relaxed casualness.

Technical problems frequently arise, presenting challenges (or nightmares) to the anthropological specialists who are charged with the duty of "preserving Polynesian culture" at the PCC. Health and safety regulations, building codes, budgetary concerns, bureaucracy, and sometimes misguided actions of well-intending persons often prevent a fully authentic representation of culturally correct details. For some, it is still painful to recall the episode in which an old Samoan double canoe of exquisite

Plate 3. A casual discussion of traditional Tongan house construction. (Photo by Noel McGrevy)

construction showing the beautiful markings of native-grain wood was trimmed down fore and aft and painted in a bright combination of light-blue and lemon yellow "so that it would better catch the tourists' eye." Or, there was a "near disaster" when at the last moment it was discovered that a priceless piece of Hawaiian *tapa* (bark cloth) was about to be used as a tablecloth at a staff party where punch and Chinese food (with its many delicious but viscid sauces) were to be served.

To upgrade the overall authenticity of the PCC, the Center employs one full-time cultural specialist and has recently acquired the half-time services of a BYU-Hawaii faculty member on indefinite loan to augment the cultural operation. Scholars and highly-respected representatives from Polynesian cultures are also called upon for their insights. The individuals selected to supervise each of the seven cultural demonstrations, or "villages," are, whenever possible, proven experts in their own ethnic cultural background and are given a wide latitude of options concerning the presentations in their areas.

In spite of the conscious effort now being made to improve the PCC, continuing problems exist, some of which arise from naïve or uninformed tourists' expectations. Many visitors have preconceived ideas of what Polynesia "should be" and are sometimes disappointed when their expectations are not met. Some visitors are critical because no one lives in the houses at the center. One vistor, who claimed to be a trained social scientist, observed that the women were "over-dressed," that there was not one bare-breasted woman at the Center! This person should have known that in all but the most remote parts of Polynesia, such attire (or lack of it) is not to be found today, and it would now be offensive and personally embarrassing for the women to dress (or undress) in such a manner.

Another legitimate criticism that is very difficult to resolve is the time or period theme. What date or era should the exhibits portray? In the past two to three hundred years, all of the Polynesian Islands have undergone rapid, sometimes drastic, cultural change. It is virtually impossible to place all of the buildings, costumes, material items, and live demonstrations (dances, songs, and games) within the same specific time-frame. The PCC tried to tie all portions of "village" exhibits into a functionally integrated whole, with full realization that an artifact might be removed two hundred years in authenticity from the house where it is located. Suggestions have been made to expand the Center and provide three or four clusters of buildings in each "village" to represent change through time. This task would be monumental and far transcend the original intent of the PCC. The best solution to date is to have the tour guides alert the visitors that such discrepancies do exist and point them out.

The large number of visitors per day makes it impossible to give a detailed representation of all aspects of the various Polynesian cultures. The basic emphasis is on the material culture (houses, canoes, and artifacts) and the performing arts (singing and dancing). The ideology, social organization, and world view of each culture—so important to their personal life-style—is painfully absent. Only some general allusions to the nonmaterial aspects of Polynesian life are made. This is not a fault of the PCC, but merely a fact of life. As mentioned above, a detailed description of this component of Polynesian culture would require more time than the workers can give or the average visitor is willing to expend. However, individuals with deeper interests are welcome to remain in a "village" and chat with staff on duty in the exhibit. Some specialized presentations are now available to interested groups and a broader offering is planned for the future. Thus, members of a study group may spend more time at the Center as serious students of culture rather than merely interested spectators.

As a cultural model or "living museum," the Center uses a thematic approach which concentrates on certain dynamic and tangible aspects of culture. In an effort to make the visit more meaningful, each of the "villages" has developed some specific activity such as husking a coconut, learning to use a certain percussion instrument, involvement in a game of skill, or performing a dance that encourages tourist participation—all popular with visitors. The PCC is learning from its past mistakes and is now, more than ever, attempting to allay as many criticisms and deficiencies as possible. Special training sessions are held for workers who are involved with tourists on a face-to-face basis. (Not all Polynesians have an in-depth knowledge of the traditions and culture of their own specific ethnic group, and few workers have more than a superficial understanding of the culture of the other groups represented at the Center.) These training programs are designed to give guides, "villagers," and other personnel a basic understanding of the material culture, historical development, and contemporary situation of the societies represented at the facility. The sessions also help to develop personal confidence and self-assurance in greeting and instructing the daily crowds.

The Economic Impact of the Model Culture

The Polynesian Cultural Center and its sister institution Brigham Young University–Hawaii operate closely together as the two major sources of employment in Laie. Both institutions receive tax-exempt status: the BYU–H because it is a private college, and the PCC because of its deep involvement in supporting BYU–H through student employment arrangements and direct financial subsidies to the college. For the past three years, the PCC has given annually more than one million dollars in unrestricted funds to BYU–H. In addition, the college receives nearly us$100,000 annually to upgrade the research and instruction capabilities of its faculty. Also, funds from the Center support nearly one hundred students at BYU–H who are employed at the college and who, except for this financial support, have no relationship whatever with the PCC. Further as mentioned earlier, more than five hundred BYU–H students are directly employed by the Center. In total, the PCC generated in 1975 about us$1.6 million in benefits to the BYU–H and its students. In addition, the Center disburses about us$2.5 million in salaries and wages, paid principally to residents of Laie and adjacent communities.

The economic impact of the PCC extends beyond Laie and surrounding communities. The leader of the Tongan "village" reported that all full-time adult workers send in excess of us$100 per month to their families or private bank accounts in their home islands, and help to offset the deficit trade balance (Urbanowicz, chapter 5). When asked why so much money is sent abroad, especially in light of the high cost of living in Hawaii, this fine Tongan gentleman replied 'Autō e manu ki tokū, or "At sunset the birds return to Toku [an island in Tonga]," paraphrased to mean, "In his heart and in the heart of all good Tongans, there is only one home, Tonga," and his relatives there need the money more than he does in

Hawaii. Although no other group reported that *all* their full-time employees send money to their respective homelands, the practice is common.

The skills learned at the Center also benefit the students regardless of their success at the college. The PCC may sometimes appear to be a "tropical state fair" with dozens of light-hearted, smiling persons "doing their own thing," but to be genuine and enthusiastic, eager to please, and quick to smile day after day, regardless of one's inner pressures, is a highly-prized skill. The poise and confidence gained by the workers, especially the college students, will probably stand them in good stead wherever they go. Also, the knowledge gained in becoming familiar with rapidly vanishing aspects of their culture will undoubtedly prove valuable, making these persons "cultural repositories" of an otherwise scarce and dying cultural tradition.

It would be erroneous to suggest that the Polynesian Cultural Center benefits only individuals who want to become more appreciative of their traditional heritage, or that the Center provides secure economic positions only for those who could not otherwise cope with the more demanding way of life of the mid-twentieth century. For better or worse, the economic and social realities of our era have become a fact of life throughout all of the islands of Polynesia. The question is not "if" Polynesia will change, but "how" it will resolve the changes that are occurring. The PCC is a large-scale operation requiring a wide variety of professions and skills, and through cooperation with BYU–H, the Center turns out top-quality entertainers and others skilled in the material crafts of Polynesia. Behind the scenes, students are involved with diverse, work-related experience, such as personnel management, accounting, commercial art, carpentry, foods and nutrition, secretarial skills, public relations, printing, electronics, police and security, travel ticketing, purchasing and supply, and auto mechanics.

The Center employs a large number of persons in varied occupations including highly-trained professional administrators and knowledgeable experts of specific cultures supervising the work in the respective "villages," and Laie housewives looking for a supplemental family income. Through rational planning and cooperation, the PCC can satisfy the needs of the curious tourist as well as provide for the enrichment and improvement of its employees, and thus fulfill the three-fold purpose for which it was created.

The overall effect of visitor contact at the PCC is not as great as some might imagine. The tourists are no more an imposition to the worker in one of the "villages" at the Center than a guest at a hotel is to the desk clerk or a diner is to a restaurant worker. Hospitality is good business, and it does not hurt to smile. When the working day is over, the Center employees return to their dorms and homework, or to their homes and families, and are undisturbed by outsiders until the next day's group arrives.

The workers at the PCC are not unfamiliar with tourists. For employees who originate from such places as Fiji, Tahiti, and especially Hawaii, the tourist has been a familiar fact of life for as long as they can remember. Even those from Samoa, Tonga, and Rotorua in New Zealand learned to accept and tolerate tourists long before they began their work at the Center. For most employees, this contact with and acceptance of foreigners commenced in their home areas by the presence of missionaries, educators, and administrative officials. Because of life-long contacts with persons not of one's culture, together with the experience gained at the PCC, most workers are much more at ease and familiar with the visitor than is the converse. Many employees have been to Mainland U.S.A. as visitors, as Mormon missionaries, or in the military service. And, as the result of the LDS missionary program, some workers have been to Asia, Latin America, or even Europe and have gained a high degree of fluency in the languages of these respective areas. It is always a source of amusement to see the look on visitors' faces when a worker, dressed in traditional attire, approaches a group of Japanese tourists and begins to freely converse with them in Japanese. The workers at the PCC take obvious pride in their cultural heritage, and most of them appreciate the fact that through the medium of the model village they can present that which they deeply treasure and value to visitors in a positive context unfettered by the lights of Waikiki or the Hollywood makeup artist.

One interesting side effect of the multiethnic nature of the PCC is the opportunity it affords for persons from other Polynesian areas to live in Hawaii or for local Hawaiians to have Fijians, Tongans, and New Zealanders as neighbors. The average employee has little opportunity to interact meaningfully with a tourist at the Center, but he may live next door to people whose original home is thousands of miles distant. A genuine intercultural exchange takes place in this context, and those who benefit most from this experience are not the transient tourists, but the PCC workers themselves.

Laie was initially a "company town" with the Mormon Church (rather than a factory) as the center of power. Before the establishment of the PCC, relatively few visitors came to Laie except for kinship and religious purposes. Now all that has changed. Hawaii is receiving in excess of two million visitors annually, and half of them visit the PCC. However, the facility is equipped to handle large numbers of guests during the full course of the day, so that there is very little tourist "spill-over" into the community at large. In fact, the frequent outpouring of anti-tourist sentiment found in so many other communities of Hawaii is conspicuously absent among the permanent, long-term residents of Laie. How-

ever, during my twelve-years residence in the community I have observed, as the result of the location of the Center in Laie, a marked
increase in income and the material welfare of its inhabitants; and tourism
per se has not significantly or directly disrupted local life-styles. (A job at
the Center is substantively little different than is any other occupational
task. A job as a mechanic, secretary, or commercial artist at the PCC
varies little from the same job anywhere else).

The Polynesian Cultural Center is successful as a "model culture" in
Laie's social context in two principal ways. First, as outlined extensively
above, it is the reconstruction of the exotic, more popular elements of
Polynesia and puts "on stage" for the visitors selected aspects of Polyne-
sian life, especially in the realm of material culture and aesthetics, which
are not now the normal way of life in Laie, Hawaii, or anywhere else in
Polynesia. (No one in Hawaii still lives in a thatched hut; the outboard
motor and Bruce Lee-type Kung Fu films are making their imprint in the
Marquesas Islands; and commercial television is beamed daily to the
Manu'a Group in Samoa).

The second principal justification for considering the PCC to be an
adequate "model culture" is that the presence of visitors does not interfere
with the daily lives of the people of Laie. Students attend grade school, a
college functions effectively, the bank opens and closes; in general,
people work *away* from the prying eyes of the tourist. Basic local values
are not disrupted, and neither does the "model culture" disrupt the strong
religious orientation of the community. Because it is a church-sponsored
institution, the PCC actually serves to enhance Mormon norms and values
by not operating on Sunday and by giving release-time consideration for
persons having special church-related assignments. In fact, the location of
the PCC at the edge of Laie, rather than in the middle of the community,
ensures much less interference with local habits than in similar "model
cultures" such as Leavenworth, Washington; Cherokee, North Carolina;
or, Rothenburg-ob-der-Tauber in Germany. The relationship between
Laie, the PCC and BYU–H is somewhat analogous to Oberammergau—a
town that, for religious purposes, becomes host to short-term guests once
every decade for the world-renowned Passion Play. The people of this
small community in the German Alps are thoroughly modern and live
similar to the life-style in other villages in the region. Their involvement
with mass tourism reinforces rather than disintegrates their sense of
community and cohesion.

The overall impact of the "model culture" of the PCC in the lives of the
workers, especially the students, has the following consequences that may
be both positive and negative in nature. First, their involvement at the
Center affords them the opportunity for an education that, in many cases,
could not otherwise be financed. However, because of the often vast

distances from home and the necessity for reduced course loads because of working and church-related assignments, it is not uncommon for a student to undergo a long-term separation from home and family, but a sense of total isolation seldom occurs because the extended family is still quite effective in most Polynesian societies. A student often has a fellow member of his family at school, or an older sibling or other close relative may have immigrated to Laie or a nearby community. A second, and important, feature of the "model culture" is that many students who previously had little direct contact with their cultural heritage now have their ethnic identity reinforced through their association with the Center. This has been especially true for students from New Zealand, French Polynesia, and Hawaii, as well as for migrant families from such areas as Samoa and Tonga whose children have little opportunity for encultura- tion within their original ethnic group. Exposure to Polynesian culture other than one's own is a third aspect of the model culture nature of the PCC. By close association with persons from a common cultural heritage, a great wealth of information is exchanged and absorbed on an informal, unstructured, one-to-one basis. As a result, students often request the opportunity to become involved with another group. Similarly, students who are ethnic minorities in their homelands (e.g., East Indians from Fiji, Filipinos from Hawaii, and Chinese from French Polynesia) have an opportunity, often for the first time in their lives, to cross the cultural line and gain insight and even participate in the dominant culture. At home, these doors to intercultural communication are frequently closed, if not barred. The fourth result of this "model culture" is the fact that students from the less-developed realms of Polynesia who come to BYU–H and the PCC live in the urban cosmopolitan cultural milieu of modern Hawaii, with wide exposure to Western values and technology. But, the very fact of residing in Hawaii may well lead to a fifth feature: many students receive a distorted atypical view of the modern world. Hawaii is one of the premier tourist resort areas of the world, and Oahu also has one of the highest concentrations of military personnel-per-population-size in Amer- ica. As a result, the students from elsewhere in Polynesia see many people with a lot of time and money on their hands. Their view of reality is not corrected by looking inwardly at Laie either, because the Mormon Church plays such an overwhelming, dominant role in shaping commu- nity affairs and local norms. Few students get a fair chance to see the broad spectrum of "mainstream" America. A sixth feature is the fact that students gain skills in tourism, the performing arts, and other work experience, which can at a later time prove to be of worth in their homeland or in their private lives. Seventh, their involvement at the PCC enables them to do what few college students can elsewhere—earn extra funds to send home to their families, thereby enhancing their image among their family and as members of their community. This involvement in the financial and social structure also serves to validate their church membership by showing that an LDS student in Hawaii can still be an asset to the home community. Also, the student's comparative affluence, derived from mass tourism, may reinforce the financial potential of tourism at home (cf. V. Smith's reference to Point Hope, Alaska, in chapter 3). As a last feature, after years of student catering to the superficial "smile all the time" expected at the PCC, there is a real danger that some of the more pressing problems of one's homeland might be overlooked, or that the partial image of the culture that is daily portrayed will, in fact, become the cultural reality of the hosts. Either eventuality would greatly diminish the overall potential of the Center to be more than a "tropical amusement park" and should be carefully considered in evaluating its impact.

A Model Culture in a Real World

The Polynesian Culture Center is a highly successful social and economic operation that is effectively meeting the multiple needs for which it was, rather daringly, conceived. However, the problems encountered in any large establishment are to be found at the PCC, including labor disputes, differences of opinion, problems in communications, personality clashes, and other difficulties that occur when large numbers of persons work together. Despite their existence, I believe that the task of presenting diverse Polynesian cultures on a mass scale has been highly successful, and that the problems are only minimally apparent to the paying guest.

Anyone contemplating the establishment of a facility such as the Polynesian Cultural Center must fully consider the range and multitude of problems. Because of the large number of employees (over eight hundred), the cultural differences, and the high volume of visitors each day, the management of a model culture must be acutely aware of the problems as they arise and must act quickly to meet and solve problems, real or imagined, as they emerge. Pressures from within the institution, as well as from those outside the direct sphere of operation, can make management a difficult task. By dealing with "in house" problems as they arise and trying to create a feeling of rapport with the working staff, administrators can be free to deal with outside concerns such as transportation companies, labor unions, sales and promotion groups, tour agencies, and other parties exerting their special pressures to gain preferential treatment from the Center.

Possibly a prerequisite in maintaining a sense of cooperation and cohesion is a spirit of dedication and cooperation. The PCC has a definite advantage in the common Latter-day Saint affiliation of most of the personnel at the Center, which tends to minimize conflict and reinforce understanding. This is not to say that service problems do not arise, but when problems do arise, cultural and personnel differences that might otherwise prove to be irreconcilable can be dealt with beginning from a basic philosophical orientation as Mormons, which often transcends cultural differences.

The Polynesian Cultural Center is fortunately located on an island that is one of the busiest tourist centers of the world. Its popularity is well established, but it is doubtful if it could be as successful if it were located elsewhere, other than on Oahu in the state of Hawaii. It is not unique as a cultural center. Other centers such as Rotorua in New Zealand, Orchid Island in Fiji, or the cultural center in Ponape exist and prove to be popular local attractions. But, as is the case of the Polynesian Cultural Center, these "model culture" centers generally draw visitors *after the fact*. The centers are visited because the guest has been drawn to the area by one of the various types of tourism: recreational, ethnic, or cultural. The Polynesian Islands are too remote to hope for model culture exhibits to pull in clientele on their own merits. Even the PCC in its active promotional efforts in the United States, Canada, and Japan, plays heavily on the theme ". . . when in Hawaii, visit us." Places such as French Polynesia, Micronesia, Samoa, and Tonga, which are contemplating a rapid thrust into tourism and resort development, may well be advised to explore the potential of a "model culture" site, but such endeavors should also be realistically planned within the rational bounds of potential, and probably operational costs. A serious miscalculation in either of these two areas could seriously jeopardize the successful longevity of such an undertaking.

Brigham Young University-Hawaii

Part V

Touristic Studies in Anthropological Perspective

THERON NUÑEZ

Since its beginning little more than a decade ago, the study of tourism by anthropologists has been characterized largely by serendipity. This, however, is not an irony, for many of the now traditional and established interests of anthropologists derive from fortuitous observations or accidental "discoveries" while researching other or unrelated topics or problems. For the last ten years, anthropologists have gone to study other things or other people and almost everywhere have discovered tourists.

Why then have anthropologists only recently found tourism of scholarly interest? The answer, I think, lies in the observation that the study of tourism finally has become respectable. That is to say, anthropologists have been aware for many years of the impact of tourism on indigenous societies but may have refrained from publishing their observations in systematic form because the study of tourism was somehow not considered "proper" or within the traditional purview of the discipline. This volume clearly demonstrates the demise of that view and the acceptance of tourism as a legitimate field of inquiry under a variety of traditional anthropological rubrics. What follows, then, is an examination of those approaches that have been used or might be used in modified form to further the study of tourism.

The acculturation model is the most obvious. Anthropologists have known for more than a half century many of the things likely to eventuate when different cultures come into contact, and this knowledge can readily apply to contact between tourists and indigenous, or "host," societies. Acculturation theory explains that when two cultures come into contact of any duration, each becomes somewhat like the other through a process of borrowing. However, the nature of the contact situation, the distinctive profiles of the contact personnel, different levels of sociocultural integration, numerical differences in the populations, and other variables typically result in asymmetrical borrowing. Furthermore, acceptance or

rejection of alien traits or artifacts conditioned by the foregoing considerations may have far-reaching indirect consequences because the functional model of societies explains that a perturbation of one aspect of a
social system is likely to disturb or change other aspects.

Tourists are less likely to borrow from their hosts than their hosts are
from them, thus precipitating a chain of change in the host community.
The notion that people in more or less continuous, first-hand, face-to-face
contact become more like each other should not be ignored just because
tourists come and go. A tourist clientele tends to replicate itself. As a host
community adapts to tourism, in its facilitation to tourists' needs, attitudes, and values, the host community must become more like the
tourists' culture. That is what tourists in search of the exotic and "natural"
vacation setting mean when they say that a place has been "spoiled" by
tourism, i.e., those who got there before them and required the amenities
of home. Anthropologists are often in the forefront of those who deplore
the dilution and adulteration of traditional cultures, what Mexican
intellectuals have called the *Cocacolaización* of the native way of life.
However, the alteration of one culture by another has always been a fact
of existence. Some societies have remained in relative isolation from
others for long periods of time, but in this century virtually no community
is immune from outside contact, and the tourist is more ubiquitous than
any other kind of representative of other cultures. Although anthropologists decry, as they should, the exploitation of any people by another, they
should realize better than most that communities dedicated to tourism
from an economic point of view must maximize the exploitation of the
tourist clientele to the fullest. The ethical question is who or how many
profit from the exploitation, which I will address later.

Perhaps the most striking example of the asymmetry in host-guest
relationships is to be found in linguistic acculturation in which the usually
less literate host population produces numbers of bilingual individuals,
while the tourist population generally refrains from learning the host's
language. The cadre of bilingual individuals in a tourist-oriented community or country are usually rewarded. The acquisition of a second
language for purposes of catering to tourists often results in economic
mobility for people in service positions. Interpreters, tour guides, bilingual waiters, clerks, and police often are more highly compensated than
the monolinguals of their communities. In the history of acculturation
phenomena, rarely has a community, a country, or a culture been a
willing host but rather has had another people and aspects of another way
of life foisted or forced upon them.

Today, however, tourists are literally being invited, encouraged, and
enticed to bring themselves and their alien ways even to places and
countries where their countrymen have but recently been ejected by

revolution or rejected by successful independence movements. In the modern world, the underdeveloped or developing nations are those most often encouraging and promoting tourism. Within the last few decades, many newly independent countries and some emerging from relative feudal isolation into a wider world have realized that their competitive status in a world money economy is precarious at best. Tourism is seen as an avenue, along with others, depending on the country's resources, toward development and modernization. This situation indicates an interesting irony: in order to survive and perpetuate their cultural identity and integrity, emerging new nations or quite traditional cultures caught up in a competitive world economy encourage and invite the most successful agents of change (short of political or military agents) active in the contemporary world. This kind of initiative on the part of a host culture introduces a novel variable into the traditional equation of acculturation.

Finally, the anthropological study of tourism, with some exceptions contained in this volume, has followed the same ontogeny as the study of acculturation. Historically, anthropologists were interested in the effects or results of contact between what were usually called dominant and subordinate cultures, but this generally meant that they focused almost exclusively upon changes in the subordinate culture or with sifting, after the fact, which culture traits were of indigenous origin and which were alien. Only as acculturation theory became more sophisticated did the functional nature of acculturation become more apparent, and then anthropologists understood that they must examine both parties within the situational nature of contact if more complete understanding of the phenomenon were to be approached. This is the sequence that has been generally followed in the more specific studies of tourism, and we are just now beginning to realize that the tourists themselves, the donor personnel as representatives or agents of an alien culture (although never fully representative of it) must also be studied.

The varieties of cultural and social change that are likely to occur with the advent of tourism are obviously going to affect the lives of individuals in the host cultures more radically than those of the transient cultures. I would suggest that the traditional approaches of innovation theory and personality theory within anthropology are applicable here.

Many anthropologists agree that two classes of individuals are likely to be innovators within their own communities and/or the first to accept and possibly promulgate an alien trait or behavior. These classes of people have been described as those who hold traditional positions of prestige within their communities and those who are somehow culturally marginal. There is also some scholarly agreement among those who study culture change that traditionally prestigious individuals may be successful innovators when a community is undergoing gradual, orderly change, whereas culturally marginal individuals are more likely to be innovators during periods of rapid, stressful change. This thesis involves a number of assumptions: that prestige is often related to leadership, that traditional leadership at the community level is usually conservative and respected, that an innovation advocated by a prestigious traditionalist may be emulated with little risk so long as such changes involved occur in a more or less gradual and orderly fashion; conversely, marginal individuals are less often prestigious in traditional societies, less often are associated with leadership, less likely to be emulated, etc. However, a further assumption is that the above holds true so long as successful leadership provides solutions to the mundane problems of existence, so long as the *status quo* or gradual change is existentially satisfying to the community. It is assumed that during periods of rapid, stressful culture change traditional leadership may fail to innovate in the solution of problems or be unwilling to integrate novelty within community norms, whereas culturally marginal individuals, being less conservative, perhaps more imaginative, may assume positions of leadership and may become successful innovators during periods of accelerated, disquieting change.

The foregoing may be an oversimplification of a body of anthropological thought, but I submit that for the study of tourism this outline does have heuristic merit. The advent of tourism, either at the community or national level, occurs almost invariably during periods of rapid change or precipitates rapid change. Elements within national governments may make policy commitments to the promotion and development of tourism as a quick expedient to shore up a quaking economy, and a local community may be "discovered" overnight as one of the "last" unspoiled tourist meccas. This is the arena for the marginal individual to appear in as a leading performer.

Now, the term "marginal man" has meant many things to many social scientists. It has meant psychologically marginal, biologically marginal, economically marginal, and biographically marginal—in other words, an individual who differs from some cultural norm or norms and who behaves and is treated accordingly. I would submit that some forms of marginality are likely to allow some individuals to adapt more readily than others to the stresses and changes brought on by tourism and that they may therefore become the more successful innovators with a potential for economic and social mobility and possibility leadership. The kind of marginal individual I have in mind is what has come to be called the culture broker. It is a matter of being able to turn to advantage his or her marginality, demonstrating that entrepreneurship, for example, may be more adaptive than traditional economic subsistence pursuits. The marginal individual is one who may be psychologically inclined or motivated to cope with anxieties creatively, perhaps becoming bilingual. Or, he or she may have had more previous exposure than others to education, travel, bi-cultural or bi-racial experience. This does not mean to say that all marginal individuals within a culture or a community will emerge as successful innovators or will better adapt to change than nonmarginals. I think it is a matter of probabilities to be computed in terms of local or cultural variables in equation with the touristic situation and its personnel. But it is clear that in most situations a handful of people, no more economically or intellectually advantaged than their peers, appear to emerge as culture brokers. They learn the necessary second or third language; they change occupations from subsistence or salaried to entrepreneurial; they migrate to potential or developing resort areas, etc.; and, if they are successful, they are emulated by the previously less daring.

One is tempted at this juncture to speculate that if we had a full operational picture of the development of tourism from its incipient phase to full-blown established resort status that we might often find "revitalization" theories metaphorically apt, with previously marginal individuals becoming prophets or proselytizing disciples and becoming, with the advent of a new "steady state," the prestigious community leadership, attempting to revive or pressure that which attracted tourists in the first place and acting conservatively in the face of further development.

When the anthropologist is involved in empirical field research, however, he is usually concerned with the daily round of life and the annual cycles of events that engage the whole community or the largest segments of it. His approach, traditionally, is participant observation, obtaining information from a representative range of individuals and specialized data from "key" informants. The ethnographic routine need not be varied when studying tourism at the community level, except that the tourists, be they infrequent or regular visitors or part-time residents of the community, must be taken into account. This further involves an understanding of patterns of interaction between local residents, the hosts, and individual tourists or groups of tourists. In long-established tourist centers, where tourism may properly be called an industry (i.e., Bermuda and Monaco), tourists and hosts are likely to understand each other rather fully, and patterns of interaction have become routinized and may be easily understood and interpreted by the ethnographer. However, when tourism is new or recent to a traditional community, a more difficult series of chores confronts the participant-observer.

An ethnographer new to a field site is always faced with a problem of role definition: what image does he project to the people he is there to study? If he is the sole alien present, as is often the case, he and his hosts usually work out his role definition and status within the community through a somewhat mutual trial-and-error learning experience. Both the hosts and the ethnographer try to find a place where he will "fit" certain established categories of age, sex, and demeanor. However, in a community where tourists are a factor and the subject of study as well, the ethnographer is likely to be identified with the tourist population, stereotyped and classified as a member of a group or category of outsiders. The ethnographer is, of course, almost always an outsider, but most, given a reasonable degree of training, sensitivity, and persistence, establish sufficient rapport with their informants to allow them to gain a limited insider's perspective on the community. Any attempt to study an indigenous population and a tourist population in interaction will probably require talents similar to that of the Roman rider, with a foot on each horse. To make complete, accurate, and empathetic observations of both populations will necessitate a delicate balancing act. Indeed, as some of the chapters of this volume indicate, the anthropologist is likely to be most empathetic toward the host population and even hostile to the very notion of tourism, much less wishing to be identified as a tourist. To be able to achieve a degree of mutual rapport and identity with both populations requires a kind of objectivity and toughmindedness that is often lacking in social science. It seems, then, that the investigator must, in fairness to his discipline and to his informants, be a participant-observer in both camps. Having personally done this, I have found myself playing what might be considered a boundary role, attempting to interpret each culture to representatives of the other. And since most anthropologists are educators as well as researchers, the boundary role is not only objectively sound but satisfying from a philosophical and humanistic point of view.

But what is the nature of the interaction between hosts and tourists? Their relationship is almost always an instrumental one, rarely colored by affective ties, and almost always marked by degrees of social distance and stereotyping that would not exist amongst neighbors, peers, or fellow countrymen. One has a much easier task when one studies and interprets social interaction within a "natural" community where values and attitudes are more mutually shared and understood. The greater the ethnic and cultural distance between the host and tourist personnel, the greater the confusion and misunderstanding the two groups are likely to encounter and the less natural they are likely to act. However, this is not a novelty to the anthropologist familiar with other kinds of acculturational situations.

How is the anthropologist to present his understanding and interpretation of host-tourist interaction; what models are available to him that go beyond the traditional hypotheses of acculturation? The "dramaturgical" studies of Erving Goffman come immediately to mind. Tourists and more often their hosts are almost always *on stage* when they meet in face-to-face encounters. They have prepared for their performances backstage: the tourist has read his travel brochures, consulted previous visitors, planned his wardrobe, and thumbs through his dictionary and phrase book before going on stage; his host may count the house, assess the mood of the audience, arrange the lighting and props, consult with fellow performers, and rehearse a friendly smile. These metaphors are often not far from reality. Tourists often alter their demeanor when away from home, and their hosts are likely to engage in roles designed to accommodate tourists that they would never play before their peers. A taxi driver might become an instant expert on the archaeological ruins of his region. Or a tourist might assume the airs of an aristocrat in a country where his money goes twice as far as at home. I am aware that we all wear many masks, but our performances are usually more exaggerated before an audience of strangers for whom we must perform, often to the point of obfuscation. Thus the anthropologist must attempt to find his way backstage as well as view the performance from the audience.

An overview of tourism as a subject of anthropological inquiry must contend with the range and diversity of phenomena involved. Traditionally, science has approached this kind of problem by establishing taxonomies and typologies. It is too early in the development of touristic studies to attempt an exhaustive or definitive statement. This volume represents most of what anthropologists now know about the subject. However, we have some guidelines.

Ethnic and environmental tourism have been distinguished, the latter referring to the tourists' interest primarily in the aesthetic or recreational resources of features of the environment. It should be noted that it is unlikely that great numbers of tourists may be drawn to truly inhospitable environments, regardless of how exotic or interesting the host people may be. However, such situations do exist (as in Eskimo country) and tend to result in closer than usual guest-to-host population ratio. As a consequence, tourist impact might be more severe than otherwise. Other typological categories suggest themselves: internal, domestic tourism vs. international tourism; "packaged and programed" tourism vs. individual tourism; resort tourism vs. "off the-beaten-track" tourism; religious vs. secular tourism; recreational vs. educational or "cultural" tourism; and mass vs. elite tourism. This is not intended to exhaust the list of possible alternatives and indeed suggests that various permutations of the above categories are probable. A tourist often wants to enrich his leisure and travel to the fullest. A tourist's motives will undoubtedly be reflected in his expectations and behavior within the context of the host's environment.

The chapters in this volume leave many questions unanswered, as they should, but suggest others, as they must. For example, little is known aside from rather obvious generalizations regarding communication facilities, accessibility, accommodations, and publicity as to why tourists make the kinds of choices they make between one vacation and another. Or, why do Italian, Japanese, or American tourists find different tourist areas of interest? Studies of different tourist nationalities and their predilections for locale, entertainment, recreation, souvenirs, or other ethnic groups might fall within the tradition of national character studies as well as prove interesting to students of personality and culture.

I think we yet have no clear idea of how tourists form stereotypes of their hosts, and only limited evidence of how their hosts form stereotypes of them. Nor are we certain how intergroup status relationships are shaped or shared. An understanding of these processes might shed significant light on the symbolic content of each culture, especially where a host community has the opportunity to stereotype and evaluate representatives of more than one nationality.

Not to be overlooked is the fact that some host communities are themselves multiethnic and present a culturally pluralistic profile to the tourist. Such populations may be logically expected to react differentially to tourism, positively or negatively, or one or more segments of a multiethnic community might profit or suffer at the expense of others. For example, as tourism invades Surinam on the verge of independence from the Netherlands, which peoples—the Bush Negroes, East Indians, urban Blacks, Creoles, or the Dutch—will profit or lose, and who will make the policy decisions regarding the direction and development of tourism?

And what about those countries even now committed to tourism as their principal economic activity; those governments whose budgets are tied to continued income from tourists; those communities that have abandoned traditional subsistence schemes to compete for tourist monies?

Some of the foregoing questions lead us to consider, jointly, questions of applied anthropology and anthropological ethics.

Those familiar with the Fox "action anthropology" project and the Cornell-Vicos cooperative applied program of development know that some things can be done by anthropologists to help people consolidate their goals and find means to certain ends. Those anthropologists who wish or feel that they must intervene in behalf of the welfare of the people they study should remember that changes in a local community are more often accepted or opposed in a larger context. Tourism is more often *caused* than it occurs by happenstance, and is more often welcome at the outset than rejected by potential hosts, even enough promoted for economic reasons at governmental levels little concerned with long-range results at the community level. I hope that anthropologists can isolate major economic, social, and political inequities that may be brought about by the development and promotion of tourism and attack resultant inequities through their professional associations and as individuals. And, they might well be solicited to give professional guidance to communities and governments as to the most positive means for establishing mutually agreed-upon ends. Certainly, it is ethical and probably desirable that anthropologists, given the opportunity, should suggest logical alternatives to tourism as a means of economic development.

Prudence should require, however, that the anthropological community resist the temptation to condemn tourism as unnecessarily intrusive, as exploitive, as deculturative. Who are we to say that improved roads, water purification projects, and rural electrification, as spinoffs from tourist development, are not as beneficial to, let us say, rural peasants and craftsmen as they are to their governments and to tourists? At the present state of our knowledge it is difficult to demonstrate that tourism *per se* is uniquely destructive or evil. It may be in some instances the best alternative available to a community or a country; it might also prove to be destructive of natural and human resources.

As anthropologists we would not be acting ethically, however, if we did not expose the cultural fakes and the human zoos for what they are. We must equally resist the temptation to view indigenous peoples as unable to adapt and to assimilate to a changing world. We cannot keep them as pristine pets on anthropological reservations.

It remains true that most tourists represent the "haves" of the world and that many host communities and countries are relative "have-nots." It has also been observed by a number of politically astute anthropologists that modernization and industrialization programs in developing countries, more often than not those receiving aid from Western nations, often exacerbate the *status quo*, with the rich getting richer and the poor becoming poorer. These are ultimately international problems not immediately soluble in purely anthropological terms. I raise this dilemma merely to suggest that in economic exchanges between tourists and others—although the carriers, travel agencies, and governments may profit enormously—the monies expended by tourists for goods and services at the local, community level, in the markets and bazaars, in taxies and in taverns, for meals and gratuities, may bring greater prosperity and well-being to members of the host community than they might have found possible by any other means in their lifetimes. At the risk of oversimplification, what I am suggesting is that a form of what anthropologists have called a redistributive economic system is operative here. That is, monies spent by tourists are surplus monies, redistributed by an international elite amongst those who have little opportunity for producing such surpluses. One may not ideologically approve of such a system, but one may describe it within the context of economic anthropology.

In summary, as a subject of scholarly study, tourism may be new, but it may be treated within traditional methods and theories of anthropological research for the present and will benefit from the application of more recent, more sophisticated models as data and understanding accumulate. By the time a discipline begins to attempt definitions and prepare taxonomies, as this book does, the subject has achieved legitimacy.

Although the articles in this volume and those cited in the bibliography represent the bulk of the literature concerning tourism, it is certain that many other anthropologists and other scholars have considerable unpublished data in their possession. It is hoped that this effort will encourage them to bring forth their findings and to extend their research in this area. As sufficiently more substantive data accumulate, more elegant and precise theoretical postulates may replace these preliminary observations.

University of Florida

Reference List and Bibliography

Acknowledgment is due Lary Dilsaver, Nelson Graburn, Ian Matley, DiAnne Reid Ross, and Brian Farrell whose respective bibliographies were referenced.

Asterisked references are essentially nontouristic in content.

Adams, J. 1972. Why the American tourist abroad is cheated: a price theoretical analysis. *Journal of Political Economics* 80 (1): 203-7.

Adams, R. McC. 1974. Anthropological perspectives on ancient trade. *Current Anthropology* 15: 239-58.

Addison, W. 1951. *English spas*. London: Batsford.

Aerni, M. J. 1972. Social effects of tourism. Letter to the editor in *Current Anthropology* 13 (2): 162.

Alexander, D. 1972. *Holiday in the Seychelles*. Cape Town/London/New York: Purnell.

Alexander, L. M. 1953. The impact of tourism on the economy of Cape Cod, Massachusetts. *Economic Geography* 29: 320-26.

Amory, C. 1952. *The last resorts*. New York: Harper and Bros.

Annis, S. n.d. The museum as a staging ground for symbolic experience. Master's thesis, University of Chicago, Dept. of Geography.

Anan'yev, M. A. 1968. *Mezhdunarodnyy turizm* (International tourism). Moscow: Izdatel'stvo "Mezhdunarodnyye otnosheniya."

Angell, R. C. 1967. The growth of transnational participation. *Journal of Social Issues* 23: 108-29.

Apter, H.
  1974. Counting the (social) cost of tourism, Part I. *The Travel Agent*. 16 December, pp. 24-29.
  1975. Counting the (social) cost of tourism, Part II. *The Travel Agent*. 6 February. pp. 54-58.

Archer, B. H. and Sadler, P. G. 1975. The economic impact of tourism in developing countries. *Annals of Tourism Research* 3 (1): 15-32.

Ash, J. 1974. To hell with paradise. *New Internationalist* (February).

Ashton, G. 1964. Tourism as culture contact: a bibliographic survey on the impact of tourism as planned economic development. Paper presented to the symposium on Tourism, Central States Anthropological Society, 14-16 May 1964, Milwaukee, Wisconsin.

Asia Travel Trade. February, 1977, p. 23.

Aspelin, P. L. 1977. The anthropological analysis of tourism: indirect tourism and political economy in the case of the Mamainde of Mato Grosso, Brazil. *Annals of Tourism Research* 3 (3): 135–60.

Badea, L. 1969. Le premier colloque national de la géographie du tourisme (Bucarest, September 1968). *Revue Roumaine de Géologie, Géophysique, et Géographie, Serie de Géographie* 13 (1): 91–93.

°Balandier, G. 1951. La situation coloniale: approche théorique. *Cahiers Internationaux de Sociologie* 11: 44–79.

Ball, D. A. 1971. Permanent tourism: a new export diversification for less developed countries. *International Development Review* 13 (4): 20–3.

Balossier, R. 1967. Approche sociologique de quelques problèmes touristiques. *Cahiers de Tourisme*, Series C., No. 3.

Balsdon, J. P. V. D. 1966. *Life and leisure in ancient Rome*. London: Bodley Head.

Barbose Y. 1970. Trois types d'intervention du tourisme dans l'organization de l'èspace littoral. *Annals de Géographie* 79: 446–68.

Baretje, R. 1969. Bibliographie touristique. In *Collection Etudes et Memoires* 22 (11): 104. Aix-en-Provence: Centre d'Etudes du Tourisme.

Baretje, R. and Defert, P. 1972. Aspects économiques du tourisme. Paris: Editions Berger-Lavrault.

Barratt, P. J. H. 1972. *Grand Bahama*. Newton Abbot: David and Charles.

Barth, F. (ed.)
   °1963. *The role of the entrepreneur in social change in northern Norway*. Bergen: Scandinavia Univ.
   °1967. On the study of social change. *American Anthropologist* 69: 661–69.

Barthes, R. 1973. *Mythologies*. London: Paladin.

Beck, B. and Bryan, F. 1971. This other eden: a survey of tourism in Britain. *The Economist* 6683: 25.9, xxiv.

Beesley, M. E. 1965. The value of time spent in traveling: some new evidence. *Economica* 32 n.s.: 174–85.

Belardinelli, E. 1970. *Problemi attuali degli approdi turistici*. Milan: Giuffrè.

Bell, T. A. 1973. The metamorphosis of Tahiti: change and tradition in a transforming landscape. *Yearbook of the Association of Pacific Coast Geographers* 35: 103–13.

Bennett, C. M. 1970. Tourism and its effect on the peoples of the Pacific. *Proceedings of the 19th Annual Pacific Area Travel Association* (PATA) *Conference*, 13–17 April 1970, Auckland, New Zealand. pp. 78–81.

°Berlyne, D. E. 1962. New directions in motivation theory. In *Anthropology and Human Behavior*. T. Gladwin and W. C. Sturtevant, eds., pp. 150–73. Washington, D.C.: Anthropological Society of Washington.

Berthoud, G. 1972. Introduction: dynamics of ownership in the circum-Alpine area. *Anthropological Quarterly* 43 (3): 117–24.

Bertolino, A. 1973. *Lezioni di economia del turismo*. Firenze: Universita degli Studi.

Blake, E. W. 1974. Stranger in paradise. *Caribbean Review* 6: 9–12.

Blake, G. W. and Lawless, R. 1972. Algeria's tourist industry. *Geography* 57: 148–52.

Bocca, G. 1963. *Bikini Beach*. London: W. H. Allen.

Bochet, G. 1971. Souvenir-hunting—. *Tam-Tam* 5: 1–3. Abidjan: Ivory Coast Information Journal, Ministry of Tourism of the Ivory Coast.

Bodine, J. 1964. Symbiosis at Taos and the impact of tourism on the Pueblo: a case of "unplanned" economic development. Paper presented to symposium on Tourism, Central States Anthropological Society, 14–16 May 1964, Milwaukee, Wisconsin.

Boek, W. S. 1964. Touring as planned economic development: coordinating diverse local interests with outside capital. Paper presented to the symposium on Tourism, Central States Anthropological Society, 14–16 May 1964, Milwaukee, Wisconsin.

°Boeke, J. H. 1953. *Economics and economic policy of dual societies as exemplified by Indonesia.* New York: International Secretariet, Institute of Pacific Relations.

Boissevain, J. 1976. Tourism and development in Malta. Paper read at the symposium on Tourism and Culture Change, American Anthropological Association, 18 November 1976, Washington, D.C.

Bonapace, U. 1968. Il turismo nella neve in Italia e i suoi aspetti geografici. *Revisita geografica italiana* 75 (2): 157–86 and 75 (3): 322–59.

Bond, M. E. and Ladman, J. R.
    1971. Tourism: a regional growth phenomenon. *Rocky Mountain Social Science Journal* 8 (2): 23–32.
    1972. Tourism: a strategy for development. *Nebraska Journal of Economics and Business* 2 (1): 37–52.
    1974. The tourist industry: what impact on Arizona? *Arizona Business* 20: 20–26.

°Boon, J. A. 1974. The progress of the ancestors in a Balinese temple group. *Journal of Asian Studies* 34 (1): 7–25.

Boorstin, D. 1962. *The image, or what happened to the American dream.* New York: Atheneum.

Bornet, B. 1974. Tourisme et environnement: faut-il souhaiter une concentration ou une deconcentration touristique? *Les Cahiers du Tourisme,* Serie C, No. 20. Aix-en-Provence: Centre d'Etudes du Tourisme.

°Boserup, E. 1970. *Women's roles in economic development.* London: George Allen and Unwin.

Bouret, R. E. 1972. *Tourism in Puerto Rico.* San German: Inter-American University Publications.

Boyer, M. 1972. *Le Tourism.* Paris: Editions du Seuil.

Brameld, T. and Matsuyama, M. 1974. The Polynesian cultural center of Hawaii: a laboratory of educational anthropology. Paper presented to the symposium on Tourism and Culture Change, American Anthropological Association, 19–24 November 1974, Mexico City, Mexico.

°Brennan, N. 1973. Cooperativism and socialization among the Cuna Indians of San Blas. Master's thesis, Univ. of California at Los Angeles.

Brewer, J. D., 1974. Tourism, business and ethnic categories in a Mexican town. Paper presented to the American Anthropological Association, 19–24 November 1974, Mexico City, Mexico.

°Brown, J. 1970. Sex division of labor among the San Blas Cuna. *Anthropological*

Quarterly 43 (2): 57–63.

Brown, N. O. 1959. Life against death. London: Rutledge and Paul Kegan.

Bryan, W. 1957. A geographic study of the tourist industry of Mexico. Master's Thesis, Dept. of Geography, Oklahoma State Univ.

Bryden, J. 1973. *Tourism and development: a case study of the commonwealth Caribbean.* New York: Cambridge Univ. Press.

Bryden, J. and Faber, M. 1971. Multiplying the tourist multiplier. *Social and Economic Studies* 20 (1): 61–82.

Burgelin, O. 1967. Le tourisme juge. *Communications* 10: 65–97. Special edition, Vacances et tourisme.

Burkart, A. J. and Medlik, S. 1974. *Tourism: past, present and future.* London: William Heinemann Ltd.

Burn, H. P. 1975. Packaging paradise—the environmental costs of international tourism. *Sierra Club Bulletin* 80 (5): 25–28.

Burnet, M. L. 1970. Pays en voie de developpement et tourisme. *Bulletin de l'Association des Géographes Francais.* Pp. 377–8.

Burton, T. L. 1971. *Experiments in recreation research.* London: Allen and Unwin.

Butler, R. W. 1974. The social implications of tourist development. *Annals of Tourism Research* 2 (2): 100–114.

Caribbean Ecumenical Consultation for Development. 1971. *The role of tourism in Caribbean development.* Study Paper No. 8. Bridgetown, Barbados.

*Caro Baroja, J. 1968. Mascaradas y alardes' de San Juan. In *Estudios sobre la vida tradicional española.* J. Caro Baroja, ed. Barcelona: Ediciones Peninsula, pp. 167–82.

Carone, G. 1959. Il turismo nell'economia internazionale. Milan: Giuffrè.

Carpenter, B. R. 1962. Puerto Rico's tourist industry. *Annals of the Association of American Geographers* 52: 323–24, abstract.

Carpenter, E. 1972, 1973. *Oh, what a blow that phantom gave me!* New York: Holt, Rinehart and Winston.

Castro Farinas, J. A. 1969. Los medios de communication social y el desarrollo del turismo. *Estudiant Information* 9 (1): 55–71.

Cazes, G.
    1968. Le development du tourisme à la Martinique. *Cahiers d'Otre Mer* 21 (83): 225–26.
    1972. Tourisme, developpement et amenagement: l'example de Puerto Rico. *Les Cahiers du Tourisme,* Serie B, No. 16. Aix-en-Provence: Centre d'Etudes du Tourisme.

Chen, P. 1972. Social pollution—with special reference to Singapore. *NYLTI Journal* (Singapore). May, Pp. 117–25.

Chesnutwood, C. M. 1958. Computing a qualitative tourist industry index. *Annals of the Association of American Geographers* 48: 356, abstract.

Chirstaller, W.
    1955. Beitrage zu einer geographie des fremdenverkehrs. *Erdkunde* 9 (1): 1–19.
    1964. Some considerations of tourism of Europe: the peripheral regions— underdeveloped countries—recreation areas. *Papers of the Regional Science Association* 12: 95–105.

Chiti, M. P. 1970. Profilo pubblico del turismo. Milan: Giuffrè.

Clement, H. G. 1961. *Future of tourism in the Pacific and Far East.* U.S. Department of Commerce. Washington, D.C.: U.S. Government Printing Office.

Cleveland, H.; Mangone, C. J.; and Adams, J. C. 1960. *The overseas Americans.* New York: McGraw-Hill.

Cohen, E.
    1971. Arab boys and tourist girls in a mixed Jewish Arab community. *International Journal of Comparative Sociology* 12 (4): 217–33.
    1972. Toward a sociology of international tourism. *Social Research* 39: 164–82.
    1973. Nomads from affluence: notes on the phenomenon of drifter-tourism. *International Journal of Comparative Sociology* 14 (1–2): 89–103.
    1974. Who is a tourist? *Sociological Review* 22 (4): 527–53.
    1976. *Tourism in the Pacific Islands.* Exchange Bibliography #1155. Monticello, Ill.: Council of Planning Librarians.

Cohen, Y. 1974. Comment. *Current Anthropology* 15: 250–51.

Coker, J. A. 1950. Tourism and the peasant in the Grisens. *Scottish Geographical Magazine* 66: 107–16.

Cole, J. W. 1972. Cultural adaptation in the eastern Alps. *Anthropological Quarterly* 45 (3): 158–76.

Cole, R. G. 1972. Sixteenth-century travel books as a source of European attitudes toward non-white and non-western culture. *Proceedings of the American Philosophical Society* 116 (1): 59–67.

Colenutt, R. J. 1969. Modelling travel patterns of day visitors to the countryside. *Area* 2: 43–47.

Colley, G. 1967. International tourism today. *Lloyds Bank Review* 85: 29–41.

Colloque d'Antrans—Grenoble. 1973. Tourisme et emploi dans les Alpes. *Revue de Géographie Alpine* 61 (4): 509–70.

Cooper, C. E. 1947. Tourism. *Journal of Geography* 41: 115–20.

Cosgrove, I. and Jackson, R. 1972. *The geography of recreation and leisure.* London: Hutchinson.

Cowan, G. 1975. Cultural impact of tourism with particular reference to the Cook Islands. In *A new kind of sugar: tourism in the Pacific.* B. R. Finney and K. A. Watson, eds., pp. 79–86. Honolulu: East-West Cultural Learning Institute.

Crampson, L. J. and Tan, T. K. 1973. A model of tourism flow into the Pacific. *Revue de Tourisme* 3: 98–104.

Crocombe, R.
    1972. Preserving which tradition? the future of Pacific cultures. *Pacific Perspective* 1 (1): 1–5 and 1 (2): 28–49.
    1973. *The new South Pacific.* Rutland, Vermont: Charles E. Tuttle Co., Ltd.

Crowley, D. J. n.d. Tourism in Ghana. *Insight and Opinion* 6 (2): 109.

Crystal, E. 1976. Ceremonies of the ancestors. *Pacific Discovery* 29 (1): 9–18.

Cullinan, T. n.d. *Non-tourism in Latin America.* Menlo Park: Stanford Research Institute.

Curti, G. P. 1962. The isle of Man: geographical factors in the evolution of a political enclave. *Annals of the Association of American Geographers* 52: 327, abstract.

Danilova, N. A. 1973. Klimat pribaltiki i prodolzhitelnost' perioda, blagopriyatnogo dlya turizma (Climate of the Baltic area and duration of the period favorable to tourism). In *Geografiya i turism*. S. A. Kovalov et al., eds. Voprosy Geografii, vol. 93. Moscow: Izdatel'stvo "Mysl."

Deasy, G. F. and Griess, P. R. 1966. Impact of a tourist facility on its hinterland. *Annals of the Association of American Geographers* 56 (2): 290–306.

Demory, Barbara, 1976. The tourist as guest. Paper read at the symposium on Tourism and Culture Change, American Anthropological Association, 18 November 1976, Washington, D.C.

Desplanques, H. 1973. Une nouvelle utilization de l'èspace rurale en Italie: l'agritourisme. *Annales de Géographie* 82 (450): 151–63.

Devons, E. 1961. World trade in invisibles. *Lloyds Bank Review* 60 n.s.: 37–50.

DeVries, P. J. 1972. From plantation to tourism: social and economic change in Montserrat, West Indies. Paper read to the Canadian Sociological and Anthropological Association, May 1972.

Dilsaver, L. M. 1976. Tour planning as a role for geographers in international tourism. Master's thesis, Dept. of Geography, California State Univ., Hayward.

Donehower, E. J. 1969. The impact of dispersed tourism in French Polynesia. Master's thesis, Univ. of Hawaii.

Dower, M.
    1965. Fourth wave: the challenge of leisure. *Architect's Journal* (20 January).
    1973. Recreation, tourism and the farmer. *Journal of Agricultural Economics* 24: 465–77.

Doxey, G. V. and Associates. 1971. *The tourist industry in Barbados: a socio-economic assessment*. Kitchener, Ontario: Dusco Graphics.

Driss, A. 1969. La planification touristique et son integration, dans les pays en voie de developpement. *Rapport sur le Seminaire Tourisme et Developpement* 16 May–6 June 1969, Berlin, Germany.

Duchet R. 1949. *Le tourism a travers les ages*. Paris: Vigot Freres.

Dumazedeir, J. 1967. *Towards a society of leisure*. New York: Free Press.

Dunkle, J. R. 1950. The tourist industry of southern California: a study in economic and cultural geography. Master's thesis, Dept. of Geography, Univ. of California, Los Angeles.

Dupront, A. 1967. Tourism et pelegrinage, reflexions de psychologie collective. *Communications* 10: 97–121.

Durand, M. G. 1966. Une ênquete sur le tourism social et familial. *Revue de Geographie Alpine* 54 (1): 73–95.

°Durkheim, E. 1912. *Elementary Forms of Religious Life*. London: Allen and Unwin.

Edelmann, K. M. F. 1975. Major problems of tourism growth in developing countries. *Annals of Tourism Research* 2 (1): 33–43.

Edgell, M. C. R. and Farrell, B. H., eds. 1974. *Themes on Pacific Lands*. Western Geographical Series, vol. 10. Victoria, British Columbia: Univ. of Victoria.

Egan, M. 1967. *The visitor industry in American Samoa*. Report for the Hawaii Visitors Bureau, Honolulu.

Eiselin, E. 1955. A tourist-geographer visits Iquitos, Peru. *Journal of Geography* 55: 176–82.

Enzenberger, H. 1962. *Einzelheiten*. Frankfurt-am-Main: Suhrkamp Verlag.

Erbes, R. 1973. *International tourism and the economy of developing countries*. Paris: OECD Development Centre.

Eriksen, W. 1968. Zur geographie des fremdenverkehrs in Argentinien. *Die Erde* 99: 305-26.

Evans, N. H.
   1970. Tourist contact and culture change in the Banderas Valley, Nayarit and Jalisco, Mexico. Master's thesis, Long Beach State Univ.
   1976. Tourism and cross-cultural communication. *Annals of Tourism Research* 3 (4): 189-98.

Fabiane, D. 1971. Information sources on international travel and tourism. *The Professional Geographer* 23 (3): 234-36.

Fanon, F. 1968. *The wretched of the earth*. New York: Grove Press.

Farber, M. 1954. Some hypotheses on the psychology of travel. *The Psychoanalytic Review* 41: 267-71.

Farrell, B. H. 1974. The tourist ghettos of Hawaii. In *Themes on Pacific lands*. M. C. R. Edgell and B. H. Farrel, eds., pp. 181-221. Western Geographical Series. Victoria, B.C.: Univ. of Victoria.

Fieguth, W. 1967. Historical geography and the concept of the authentic past as a regional resource. *Ontario Geography* 1: 55-60.

Field, J. A., Jr. 1971. Transnationalism and the new tribe. *International Organization* 25 (3): 353-72.

Finney, B. R. 1973. *Polynesian peasants and proletarians*. Cambridge, Mass.: Schenkman.

Finney, B. R. and Watson, K. A. 1975. *A new kind of sugar; tourism in the Pacific*. Honolulu: East-West Culture Learning Institute.

Force, R. W. 1975. Tourism and change: stimulation and recreation. Paper read at the Pacific Science Congress, August 1975, Vancouver, B.C.

Force, R. W. and Bishop, B., eds. 1975. *The impact of urban centers in the Pacific*. Honolulu: East-West Culture Learning Institute.

Forster, E. 1923. *Room with a view*. New York: Knopf.

Forster, J. 1964. The sociological consequences of tourism. *International Journal of Comparative Sociology* 5 (12): 217-27.

Fox, M. 1975. The social impact of tourism—a challenge to researchers and planners. In *A new kind of sugar: tourism in the Pacific*, B. R. Finney and K. A. Watson, eds., pp. 27-47. Honolulu: East-West Culture Learning Institute.

Francillon, G. 1974/75. *Bali: tourism, culture and environment*. Report No. SHC-75/WS/17. Bali, Indonesia and Paris: Universitas Udayana and UNESCO.

Francke, L. 1976. Sun spots. *Newsweek*. January 5, pp. 44-50.

Fraser, R. 1973. *Tajos: the story of a village on the Costa del Sol*. New York: Pantheon.

Friedheim, E.
   1976a. Turista: the medical battle begins. *The Travel Agent* 143 (8): 82-83.
   1976b. Turista war: a win is possible. *The Travel Agent* 143 (9): 74-75.

Friedl, J.

1972. Changing economic emphasis in an alpine village. *Anthropological Quarterly* 43 (3): 145–57.

1973. Benefits of fragmentation in a traditional society: a case from the Swiss Alps. *Human Organization* 32 (1): 29–36.

Friends of Micronesia. 1973. Tourism: a special report. *Newsletter* 3: 4 Berkeley, California.

Fukunaga, L. 1975. A new sun in North Kohala. In *A new kind of sugar: tourism in the Pacific*, B. R. Finney and K. A. Watson, eds., pp. 199–228. Honolulu: East-West Culture Learning Institute.

Gamper, J. A. 1974. The influence of tourism on ethnic relations in southern Austria. Master's thesis, Dept. of Anthropology, California State University, Hayward.

Gaulis, L. and Creux, R. 1975. *Pionniers Suisses de l'hotellerie*. Paudex (Suisses): Editions de Fontainemore.

Gearing, C. E., Swart, W. W. and Var, T., eds. 1976. *Planning for tourism development*. New York: Praeger.

Gebhardt, R. 1976. Blacktop bid for the tourist: how the road came to Baja. In Travel and Resort Section, *New York Times*, 18 January 1976.

Geddes, L. 1966. The tourist industry today. *Journal of the Royal Society of Arts* 114: 448–59.

Geertz, C.
  ° 1957. Ethos, world view, and the analysis of sacred symbols. *Antioch Review* 17: 4.
  ° 1959. Form and variation in Balinese village structure. *American Anthropologist* 61: 911–1001.
  ° 1963a. *Agricultural involution*. Berkeley: Univ. of California Press.
  ° 1963b. *Peddlers and princes*. Chicago: Univ. of Chicago Press.
  ° 1966. Religion as a cultural system. In *Anthropological approaches to the study of religion*, M. Banton, ed., pp. 1–46. London: Tavistock.
  ° 1972. Deep play: notes on the Balinese cock fight. *Daedalus* 101: 1–37.

Geographical Review 25: 507–9 (1936). Some geographical aspects of tourism.

Gerakis, A. S. 1966. Economic man; the tourist. *Finance and Development*, maart.

Gerassi, J. 1963. *The great fear: the reconquest of Latin America by Latin Americans*. London: Macmillan.

Geshekter, C. 1976. Tourism and African underdevelopment. Paper read at the symposium on Tourism and Culture Change, American Anthropological Association, 18 November 1976, Washington, D.C.

Gillmor, D. C. 1973. Irish holidays abroad: the growth and destinations of chartered inclusive tours. *Irish Geography* 6 (5): 618–25.

Ginier, J.
  1964. Quelques aspects du tourism americain en France. *Annales de Geographie* 73 (397): 297–318.
  1965. *Geographie Touristique de la France*. Paris: Societe d'Edition d'Enseignement Superieur.
  1969. *Les touristes etrangers en France pendant l'été*. Paris: Genin.

° Gluckman, M. 1947. Malinowski's "functional" analysis of social change. *Africa* 17: 106–21.

Goethe, J. W. 1962. *Italian journey (1786–88)*. New York: Pantheon

Goffman, E.
  1959. *The presentation of self in everyday life*. New York: Doubleday.
  1967. *Interaction ritual*. New York: Doubleday.

Goldstein, V. 1975. Planning for tourism on the island of Hawaii: the effects of tourism on historical sites and culture. In *A new kind of sugar: tourism in the Pacific*, B. R. Finney and K. A. Watson, eds., pp. 161–64. Honolulu: East-West Culture Learning Institute.

Gooding, E. G. B. 1971. Food production in Barbados, with particular reference to tourism. In *The tourist industry in Barbados*. Report for G. V. Doxey and Associates. Kitchener, Ontario: Dusco Graphics.

Graburn, N. H. H., ed. 1976. *Ethnic and tourist arts: cultural expressions from the fourth world*. Berkeley and Los Angeles: Univ. of California Press.

Graves, C. 1957. *Royal riviera*. London: Heinemann.

Graves, R. and Hodges, A. 1973. *The long weekend*. London: Penguin.

Gray, H. P.
  1970. *International travel–international trade*. Lexington, Mass.: D. C. Heath and Co.
  1974. Towards an economic analysis of tourism policy. *Social and Economic Studies* 23 (3): 386–97.

Gray, R. D. 1967. *Goethe: a critical introduction*. London: Cambridge Univ. Press.

Greenwood, D. J.
  1970. *Agriculture, industrialization and tourism: the economics of modern Basque farming*. Ann Arbor: University Microfilms.
  1972. Tourism as an agent of change: a Spanish Basque case. *Ethnology* 11: 80–91.
  1976. Tourism as an agent of change. *Annals of Tourism Research* 3 (3): 128–42.

Gubler, W. H. 1967. Las Vegas: an international recreation center. M. A. Thesis. Salt Lake City: University of Utah.

Haden-Guest, A. 1972. *Down the programmed rabbit hole*. London: Hart-Davis, Macgibbon.

Hall, S. 1969. Hippies: an American moment. In *Student Power*, J. Nagel, ed. Dondon: Merlin.

°Hallowell, A. I. 1957. The backwash of the frontier: the impact of the Indian on American culture. In *The Frontier in perspective*, W. D. Wyman and C. B. Kroeber, eds. Madison: Univ of Wisconsin Press.

Hannah, W. 1972. Bali in the seventies; Part I: cultural tourism. *American Universities Field Staff Reports*, Southeast Asia Series 20: 2.

Harrigan, N. 1974. The legacy of Caribbean history and tourism. *Annals of Tourism Research* 2 (1): 13–26.

Hasselblat, W. B. 1973. Tourist promotion in developing countries. *Intereconomics* 8: 241–44.

Hawaii Architects and Engineers, Inc. 1968. *Cultural considerations for planning in Micronesia*. Honolulu.

Hawkins, I. 1973. Tourism changes for Europe. *West Indies Chronicle* Aug 1973, pp. 317–19.

Helms, M. 1970. Matrilocality, social solidarity and culture contact: three case histories. *Southwest Journal of Anthropology* 26: 197–212.

Hendee, J. C. 1975. Sociology and applied leisure research. *Annals of Tourism Research* 2 (3): 155–63.

Hennessey, J. 1975. Increasing competition in tourism. *Eastern Economist* 61 (3): 12–33.

Herrera, F. 1972. Aspectos del desarollo economico y social de los Indies Cunas de San Blas, Panama. *American Indigena* 32 (2): 187–95.

Heutz de Lemp, C. 1964. Le tourisme dans l'archipel des Hawaii. *Cahiers d'Outre Mer* 17 (65): 9–57.

Hibbert, C. 1969. *The grand tour.* London: Weidenfeld and Nicolson.

Hicks, B. 1976. Perceptual conflict as the snake in a tourist's paradise. Paper read at the symposium on Tourism and Culture Change, American Anthropological Association, 18 November 1976, Washington, D.C.

Hill, A. 1971. Tourism in Africa: Africa's tourist growth confounds the experts. *African Development* 5: 75.

Hillendahl, W. H.
> 1971. Economic rate of return of tourism. Paper read to the third travel research seminar, Pacific Area Travel Association, 10 November 1971, Singapore.
> 1973. Political and economic variations in the world and their effect on travel. Paper read to the fifth travel research seminar, Pacific Area Travel Association, 16 October 1973, Suva, Fiji.

Hiller, H. L.
> 1974a. Where is tourism traveling? *Journal of Interamerican Studies and World Affairs,* 16 (4): 508–15.
> 1974b. Caribbean tourism and the university. *Caribbean Educational Bulletin* 1 (1): 15–22.
> 1974c. Commentary on things tourismic. *Caribbean Review* 6 (4): 8 and 50–52.
> 1975. The organization and marketing of tourism. In *A new kind of sugar: tourism in the Pacific,* eds. B. R. Finney and K. A. Watson, pp. 237–46. Honolulu: East-West Culture Learning Institute.

Hills, T. L. and Lundgren, J. 1974. The impact of tourism. Paper read at the International Geographical Union Regional Meeting, December 1974, Palmerston North, New Zealand.

Himan, H. C. 1969. Tourism and economic development: the British Honduras case. *Overseas Research Center—Developing Nations,* Monograph 1.

Hudson, E. 1973. *Vertical integration in the travel and leisure industry.* Paris: Institute de Transport Aerien.

°Hughes, C. C. 1960. *An Eskimo village in the modern world.* Ithaca: Cornell Univ. Press.

Huizinga, J. 1950. *Homo Ludens: a study of the play element in culture.* Boston: Beacon.

Hutson, J. 1971. A politician in Valloire. In *Gifts and poison,* F. G. Bailey, ed., pp. 68–96. New York: Shocken Books.

Idacipta, P. T. 1976. Master plan for South Sulawesi tourist development. In

Rencana Induk Pengembangan Pariwisata Sulawesi Selastan, vol. 2. Djakarta: Government Printing Office.

Inkeles, A. 1969. Making men modern: on the causes and consequences of individual change in six developing countries. *American Journal of Sociology* 78: 208–25.

Inskeep, E. L. 1975. Physical planning for tourist development. In *A new kind of sugar: tourism in the Pacific*, B. R. Finney and K. A. Watson, eds., pp. 247–52. Honolulu: East-West Culture Learning Institute.

International Union of Official Travel Organizations (IOUTO)

    n.d. *Bilateral tourist policies for the establishment of joint programmes.*

    n.d. *Charter for development and protection of tourist resources study.*

    n.d. *Factors determining selection of sites for tourism development.*

    n.d. *Guidelines for the preparation of promotional plans.* Manual.

    n.d. *Long-term effectiveness of tourist promotional campaigns.*

    n.d. *Pilot study on long-term forecasts.*

    n.d. *Pilot study on the relations between infrastructure policies and tourist plant and development policies.*

    n.d. *Potential international supply of tourism resources.*

    1972. Tourism's role in economic development. *Travel Research Journal* 2: 3–22.

    n.d. *Tourist planning.*

    n.d. *Tourist publicity.*

Jackson, J. B. 1963. Rise and fall of tourism in the southwest. *Annals of the Association of American Geographers* 53: 599, abstract.

Jackson, R. T.

    1969. Uganda's place in world tourism. *Seminar Papers.* Nairobi: Makerere University College, Dept. of Geography.

    1973. Problems of tourist industry development on the Kenyan coast. *Geography* 58 (1): 62–5.

Jafari, J.

    1973. Role of tourism on socio-economic transformation of developing countries. Master's thesis, Cornell Univ.

    1974a. The components and nature of tourism: the tourist market basket of goods and services. *Annals of Tourism Research* 1 (3): 73–90.

    1974b. Socio-economic costs of tourism to developing countries. *Annals of Tourism Research* 1 (7): 227–63.

    1975. Creation of the inter-departmental World Tourism Organization. *Annals of Tourism Research* 2 (5): 237–46.

Johnson, R. B. 1976. Tourism in Tonga: a case study. Paper read at the symposium on Tourism and Culture Change, American Anthropological Association, 18 November 1976, Washington, D.C.

Jones, S. B. 1933. Mining and tourist towns in the Canadian Rockies. *Economic Geography* 19: 368–78.

*Jopling, C. 1974. Women's work: a Mexican case study of low status as a tactical advantage. *Ethnology* 13 (2): 187–95.

Jursa, P. E. and Winkates, J. F. 1974. Tourism in Ethiopia: a case study. *Issue* 4 (1): 45–9.

Kanywanyi, J. L. 1973. Tourism benefits the capitalists. In *Tourism and Socialist Development*, I. G. Shivji, ed., pp. 52–65. Tanzanian Studies No. 3. Dar es Salaam: Tanzania Publishing House.

Kaplan, M. 1960. Leisure in America: a social inquiry. New York: John Wiley and Sons.

Kaviolis, V. 1970. Post-modern man: psychological responses to social trends. *Social Problems* 17 (4): 435–48.

Kayser, B. 1962. La Geographie appliquée au tourisme. *Colloque National de Geographie Appliquee*, Strasbourg 1961. Paris: Edition du Centre National de la Recherche Scientifique.

Keller, A. 1970. He said: "Tourists never take the mail boat:—that clinched it. *New York Times* Section 10, 24 May 1970.

Kemper, Robert V. 1976. Tourism and regional development in Taos, New Mexico. Paper read at the symposium on Tourism and Culture Change, American Anthropological Association, 18 November 1976, Washington, D.C.

Kent, J. 1972. *Solomon Islands*. Newton Abbot, Eng.: David and Charles.

Kent, N.
    1971. Escape mecca of the world. *Hawaii Pono Journal* 1(4): 32–58.
    1975. A new kind of sugar. In *A new kind of sugar: tourism in the Pacific*, B. R. Finney and K. A. Watson, eds., pp. 169–98. Honolulu: East-West Culture Learning Institute.

Keogh, B. M. 1969. The role of travel in the recreational day-trip. Master's thesis. London, Ontario: Univ. of Western Ontario.

°Khury, F. 1968. The etiquette of bargaining in the Middle East. *American Anthropologist* 70: 698–706.

Kloke, C. 1975. South Pacific economies and tourism. In *A new kind of sugar: tourism in the Pacific*, B. R. Finney and K. A. Watson, eds., pp. 3–26. Honolulu: East-West Culture Learning Institute.

Knebel, H. J. 1960. *Soziologische strukturwanderlungen im modernen tourismus*. Stuttgart: F. Enke Verlag.

Koch, A. 1966. *Fremdenverkehr als entwicklungshilfe*. Munchen: Jahrbuch fur Fremdenverkehr.

Koning, H. 1974. Travel is destroying a major reason for travelling. *The New York Times*. Sunday, 17 November 1974.

Krause W. and Jud, G. D. 1973. *International tourism and Latin American development*. Studies in Latin American Business No. 15. Austin: Univ. of Texas, Graduate School of Business.

Krippendorf, J. 1973. Le tourism à la croissance zéro. *Revue de Tourisme* 2: 59–65.

Krizan, B. 1971. The economic impact of tourism on the American Virgin Islands. Master's thesis, Southern Illinois Univ.

Kruschke, E. R. 1974. Tourism and the energy crisis. Paper read at the symposium on Tourism and Culture Change, American Anthropological Association, 19–24 November 1974, Mexico City, Mexico.

Labor, G. 1969. Determinants of international travel between Canada and the U.S. *Geographical Analysis* 1 (4): 329–36.

Lamborn, B. N. A. 1974. Energy economics of tourist travel. *Florida Environmental and Urban Issues* 1: 4–5.

Lancaster, J. R. and Nichols, L. L. 1971. *A selected bibliography of geographical references and related research in outdoor recreation and tourism, 1930-71.* Exchange Bibliography #190. Monticello, Ill.: Council of Planning Librarians.

Lane, L. W. Jr. 1975. Tourism: a sound economic partner and a good environmental influence. Paper read to the New Zealand National Travel Association Seminar, 9 April 1975, Wellington, New Zealand.

Lansing, J. 1968. The effects of migration and personal effectiveness on long distance travel. *Transportation Research* 2: 329-38.

°Lansing, J. S. 1973. *Evil in the morning of the world: phenomenological approaches to a Balinese community.* Ann Arbor: Univ. of Michigan Center for South and Southeast Asian Languages.

Larrabee, E. and Meyersohn, eds. 1952. *Mass leisure.* Glencoe: Free Press.

Latouche, R. 1963. Un colloque scientifique sur le tourisme à Nice. *Revue de Geographie Alpine* 51 (2): 369-70.

Lavery, P. Resorts and recreation. In *Recreational geography*, P. Lavery, ed., pp. 167-96. New York: Wiley and Sons.

Leach, E. R. 1961. Time and false noses. In *Rethinking anthropology*, E. R. Leach, ed., pp. 132-36. London School of Economics, Monographs in Social Anthropology No. 22. London: Athlone Press.

Le Fevre, T.
    1975a. Who gets what from tourists? In *A new kind of sugar: tourism in the Pacific*, B. R. Finney and K. A. Watson, eds., pp. 101-10. Honolulu: East-West Culture Learning Institute.
    1975b. Making do with leftovers from Pacific tourism. In *The Pacific Way*, S. Tupounina, R. Crocombe, and C. Slatter, eds., pp. 215-21. Suva, Fiji.
    1975c. Rarotonga airport: a preliminary view of the possible balance sheet. In *A new kind of sugar: tourism in the Pacific,* eds. B. R. Finney and K. A. Watson, eds., pp. 87-100. Honolulu: East-West Culture Learning Institute.

Lee, R. L. 1974. Who owns boardwalk?: the structure of control in the tourist industry of Yucatan. Paper read at the American Anthropological Association, 19-24 November 1974, Mexico City, Mexico.

Lerner, D. 1958. *The passing of traditional society.* Glencoe: The Free Press.

Leugger, J. 1958. Weitere soziologische aspekte des fremdenverkehrs. *Revue de Tourisme* 13 (1): 9-16.

Levitt, K. and Gulati, I. 1970. Income effect of tourist spending: mystification multiplied; a critical comment on the Zinder Report. *Social and Economic Studies* 19 (3): 325-43.

Lewis, G. 1972. *The Virgin Islands.* Evanston: Northwestern Univ. Press.

Lickorish, L. J. 1970. Tourism. In *World airports: the way ahead*, pp. 110-19. London: The Institute of Civil Engineers.

Lickorish, L. J. and Kershaw, A. G. 1958. *The travel trade.* London: Mackay and Co.

Liegeois, F. and Magis, J.
    1967a. Le tourism: fait sociologique. *Ethnie Francaise.* March–April, pp. 13-18.
    1967b. Tourisme: nouvelle demension social (le). *Documents CEPESS* 6 (5): 3-125.

Light, I. 1974. From Vice District to tourist attraction: the moral career of American Chinatowns. *Pacific History Review* 43 (8): 367–94.

Lockefeer, H. 1974. Derde wereld ziet nadelen van toerisme. *Volkskrant* 29.

°Loeb, L. D. 1970. *The Jews of southwest Iran: a study of culture persistence.* Ann Arbor: University Microfilms.

Loki, M. 1975. How Fijians can benefit from tourism and how to milk the tourists. In *The Pacific way*, S. Tupouniua, R. Crocombe, C. Slatter, eds., pp. 222–26.

Loukissas, P. J. 1975. Tourism and environmental conflict: the case of the Greek island of Mykonos. Paper read at the symposium on Tourism and Culture Change, American Anthropological Association, 6 December 1975, San Francisco, California.

Lowenthal, D.
     1962. Tourists and thermalists. *Geographical Review* 52 (1): 124–27.
     1962–63. Not every landscape pleases. *Landscape* 13 (2): 19–23.

Lundberg, D. E.
     1971. Why tourists travel. *Cornell Hotel and Restaurant Administration Quarterly* 11 (4): 75–81. Ithaca: Cornell Univ., School of Hotel Administration.
     1974. *The tourist business.* Boston: Cahners.

Lundgren, L. O. J. 1973. The development of the tourist travel systems. *Revue de Tourisme* 28 (1): 2–14.

MacCannell, D.
     1973. Staged authenticity: arrangements of social space in tourist settings. *American Journal of Sociology* 79 (3): 589–603.
     1976. *The tourist: a new theory of the leisure class.* New York: Schocken Books, Inc.

Macaulay, R. 1949. *Fabled shore.* London: Hamish Hamilton.

Madden, M. S. and Cohn, S. L. 1966. The legal status and problems of the American abroad. *Annals of the American Academy of Political and Social Science* 368: 119–31.

°Magubane, B. 1973. The Xhosa in town, revisited urban anthropology: a failure of method and theory. *American Anthropologist* 75: 1701–15.

°Malinowski, B. 1945. *Dynamics of culture change.* New Haven: Yale Univ. Press.

Mann, T. 1930. *Death in Venice.* New York: Knopf.

Manning, F.
     1973. *Black clubs in Bermunda: ethnography of a play world.* Ithaca: Cornell Univ. Press.
     1974. Cup match and carnival: secular rites of revitalization in decolonizing, tourist-oriented societies. Paper presented to Burg Wartenstein Symposium 64. New York: Wenner-Gren Foundation for Anthropological Research.

Marcuse, H. 1968. *Eros and civilization.* London: Sphere.

Mark, S. M. 1975. Tourism and quality growth in the Pacific area. In *A new kind of sugar: tourism in the Pacific*, B. R. Finney and K. A. Watson, eds., pp. 147–52. Honolulu: East-West Culture Learning Institute.

Marnham, P. 1971. *The road to Katmandu* London: Macmillan.

Mathews, H. G. 1975. International tourism and political science. *Annals of Tourism Research* 2 (4): 195–204.

Matley, I. M. *The geography of international tourism.* Association of American Geographers Resource Paper 76–1.

Matznetter, J. (ed.)

   1974a. *Studies in the geography of tourism.* Frankfurt am Main: J. W. Goethe-Universitat.

   1974b. Reports of working groups: geography of tourism and recreation. *I.G.U. Bulletin* 25 (1): 7.

°Mauss, M. and Mauss, H. H. 1898. Essaie sur la nature et la fonction au sacrifice. *L'Année Sociologique* 2: 29–138.

May R. J. 1975. Tourism and the artifact industry in Papua New Guinea. In *A new kind of sugar: tourism in the Pacific*, B. R. Finney and K. A. Watson, eds., pp. 125–34. Honolulu: East-West Culture Learning Institute.

McEachern, J. and Towle, W. L. n.d. *Ecological guidelines for island development.* Morges, Switzerland: International Union for Conservation of Nature and Natural Resources.

Mead, W. E. 1914. *The grand tour in the eighteenth century.* New York: Benjamin Blom, Inc.

McGrevy, N. L. 1975. The polynesian cultural center: a model for cultural conservation. Paper read at the symposium on Tourism and Culture Change, American Anthropological Association, 6 December 1975, San Francisco, California.

McGuire, J. W. 1963. *The future growth of Hawaiian tourism and its impact on the state and on the neighbor islands.* Honolulu: Univ. of Hawaii, Economic Research Center.

McIntosh, R. W. 1972. *Tourism principles, practices and philosophies.* Columbus: Grid.

McKean, P. F.

   1972. Tourist-native interaction in paradise: locating some partial equivalence structures in Bali. Paper read at the 71st Annual meeting, American Anthropological Association. Forthcoming in *Masyarakat Indonesia* (Indonesian Society), Jakarta.

   1976a. Tourism, Culture Change and Culture Conservation. In *World anthropology: ethnic identity in modern Southeast Asia*, D. Banks, ed. Mouton: The Hague.

   1976b. An anthropological analysis of the culture-brokers of Bali: guides, tourists, and Balinese. Background paper for the UNESCO/WORLD BANK seminar on the socio-cultural impacts of tourism, 7–11 December 1976, Washington, D.C.

   °1977. From purity to pollution? a symbolic form in transition: the Balinese ketjak. In *The imagination of reality: symbol systems in Southeast Asia*, A. Becker and A. Yengoyan, ed. Tucson: Univ. of Arizona Press.

McKim, P. n.d. *The London youth culture: a study of social non-structure.* Ann Arbor: Microfilms.

McLeod, E. M. 1974. Bibliography of studies and documents on Caribbean tourism. Appendix VII, Volume 6: *Tourism, Carribbean Regional Study.* International Bank for Reconstruction and Development, Washington, D.C.

Medlik, S. 1966. *Higher education and research in tourism in western Europe.* London: Univ. of Surrey.

Medlik S. and Middleton, V. T. C. 1973. The tourist product and its marketing implications. *International Tourism Quarterly* 3: 28–35.

Meinke, H. 1968. *Turismus und wirtschaftlichen entwicklung*. Göttingen: Van den Hoek und Ruprecht.

Mercer, D. C.

  1970a. The geography of leisure: a contemporary growth point. *Geography* 55: 261–73.

  1970b. Discretionary travel behavior and the urban mental map. *Australian Geographical Studies* 9 (2): 133–43.

  1970c. The role of perception in the recreation experience: a review and discussion. *Journal of Leisure Research* 3: 261–76.

Meriaudeau, R. 1963. Les stations de sports d'hiver en Suisse, en Autriche et en Allemagne meriodionale. *Revue de Géographie Alpine* 51 (4): 675–718.

Merlini, G. 1968. Problemi geografici del turismo in Italia. *Bollettino della Società Geografica Italiana*, Series IX, 9 (1–3): 1–30.

Merlo. L. 1959. Aspetti ed evoluzione del turismo sociale. *Civitas* 10 (2): 38–43.

Michener, J. A. 1973. *The drifters*. London: Corgi.

Micssec, J. M. 1972. La croissance du tourism en Tunisie. *L'Information Geographique* 36 (4): 169–78.

Middleton, V. 1972. Development and trends in travel to Britain. *British Tourist Authority, Research Newsletter* No. 5 (Summer 1972), pp. A–D.

Milner, G. B. 1972. Samoan lesson. *New Society*, volume 27, July 26, 1972.

Mings, R. C.

  1966. The role of the commonwealth government in the growth and development of the Puerto Rico tourist industry. Ann Arbor: University Microfilms.

  1969. Tourism's potential for contributing to the economic development in the Caribbean. *Journal of Geography* 68: 173–77.

  1970. Research on the tourist industry in Latin America: its present status and future needs. In *Geographic Research in Latin America*, B. Lentnek, R. L. Carmin, and T. L. Martinson, eds., pp. 315–23. Proceedings of the Conference of Latin American Geographers, vol. 1.

  1974. *The tourist industry in Latin America: a bibliography for planning and research*. Exchange Bibliography #614. Monticello, Ill.: Council of Planning Librarians.

Mitchell, F. H.

  1968a. *The costs and benefits of tourism in Kenya*. Report to the Kenya Tourist Development Corp. Nairobi, Kenya: Univ. College, Institute for Development Studies.

  1968b. *The impact of tourism on national income*. Nairobi, Kenya: Univ. College, Institute for Development Studies, Staff Paper No. 30.

  1970a. The value of tourism in East Africa. *East African Economic Review* 1 (2): 1–21.

  1970b. Evaluating the role of tourism in Tanzanian development. In *Tourism and Socialist development*, I. G. Shivji, ed., pp. 23–24. Dar es Salaam: Tanzania Publishing House.

Mitchell, L. S. 1969. Recreational geography: evolution and research needs. *The*

Professional Geographer 21 (2): 117-19.

Mitford, N. 1959. The tourist. *Encounter* 13 (3): 3-7.

Moir, E. 1964. *Discovery of Britain: The English tourists, 1540-1840.* Fernhill House Ltd. Distributed by Humanities Press, Highland, N.J.

Moore, K. 1970. Modernization in a Canary Island village: an indicator of social change in Spain. *Journal of the Steward Anthropological Society* 2: 19-34.

Moreno, O. 1974. Las limitaciones en el desarrolle turistico. *Comercio Exterior* 25 (3): 308-14.

Moret, Rmo. R. Joseph. 1763. *Empeños del valor, y bizarros, desempeños, o sitio de Fuenterrabia.* Manuel Silvestre de Arlequi, translotor. Joseph Miquel de Esquerro, Impressor de los Reales Tribunales de Navarra, originally written 1654, facsimile edition published by the Ministerio de Información y Tourismo de España, Industrias Gráficas Valverde, San Sebastián, 1968.

Morrison, H. B. 1972. *The golden age of travel.* Reprint of 1951 edition. New York: American Museum of Science Books.

Mozoomdar, A. 1974. Tourism and the BOP in a developing country. International Union of Official Travel Organizations (IOUTO) Seminar Paper.

Murdie, R. A. 1965. Cultural differences in consumer travel. *Economic Geography* 41 (3): 211-33.

Murphy, P. E. and Rosenblood, L. 1974. Tourism: an exercise in spatial search. *Canadian Geographer* 18 (3): 201-10.

Nagenda, J. 1969. Parading the primitive to woo tourists. *African Development* 3 (8): 15.

Naibavu, T. and Schutz, B. 1974. Prostitution: problem or profitable industry. *Pacific Perspective* 3 (1): 59-68.

Narduzzi, N. 1973. Prevision de la demande et formation du capital dans le domaine du turisme. *Revue de Tourisme* 2: 74-76.

Noronha, R. 1976. Review of the sociological literature on tourism, with Annex I: Sociological Literature, summaries. Washington, D.C.: World Bank.

Nash, D. 1970. *A community in limbo: an anthropological study of an American community abroad.* Bloomington: Indiana University Press.

National Tourism Resources Review Commission.
    1973. *Destination USA.* Volume 1, Summary Report. Washington, D.C.: U.S. Government Printing Office.
    Domestic tourism: its economic characteristics. Volume 2, Summary Washington, D.C.: U.S. Government Printing Office.
    The economic impact of tourism. Volume 5, Special Studies. Washington, D.C.: U.S. Government Printing Office.

Nayacakalou, R. 1972. The leasing of native land for tourist plant development in Fiji. In *Change and development in rural Melanesia*, pp. 151-58. Canberra: A.N.U. Research School for Pacific Studies.

Naylor, J. 1967. Tourism—Spain's most important industry. *Geography* 5 (1:234): 23-40.

Nieto, J. 1976. *Tourism: its penetration and development on a Spanish island.* Ann Arbor: University Microfilms.

Nolan, S. D. 1975. Variations in travel behavior and the cultural impact of tourism Paper read at the symposium on Tourism and Culture Change, American

Anthropological Association, 6 December 1975, San Francisco, California.

Norbeck, E. 1971. Man at play. *Natural History*. Special supplement: Play, pp. 48-53.

Nuñez, T. A.

    1963. Tourism, tradition and acculturation: weekendismo in a Mexican village. *Ethnology* 2 (3): 347-52.

    1964. Authority versus anarchy: the impact of urban tourism on a rural milieu in Mexico. Paper read at the symposium on Tourism, Central States Anthropological Society, 14-17 May 1964, Milwaukee, Wisconsin.

Organization for Economic Cooperation and Development. 1974. *Tourism policy and international tourism in OECD member countries*. Paris: OECD.

Ogilvie, F. W.

    1933. *The tourist movement*. Staples Press.

    1934. Tourist traffic. *Encyclopedia of Social Sciences* 13: 661-64. New York: Macmillan.

O'Loughlin, C.

    1967. *Economic and political change in the Leeward and Windward Islands*. New Haven: Yale Univ. Press.

    1970. Tourism in the tropics: lessons from the West Indies. *Insight and Opinion* 5 (2): 105-10.

Ossipow, P. W. 1963. Le role de l'automobile dans le tourisme. *Tourist Review* 18: 17-24 and 61-73.

Ouma, J. P. B. M. 1970. *Evolution of tourism in East Africa (1900-2000)*. Nairobi, Dar es Salaam, Kampala: East African Literature Bureau.

Pacific Area Travel Association (PATA)

    1969a. Creating a destination area. Study presented at the 9th Workshop of PATA, 24 January 1969, Chiengmai, Thailand.

    1969b. The fundamentals of travel research. Hong Kong Travel Research Seminar, 20-22 October 1969, Hong Kong.

    1973. The total travel experience. PATA 4th Travel Research Seminar, October 1973, Fiji.

Packer, L. V. 1974. *Tourism in the small community: a cross-cultural analysis of developmental change*. Ann Arbor: University Microfilms.

Parkes, J. 1925. *Travel in England in the seventeenth century*. London: Oxford Univ. Press.

Parsons, J. J. 1973. Southward to the sun: the impact of mass tourism on the coast of Spain. *Yearbook of the Association of Pacific Coast Geographers* 35: 129-46.

Pearce-Sales, J. 1959. *Travel and tourism encyclopaedia*. London: Blandford.

Pearson, R. 1957. The geography of recreation on a tropical island: Jamaica. *Journal of Geography* 56: 12-22.

Pelegrino, D. A. 1972. *An annotated bibliography on leisure*. Exchange Bibliography #345. Monticello, Ill.: Council of Planning Librarians.

Perez, L. Jr. 1973-74. Aspects of underdevelopment: tourism in the West Indies. *Science and Society* 37: 473-80.

Perpillou, A. 1966. Quelques études recèntes sur les problèmes géographiques du tourisme. *Annales de Geographie* 75 (409): 341-45.

Persaud, B. 1970. Impact of tourism. *West Indies Chronicle*, July, pp. 329–31.

Persaud, L. 1973. European tourism "not the answer." *West Indies Chronicle*, December, pp. 485–46.

Peters, M. 1969. *International tourism: the economics of the international tourist trade*. London: Hutchinson.

Pi-Sunyer, O.

    1973a. Tourism and its discontents: the impact of a new industry on a Catalan community. *Studies in European Society* 11: 11–20.

    1973b. The commercialization of leisure: fishermen and tourists in a Catalan maritime community. Paper presented to the American Anthropological Association, November 1973, New Orleans, Louisiana.

Pitt-Rivers, J. 1964. Pilgrims and tourists: conflict and change in a village of southwestern France. Paper read at the symposium on Tourism, Central States Anthropological Society, 14–16 May 1964, Milwaukee, Wisconsin.

Pittock, A. B. 1967. Aboriginese and the tourist industry. *Australian Quarterly* 39 (3): 87–95.

Planina, J. 1962. Turizem kot druzbena en ekonomska kategarija. *Economisk Revy* 13 (1): 29–37.

Polson, F. T. 1973. The social and cultural impacts of tourism development in Micronesia and on Wuvulu Island. Master's thesis, Dept. of Urban Planning, University of California, Los Angeles.

Pool, I., Keller, S. and Bauer, R. A. 1956. The influence of foreign travel on political attitudes of American businessmen. *Public Opinion Quarterly* 20 (1): 161–75.

Pope, R. H. 1964. Touristry: a type of occupational mobility. *Social Problems* 2: 336–66.

Poser, H. 1939. Geographische studien uber den fremdenverkehr im riesengebirge: ein beitrag zur geographischen betrachtung des fremdenverkehrs. *Abhandlungen der Gesellschaft der Wissenschaften zu Gottingen, Mathematisch-Physikalishe Klasse*, Dritte Folge, Heft 20, pp. 1–173.

Pospisil, L. 1975. Tyrolean peasants of Obernberg. Paper read at the conference of the Wenner-Gren Foundation, August-September 1975, Burg Wartenstein, Austria.

Pouris, D. and Beerli, C. 1963. *Culture and tourism*. Paris: Organization for Economic Cooperation and Development.

Press, I. 1969. Ambiguity and innovation: implications for the genesis of the culture broker. *American Anthropologist* 71: 206–17.

Pritchett, V. S. 1964. *The offensive tourist*. New York: Alfred Knopf

Pudney, J. 1953. *The Thomas Cook story*. London: Michael Joseph.

Quandt, R. E., ed. 1970. *Demand for travel: theory and evaluation*. Lexington, Mass.: Lexington Books.

Quintana, B. B. and Floyd, L. G. 1972. *Que Gitano! Gypsies of southern Spain*. New York: Holt, Rinehart and Winston, Inc.

Quirt, J. H. 1962. Airlines: profitless progress. *The Exchange* 23: 4.

Ramaker, J. G.

    1966. *Toeristen en toerisme: sociaal-economische beschouwingere over het moderne toerisme*. Assen: Van Gorcum

1973. *Le bilan touristique. Revue de Tourisme* 1: 33–34.

Rambaud, P. 1967. Tourisme et urbanisation de Campagne. *Sociologica Ruralis* 7: 311–55.

Reason, J. 1964. *Man in motion: the psychology of travel.* New York: Walker and Co.

Redcliff, M. 1973. The effects of socio-economic change in a Spanish pueblo on community cohesion. *Sociologia Ruralis* 13 (1): 1–14.

°Redfield, R., Linton, R. and Herskovits, M. 1936. Memorandum in the study of acculturation. *American Anthropologist* 38 (1): 129–52.

°Reiter, R. B. 1974. *Sexual domains and family in two communes in southeastern France.* Ann Arbor: University Microfilms.

Reiter, R. R. 1973. *The politics of tourism in two southern French communes.* Ann Arbor: University Microfilms.

Renaud, B. 1972. The influence of tourism growth on the production structure of island economies. *Review of Regional Studies* 2 (3): 41–56.

°Reynolds, P. L. 1968. *Peace Corps termination report.* San Blas, Panama: Nargana.

Ritchie, J. E. 1975. The honest broker in the cultural marketplace. In *A new kind of sugar: tourism in the Pacific,* B. R. Finney and K. A. Watson, eds., pp. 49–60. Honolulu: East-West Culture Learning Institute.

Ritter, W.
1966. *Fremdenverkehr in Europa.* Leiden: A. W. Sijthoff.
1974. Tourism and recreation in the Islamic countries. In *Studies in the geography of tourism,* J. Matznetter, ed., pp. 273–81. Frankfurt-am-Main: J. W. Goethe-Universitat.

Rivers, P.
1972. *The restless generation: a crisis in mobility.* London: Davis-Poynter.
1973. Tourist troubles. *New Society.* 1 February 1973, p. 539.

Robertson, A. 1965. The sunshine revolution. *The Geographical Magazine* 37 (12): 926–39.

Robineau, C. 1975. The Tahitian economy and tourism. In *A new kind of sugar: tourism in the Pacific,* B. R. Finney and K. A. Watson, eds., pp. 61–78. Honolulu: East-West Culture Learning Institute.

Robinson, G. W. S.
1957. Tourism in Corsica. *Economic Geography* 23: 337–48.
1972. The recreation geography of south Asia. *Geographical Review* 62: 561–72.

Roebuck, J. and McNamara, P. 1973. Ficheras and freelancers: prostitution in a Mexican border city. *Archives of Sexual Behavior* 2 (3): 231–44.

Rosenber, H., Reiter, R., and Reiter, R. R. 1973. Rural workers in French Alpine tourism: whose development? *Studies in European Society* 1 (1): 21–38.

Ross D. R. and Farrell, B. H., eds. 1975. *Source materials for Pacific tourism.* Santa Cruz: Univ. of California, Center for South Pacific Studies.

Roy, L. 1975. Planning for tourism on the island of Hawaii: the effects of tourism on natural resources, natural beauty and recreation. In *A new kind of sugar: tourism in the Pacific,* B. R. Finney and K. A. Watson, eds., pp. 165–68. Honolulu: East-West Culture Learning Institute.

Rudelius, W., Pennington, A. L. and Ross, I. 1971. Analyzing state tourism: a case study of the Midwest. *Journal of Leisure Research* 3 (4): 250-60.

Rutazibwa, G.
    1973. L'étude des problèmes de l'industries touristique. *Revue de Tourisme* 1: 30-33.
    1974. Le transports et le tourism international. *Revue de Tourisme* 3: 93-99.

Ryan, B. 1965. The dynamics of recreational development on the south coast of New South Wales. *Australian Geographer* 9 (6): 331-48.

Ryan, Jerry B. 1969. Tourism in the U.S. Virgin Islands: its growth and economic impact in the post-War period. Master's thesis. Univ. of Kansas.

Samy, J.
    1973. Who does what to whom in Pacific tourism? Paper read at the Seminar on Social Issues in Development Planning in the South Pacific, 29 November-3 December 1973, Suva, Fiji.
    1975. Crumbs from the table? In *The Pacific way*, S. Tupouniua, R. Crocombe, and C. Slatter, eds., pp. 205-14. Suva: South Pacific Social Science Association. Also in *A new kind of sugar: tourism in the Pacific*, B. R. Finney and K. A. Watson, eds., pp. 11-24. Honolulu: East-West Culture Learning Institute.

°Sanday, P. 1973. Toward a theory of the status of women. *American Anthropologist* 75: 1682-99.

Sandor, T. L. 1971. Economic analysis of resort development. *Cornell Hotel and Restaurant Administration Quarterly* 11 (4): 43-49. Ithaca: Cornell University.

Sargent, J. R. et al. 1967. The limits of tourism as a growth generator. *Development Digest* 5 (2): 82-86.

Sandru, I. 1970. Considerations sur la géographie du tourisme, avec spécial regard sur la Roumanie. *Revue Roumaine de Géologie, Géophysique, et Géographie*, Serie de Geographie 14 (1): 175-80.

Schmitt, R. C. 1968. Travel, tourism and migration. *Demography* 5 (1): 306-10.

Schouten, R. and Osgood, D., eds. 1975. *The impact of tourism on regional development: a case study of Taos, New Mexico*. Dallas; Southern Methodist Univ., Dept. of Anthropology.

Sedeuilh, M. 1974. Public health aspects of tourism. *WHO Chronicle* 28 (6): 293.

Selke, A. C. 1936. Geographic aspects of the German tourist trade. *Economic Geography* 12: 205-16.

°Seveck, C. A. 1973. *Longest reindeer herder*. Fairbanks: Arctic Circle Enterprises.

°Shatto, G. 1972. The San Blas Cuna Indian sociedad as a vehicle of economic development. *The Journal of Developing Areas* 6 (3): 383-97.

Shepard, P. 1955. The nature of tourism. *Landscape* 5 (1): 29-33.

Shivji, I. G., ed. 1973. *Tourism and socialist development*. Dar es Salaam: Tanzania Publishing House.

Sigaux, G. 1966. *History of tourism*. J. White, trans. London: Leisure Arts.

°Sikorski, K. A. 1968. Modern Hopi pottery. *Utah State University Monograph Series* 15 (2): 9-10.

Simmel, G. 1950. *The sociology of George Simmel*, K. Wolff, ed. Glencoe: The Free Press.

Simpson, J. 1975. Research for tourism in the Hawaii Visitors Bureau. In *A new kind of sugar: tourism in the Pacific*, B. R. Finney and K. A. Watson, eds., pp. 153–56. Honolulu: East-West Culture Learning Institute.

Simpson, A. 1968. *The new Europeans.* London: Hodder and Stoughton.

Sinclair, J. T. 1960. Current development of the tourist industry and its future in the economy of El Salvador. *Annals of the Association of American Geographers* 50: 346, abstract.

Sládek, G. 1966. *Zahraničný Cestovný Ruch* (Foreign Tourism). Bratislava: Vydavateľstvo Politickej Literatúry.

Smith, D. C. 1972. Issues in the economic development of Micronesia: tourism as an example. In *Micronesian realities: political and economic*, F. M. Smith, ed., pp. 218–34. Santa Cruz: Univ. of California, Center for South Pacific Studies.

Smith, V. L.

    1953. Travel geography courses for a new field. *Journal of Geography* 52 (2): 68–72.

    1961. Needed: geographically-trained guides. *The Professional Geographer* 13: 6

    °1968a. In-migration and factionalism: an Eskimo example. Paper presented to the American Anthropological Association, November 1968. Seattle, Washington.

    °1968b. *Intercontinental aboriginal trade in the Bering Straits area.* Tokyo: Proceedings of the VIII International Congress of Anthropological and Ethnological Sciences, volume 3.

    1975. Geographers and mass tourism. Paper read at the California Council for Geographic Education, 10 May 1975, Chico, California.

    1976. Tourism and culture change. *Annals of Tourism Research* 3 (3): 122–26.

Spencer, J. E. and Thomas, W. L. 1948. Hill stations and summer resorts of the Orient. *Geographical Review* 38: 637–71.

Stanfield, C. A. Jr. 1971. The geography of resorts: problems and potentials. *The Professional Geographer* 23 (2): 164–66.

Stitcher, J. H. 1964. The United States Indian Service responds to a felt need in planned tourism development. Paper presented to the symposium on Tourism, Central States Anthropological Society, 14–16 May, Milwaukee, Wisconsin.

°Stout, D. 1947. *San Blas acculturation: an introduction.* New York: Viking Fund Publications in Anthropology No. 9.

Sullivan, M. G. 1976. Tourism and anthropological perspective: criteria for successful integration in travel programs. Paper read at the symposium on Tourism and Culture Change, American Anthropological Association, 18 November 1976, Washington, D.C.

Sutton, W. A., Jr. 1967. Travel and understanding: notes on the social structure of touring. *International Journal of Comparative Sociology* 8 (2): 218–23.

Svendsen, A. S. 1969. Det moderne reiseliv og det private massekonsum av reiser og rekreasjon. *Ad Novas* 8: 124–28.

Talbot, N. 1974. A note on tourism in the West Indies. *Science and Society* 38: 347–49.

Taylor, J. L. 1953. Waikiki: a study in the development of a tourist community. Ph.D. dissertation, Clark University.

Teas, J. 1976. I'm studying monkeys: What do you do? Youth and travelers in Nepal. Unpublished manuscript.

Tempelman, G. J. and Peppelenbosch, P. 1974. Le tourisme international et les pays en voie de developpement. *Les Cahiers d'Outre Mer* 105: 77-87.

Thompson, Phyllis T. 1970. *The use of mountain recreational resources: a comparison of recreation and tourism in the Colorado Rockies and the Swiss Alps.* Ann Arbor: University Microfilms.

Thurot, Jean-Maurice. 1973. Le Tourisme tropical balneaire: le modèle Caraibe et ses extensions. Doctoral dissertation. Centre d'Etudes du Tourisme, Universite d'Aix-Marseille, France.

Todt, H. 1965. *Uber die räumliche ordnung von reisezielen.* Berlin: Duncker and Humbolt.

Tomasso, S. di. 1964. Turismo e civilta de massa. *Civitas* 15 (12): 33-47.

Tong, D. 1975. Planning for tourism on the island of Hawaii: an overview. In *A new kind of sugar: tourism in the Pacific*, B. R. Finney and K. A. Watson, eds., pp. 157-60. Honolulu: East-West Cultural Learning Institute.

Towle, E. L.

    1972. Tourism and the environment: the taxonomy of a symbiotic relationship. In *Organization of American States Information Document.* Washington, D.C.: Organization of American States.

    1973a. The role of the travel-tourism industry in international marine recreation development. Paper presented at the 9th Conference and Exposition, Marine Technology Society, September 1973, Washington, D.C.

    1973b. Tourism and its environmental impact on Baja, Mexico. Paper read at the Travel Industry Environment Conference, 22 October 1973, Ensenada, Baja, Mexico.

    1974. Tourism: a way to clean up the environment? In *Report on proceedings, 22nd annual meeting and 13th annual workshop, Pacific Area Travel Association,* 22-23 February 1973, Kyoto Japan. San Francisco: PATA.

Travel Weekly Seminar. 1974. Scholars examine travel motivation. *Travel Weekly.* August 29, pp. 6-39.

Trease, G. 1967. *The grand tour.* London: Heinemann.

Tryk, S. 1972. The people pleasing business. *New Mexico Business* (August).

Tupouniua, S., Crocombe, R., and Slatter, C., eds. 1975. *The Pacific way—social issues in national development.* Suva, Fiji: South Pacific Social Sciences Association.

Turner, E. S. 1967. *Taking the cure.* London: Michael Joseph.

*Turner, F. J. 1920. The frontier in American history. New York: Holt, Rinehart and Winston.

Turner, L.

    1974/1973. *Multinational companies and the third world.* London/New York: Allen Lane/Hill & Wang.

    1974. Tourism and the social sciences, from Blackpool to Benidorm and Bali. *Annals of Tourism Research* 1 (6): 180-205.

Turner, L. and Ash, J.
    1973. The golden hordes. *New Society* 19 (4): 126–28.
    1975. *The golden Hordes—international tourism and the pleasure periphery.*
        London: Constable.
*Turner, V. 1967. Betwixt and between. In *Forest of symbols: aspects of Ndembu
    ritual,* pp. 93–111. Ithaca: Cornell Univ. Press.
UNESCO. 1966. Resolution on the preservation and presentation of the cultural
    heritage in connection with the promotion of tourism. General Conference,
    XIVth Session, November 1966, Paris, France.
United Nations
    1963. *Recommendations on international travel and tourism.* Rome: United
        Nations Conference on International Travel and Tourism.
    1973. *Elements of tourist policy in developing countries.* United Nations
        Conference on Trade and Development (UNCTAD), United Nations,
        New York, TD/B.C. 3/89/Rev. 1 E73.II.D.3.
U.S. Department of Commerce. 1972. *A study of Japanese travel habits and
    patterns.* Washington, D.C.: U.S. Government Printing Office.
U.S. Department of Commerce, Office of Regional Development and Planning.
    1967. *Tourism and recreation: a state of the art.* Prepared by Arthur D. Little,
    Inc. Washington, D.C.: Government Printing Office.
Urbanowicz, C. 1975. Tourism+ in the Polynesian Kingdom of Tonga. Paper read
    at the Santa Cruz Pacific Seminar on the Social and Economic Impact of
    Tourism on Pacific Communities 5 May 1975, Santa Cruz, California.
*Van Gennep, A. 1914. *The rites of passage.* London: Routledge and Paul Kegan.
*Van Stone, J. W. 1955. Archaeological excavations at Kotzebue, Alaska. *Anthro-
    pological papers of the University of Alaska* 3: 75–155.
Veblen, T. 1899. *The theory of the leisure class.* New York: Macmillan.
*Vigier, P. 1963. *La seconde republique dans la region alpine.* Tomes I et II. Paris:
    Presse Universitaires de France.
Vine, P. 1973. Tourism: what priority should it get? *African Development* 7: 18.
Vogt, J. W. 1975. Wandering: youth and recreation travel behavior. Paper read at
    the symposium on Tourism and Culture Change, American Anthropological
    Association, 6 December 1975, San Francisco, California.
Ward, M. 1971. *The role of investment in the development of Fiji.* Department of
    Applied Economics Occasional Paper 26. Cambridge, England: Cambridge
    Univ. Press.
Waters, S. R. 1966. The American tourist. *Annals of the American Academy of
    Social Sciences* 388: 109–18.
Waters, S. R. and Patterson, W. D. 1976. The big picture: travel '76. *Annual Report
    World Travel Trends and Markets* 21: 1–120. New York: Travel Communica-
    tions, Inc.
Waugh, R. E. 1962. *The American traveler: more darkness than light?* Austin:
    Univ. of Texas, Bureau of Business Research.
Weiser, M. 1975. Porto Carras: super resort extraordinaire. *Travel Scene,* 15 May
    1975, pp. 25–27.
Wenkam, R.
    1974. *The great Pacific rip-off—corporate rapie in the Far East.* Chicago:
        Follett Publishing Co.

1975. The Pacific tourist blight. *Annals of Tourism Research* 3: 2.

Williams, A. J. and Zelinsky, W. 1970. On some patterns in international tourist flows. *Economic Geography* 46 (4): 549–67.

Williams, R. 1972. *The country and the city.* London: Chatto and Windus.

Winsburg, M. F. 1966. Overseas travel by American civilians since World War II. *Journal of Geography* 65 (2): 73–79.

Withington, W. A. 1961. Upland resorts and tourism in Indonesia: some recent trends. *Geographical Review* 51: 418–23.

Wolbrink and Assoc. 1973. *Physical standards for tourist development.* Honolulu: Pacific Islands Development Commission.

Wolf, E. 1973. Aspects of group relations in a complex society. In *Contemporary cultures and societies in Latin America*, D. B. Heath and R. N. Adams, eds., pp. 85–101. New York: Random House.

Wolfe, R. I.
    1964. Perspective in outdoor recreation: a bibliographical survey. *Geographical Review* 54 (2): 203–38.
    1966. Recreational travel: the new migration. *Canadian Geographer* 10: 1–14.

Wolfson, M. 1967. Governments' role in tourism development. *Development Digest* 5 (2): 20–26.

World Bank. 1972. *Tourism—sector working paper.* Washington, D.C.: World Bank.

World Council of Churches. 1970. *Leisure—tourism: threat and promise.* Geneva: World Council of Churches.

Wright, D. T. 1972. Planning and tourism. Thesis. Sydney, New Zealand: Univ. of Sydney, Dept. of Town and Country Planning.

Wright, D. L. and Stopford, J. 1972. *Note on the air inclusive tour holiday industry.* London: London Business School. Mimeo.

Yablonsky, I. 1968. *The hippie trip.* New York: Pegasus.

Yefremov, Yu. K. 1973. Geografiya i Turizm (Geography and tourism). In *Geografiya i Turizm*, S. A. Kovalev et al., eds. Voprost Geografii, vol. 93. Moscow: Izdatel'stvo "Mysl".

Young, G. 1973. *Tourism: blessing or blight?* Harmondsworth: Penguin Books.

Young, J. 1973. The hippie solution: an essay in the politics of leisure. In *Politics and deviance*, I. and L. Taylor, eds. London: Penguin Books.

Zachinyayev, P. N. and Fal'kovich, N. S. 1972. *Geografiya Mezhdunarodnogo Turizma* (Geography of International Tourism), Moscow: Izdatel'stvo "Mysl."

Zelinsky, W. 1971. The hypothesis of the mobility transition. *Geographical Review* 61: 219–49.

Zehnder, L. E. 1975. *Florida's Disneyworld: promises and problems.* Tallahassee: Peninsular Books.

Zinder, H. et al.
    1968. Essential elements of a tourist development programme: a critical commentary. Published by the author, Washington, D.C.
    1969. *The future of tourism in the eastern Caribbean.* Published by the author, Washington, D.C.

Index

Numbers in italics refer to illustrative material.